Deadly Departed:

DO'S, DON'TS, AND DANGERS OF AFTERLIFE COMMUNICATION

Jock Brocas

Published by Soul Odyssey Books
an imprint of Micro Publishing Media, INC

Soul Odyssey
B O O K S

PO Box 1522
Stockbridge, MA 01262
www.micropublishingmedia.com
Ordering Information:
Special discounts are available on quantity sales.

1st ed. ISBN 978-1-944068-77-6

CONTENTS

Dedication

I dedicate this book to my wife who is not only my best friend, my rock and my teacher, without her, I am nothing and with her, I am everything. I also dedicate it to the many professionals I have come across in my life and to all who serve spirit selflessly. I also dedicate the book to my friend and colleague Susan Tiemann who designed and restructured and worked with me on the book and my many other projects. This book has been many many years in the making and is written with love, forgiveness and compassion, the rules of life I strive to live by.

I want to ensure that you develop along with the right intentions and guidance from those of the highest order in the world of spirit, and I believe that I have given you more than enough information in this book to ensure that you become as professional and successful as you should be and that you serve humanity with the highest ethical standards

—JOCK BROCAS

Foreword By Robin Foy, Terence Palmer, PhD and Paula Fenn

Foreword
by Robin Foy

Jock Brocas is an experienced, dedicated professional medium and spiritual teacher. When our paths first crossed, the parallels between his early life and my own were incredibly similar. We both had an interest in religious matters; a 'knowing' deep within me that there was something special I had to do, but having no idea exactly what that would be.

We both had a passing interest in psychic matters - ghosts etc. - at an early age, and spent some time serving with the military.

We had long and meaningful chats with the padres at our respective bases, as well as spending some time in a contemplative or meditative state at that time.

We found the spiritual and psychic scene through early readings/messages we had and through visits to local Spiritualist churches, and we both found our soul mates - leading to happy second marriages - through our involvement with Spiritualism and Psychic Research.

We both feel a great need to keep up and help to improve the standards of mediumship in the world today, and to create a closer relationship between Science (especially quantum physics) and the spiritual community.

Both of us also understand the importance of working with higher vibrational beings in the development of mediumship and psychic phenomena.

Through my experiences, I have come to know very well the dangers involved in the development and demonstration of all forms of mediumship, due to my thirty-nine years of Psychic Research and its physical phenomena.

I have witnessed the personal ego of certain mediums who consider they are further progressed than the spirit guides are and helpers who work with them.

I have seen excellent and developed mediums lose the good standard of their Mediumship by allowing their ego to take control instead of their spirit guides and helpers. Occasionally this has led to a medium's guides and helpers abandoning them to work with another medium.

Fortunately, in my intimate involvement with physical circles over the years, I have always worked closely in harmony with circle guides and helpers - lovingly and with sincerity, and personally never experienced the negative forces that can so easily disrupt the development and demonstration of different forms of mediumship.

But it is a sad fact that psychic attacks and the dark forces in nature are a reality, and it is important to recognize what is possible and what you may encounter while developing or practicing mediumship of any kind, so that the dangerous (and not always obvious) pitfalls can be avoided.

Jock Brocas has provided an intricate guide in this book for professional mediums, developing mediums and prospective mediums alike to alert them to the important responsibilities they have to their clients during the demonstration of their mediumship. He has also devoted much time to the ever-present problems that they are likely to come across from time to time when faced with the onslaught of negative forces.

In plotting the course of navigation through the dangers of psychic and mediumistic development, Jock has demonstrated the use of his natural PHD (Psychic Homing Device) instead of 'radar' to successfully guide the spiritual ship of psychic development to its homeport - without hitting the icebergs!

This book is important to all mediums and potential mediums that are serious about avoiding the dangerous pitfalls that confront them in the demonstration and practice of their Mediumship.

Robin Foy[1],

Psychic Researcher, The Scole Experiment

---

1 Robin and Sandra Foy are Psychic Researchers who have specialised in investigating Physical Mediumship and Physical Phenomena in depth for 42 years now. Consequently, their unique experiences qualify them to be recognized as two of the most knowledgeable people in the world regarding this specialised subject. Over the years, they have sat with numerous physical mediums including: Leslie Flint, Gordon Higginson, John Squires, Geoffrey Jacobs, Colin Fry, Stewart Alexander, David Thompson, Mavis King, Paul McElhoney, Scott Milligan, Diana and Alan Bennett plus Tom and Linda Anderson (from the Freedom of Spirit group), Sandy Horsford, S. London Theatre School Circle and the Yellow Cloud Circle of Eternal Illumination, Kai Muegge of the Felix Experimental Group on a number of occasions; as well as conducting several home circles of their own for the development of physical phenomena; some of these produced very positive results. Whilst they do not class themselves as Spiritualists, or have any connection with Spiritualism as such, they do see themselves as Spiritual Scientists, and approach the important subject of Spiritual Science with a primarily scientific motivation. Robin and Sandra were also cofounders of the ISM Link of Home circles and

Deadly Departed By Jock Brocas, A Review

by Terence Palmer, PhD

I have only ever encountered two published works on the dangers that can be encountered in the world of spirit by naïve explorers into mediumship and spiritual communication. There may be more that I am unaware of. However, these two works are by Dion Fortune, who wrote Psychic Self-Defence, and David Ashworth, who wrote Dancing with the Devil. Dion Fortune is an advocate of the perspective that all matters concerning the psychology of mind and behaviour are in essence investigations into the 'occult'. This is a view that is dismissed and ignored by mainstream psychology, which, in my own practical experience, is a very big mistake.

The scientific study of the human mind is a scientific study of the occult, and those academics and scientists that choose

the New Spiritual Science Foundation. Additionally, Robin was the personal founder of the Noah's Ark Society for Physical Mediumship in 1990.(Foy, A Short History, n.d.)

to ignore this perspective are not doing the science of psychology any justice as a discipline in the search for 'truth' in human experience. The other book I am familiar with, by David Ashworth, is targeted at those who would teach 'Reiki' to the would-be spiritual healer. David goes to great lengths to educate the student and teachers of Reiki that the universe is comprised of negative and positive energies that hold each other in balance, and that to ignore the negative is, again, a serious mistake, as the naïve seeker can be seriously harmed by negative forces that could be described as 'evil' or even 'demonic'.

Both of the above-mentioned writers are warning different sections of the community about negative forces. Dion Fortune aims to educate the psychologists and David Ashworth aims to educate the practitioners of Reiki. These writers came into my awareness because I was researching for my doctorate as a psychologist. I had an urgent need to find a scientific framework that could accommodate those psychic and spiritual phenomena that I was experiencing and witnessing for myself. In my personal experiences I discovered the reality of unseen dimensions, but in academia I discovered the absurd refusal of mainstream psychology to recognise this reality. In order to satisfy the needs of my examiners to grant me a doctorate, I had to pretend that I did not really believe in such things as spirits. Therefore, obtaining a PhD on the subject of spirit possession was a delicate balancing act. So, what I did learn was that the science of psychology is not equipped to recognise the reality of the nature of human consciousness because it refuses to acknowledge that the human being is a spirit that occupies a material form.

It is an unfortunate fact of modern life that we are conditioned to dismiss the idea that spirits are real, and that the idea of spiritual forces provides us with inspiration for entertainment in films, etc., but nothing more.

Mainstream science reinforces the idea that spirits do not exist, and from the moment we fall from the womb, we are conditioned to believe that spirits are not real, but only exist in the imagination.

Medical science, and psychiatry in particular, are not equipped to heal people because they refuse to acknowledge that human beings are spirit beings encased in a material over-coat that is the physical body. Refusal to acknowledge this truth about the real nature of the human being is why the institutional health-care services in the modern world are not able to meet the demands of a sick population.

In my work as a psychologist, as a spiritual healer and as an educator, I encounter the spiritual causes of sickness on a daily basis. I ignore those diagnoses given by psychiatrists to my clients, but rather conduct my own investigations into the causes of their sickness. It is extremely rare for me to have a patient referred to me that does not have a spiritual cause for their problem. The most common findings are of what we may call Dark Force Entities (DFEs) or demons in religious language, the earthbound spirits of the deceased who remain earthbound largely though ignorance and false beliefs about a non-afterlife, and dissociated sub-personalities that are created within the psyche through trauma. These spirit entities are not imagined. They are real and they all have conscious awareness.

I have taken the time to place myself in a position where I can offer an endorsement to this book by Jock Brocas, Deadly Departed. He is a spirit medium, and his book is written for the education and guidance of aspiring mediums. He pulls no punches when he talks about the realities of spirit realms where real dangers are encountered, and, in harmony with the techniques and precautions espoused in the two aforementioned titles by Fortune and Ashworth, he gives advice and guidance on how to be prepared and protect oneself from dark forces.

Whilst reading the proof of Jock's book, I became immediately aware of its value for some of my current clients who had been hospitalised with psychosis. They had been cleared of the negative spirit intrusions and earthbound spirits, but they needed more help with the re-integration of their fragmented personalities, and they needed education in how to keep safe from more spirit intrusions.

In addition, and of primary importance in the recovery of such damaged individuals, is the care and understanding of their immediate families, care-givers and psychiatrists.

For family members who do not believe in the spirit realms because of their conditioning in the modern world, recognition that their loved-one has been a victim of psychic attack or misguided spirit communications can be very difficult to accommodate and process. Likewise, the psychiatrist who does not believe in spirits will be at a loss to understand how their patients have recovered in such a miraculous way when they know that their medications can not possibly be the reason.

This, for me, is the true value of Jock's book. Here is a book that I can recommend to my clients, their psychiatrists and their families as part of their education and understanding during the recovery process.

This is my endorsement – for anyone who needs to understand what has happened to them, to a hospitalized patient or a family member who has experienced 'mediumistic psychosis,' this book is a 'must-read'.

Terence Palmer, PhD
Author of The Science of Spirit Possession

Deadly Departed By Jock Brocas,
A Review

by Paula Fenn, M. Couns; B.A (Hons); Grad.Dip Psychoanalytic
Psychotherapy

As an experienced clinician who works within the fields
of Psychoanalytic Psychotherapy, Spiritual Regression Therapy and Spirit Release, I have seen evidence over my years of
practice that energy intrusions in the guises of possession and
obsession via dark force entities and earthbound spirits, psychic attacks and the presence of metaphysical evil are very real
phenomenon. In addition, within the depths of therapeutic encounters there are the risks of being the receptacle for split-off
unconscious energies which Jung encapsulated within his doc-
tor/patient transference matrix. In this book, Jock Brocas, with
the wisdom of personal and professional experience, shares
with clarity and authenticity, meaningful constructs to assist
the reader to understand the dark and how to mitigate against
its manifest intrusions.

I discovered very quickly as a novice Psychotherapist that
the clinical textbooks I had embraced up to that point which
carved out traditional psychological models of mental health
and offered guidance to the practitioner around how to assist
patients to move beyond their conditions contained massive
voids. If only some of the seeds which Jock aims to sprinkle

and grow had fallen before me in those early days of practice, perhaps my journey towards a deeper truth about mental and physical illness would not have been so arduous, nor detrimental to my own health as a consequence of the energy intrusions I unwittingly collected.

In order to meaningfully progress as a clinician, I needed new ways of thinking and understanding, a new language – in fact a lexicon of languages – through which to interpret disease and the soul to soul encounters experienced in the therapeutic relationship. As a consequence of continuous training in practical and conceptual fields to include energy healing and the energy body, Regression Therapy and trapped aspects of consciousness, mediumship and communicating with discarnate entities and spirit helpers, I now feel I am at least part way towards a more honest and enriched understanding of mental health and its associations with the physical body and spiritual matters. Working within this fusion of Mind, Body and Soul also necessarily bridges into the realms of discarnate entities and energies and their resonant attachments to and attacks towards human beings.

Jock Brocas very incisively states in Deadly Departed that this amalgamated trinity of Mind, Body and Soul is a spiritual force which operates as 'one'. A wholeness which recognizes our spiritual authority, our divine authority no less, over that which is dark.

But what of those who are conceptually, egocentrically or just naively 'beyond the dark'? Some find such shadowy matters all rather distasteful and operate from a preference to remain sheltered in all things light, rather than confront the often toxic and murky domains which they also necessarily occupy as incarnate humans in an opaque world with dark and light hues forge a dance of equilibrium through the field of consciousness. Ignorance is, unfortunately, not bliss. They wear this cloak at their peril and with an ill-considered choice which exposes them and their clients to intrusion; and of course, a continuance of suffering as a consequence.

As Jock says, "Discernment is a heightened awareness of the power of the soul" and offers an exaggerated intrinsic knowledge of a variety of realms of experience. But if the dark is compartmentalized out of awareness then this 'soul power' is fractured and true discernment cannot hold true. The power of spiritual authority, the tripartite 'oneness' of Mind/Body/Soul is disempowered and loses its force and thereby its innate powers to serve and protect.

I deeply admire Jock as an author, a professional and a human being. The narratives and case study vignettes in Deadly Departed exude the best kind of 'knowing' – the experiential birthed from the catalytic force of necessity to adapt in the face of adversity alongside Jock's continual developmental accumulation of conceptual wisdom. If I had discovered this book in my early years of soul-to-soul encounters, I can guarantee I would not have been so maimed by the energetic intrusions which, as an empathic and highly sensitive psychotherapist, I opened myself up to receiving. Rather than unconsciously making myself vulnerable and highly accessible to the malignant energies which are attracted to the abused, the traumatized and the personality-disordered patients I was seeing in a hospital environment I would have taken essential precautionary measures and protected myself. I would have known why? what? and how? and integrated this awareness with intentionality into a daily ritual of practice.

I highly recommend this book to any and all practitioners who work empathically within a relational field with clients – that's just about everyone from hairdressers to tarot readers – because it will inform you about energy, its multifaceted forms of intrusion and how to wisely protect yourself against its malignant effects. The world of encounter, that which is seen and unseen, can and does create bewildering affects and much confusion. But Mr. Jock Brocas is a true guide, in service to Mankind and Spirit, as he takes his readers through this labyrinth of emotions and quandaries.

Paula Fenn,
M. Couns; B.A (Hons); Grad.Dip Psychoanalytic Psychotherapy, Psychoanalytic Psychotherapist, Regression Therapist, Spirit Release Practitioner, Author, Lecturer, Researcher

"This overview of life spiritually explored will ring bells with many of you. If you do not think after reading this book that you have these innate abilities to develop, that it can make you understand yourself and others in a deeper, more loving and compassionate way, seeing this world in its reality of balanced energies, I can only say you need to read it again."

Leo Bonomo,
Professional Inspirational Clairvoyant Medium and Psychic

"I find this publication immensely useful to the wise professional mediums, developing mediums, and those looking on the outside in, beginning to awaken. It is NOT fear mongering as many will suggest. It is vigilance and heightened awareness that naughtiness and skulduggery is a possiblity in the world of spirit..."

Su Filer
R.G.Nurse. R.Midwife. Health Visitor Dip. Counsellor. Complementary Therapist.Hypnoanalyst MIAEBP. Spiritual Healer. ReikiMaster Teacher.

Author's Note

I do not claim to be an all knowing medium, yet I have been
lucky to have been guided by spirit, educated by those in
spirit and other professionals on this side of life. In my years
work ing as a professional medium, I have been faced with many
obstacles, some of which have been paranormal in nature, and
my understanding of the mechanics of the other side has been
deepened by those experiences.

I chose to write about the subject of spiritual protection or
understanding of the negative aspects from what would seem
like a religious point of view and though I was brought up a
Catholic, it just gave me a frame of reference on which to build
knowledge upon. I chose to stick to this understanding within
this book to allow a clear frame of reference and an easy way to
understand those aspects which are so often ignored. Though
in all religions and spiritual modalities, there exists a recognition of the polar opposite to love and what is good in the world
and though it may have many labels the base truth is the same
but with different perceptions. The truth will never be changed
but only its perception can be manipulated.

I do not wish the reader to agree with everything I've written. I wish only to plant seeds of knowledge that may sprout
into something that will bear fruit and help upon one's spiritual

path. Within every lesson or example in the book is an underlying truth within similar perceptions. There may be mistakes, there may be better ways to frame things, but the prime power or desire behind the book is to educate and open one's heart to the power within and of the dangers associated with the world of spirit. **This book is not finished, it never will be and will constantly be updated** and knowledge and reference is given from divine sources to be shared upon this plane of existence. I am no one special, I have knowledge which I share in love, forgiveness and compassion. If it helps one, then it helps a thousand more as the seed of knowledge will have been sown.

Jock Brocas,
September 30, 2017

Introduction

So why is it so difficult to believe in abilities that are certainly not tangible but do give scientific evidence of the reality of the presence of these supernormal abilities?, I mean, gravity is real -- and even your disbelief won't stop you falling!

This was a tremendous problem for me during my childhood due to my family predominantly being Catholic. My uncle, a monk in a monastery where I spent most of my time; my father who was very scientific in his approach and Masonic – he had to see to believe, and finally my time in the military where, unless you could touch it, the existence was a futile dream.

I remember as a young boy growing up and spending a great deal of my time on holiday in my uncle's monastery, talking with the monks and the priests – discussing theology and things of a spiritual nature like a person three times my age. I always had a spiritually inquisitive mind and often delved deeper, much deeper than many adults delve. My inquisitiveness for truth eventually led me away from manmade religion and to the world of the spirit, where you are your only judge.

Ever since I was young, I displayed psychic abilities, though these went on unnoticed or ignored. However, I often wondered how I could experience certain things, and others could not. I very rarely discussed these things, and if I ventured an opinion on something or suggested something out of the norm – it was rejected all too easily. How can you grow spiritually when no one will listen? Instead of playing normally like the other boys, I would attend mass and even had my own altar in my room. I somehow knew that there was something more beyond my own religion. I began to question and still experience these visions, dreams and Aha moments, yet never once discussed them with anyone for fear of ridicule.

I remember another occasion almost too vividly. When I was young, I watched my Gran suffer through cancer, and I knew that she was going to pass to heaven. I used to sing to her when she was ill in bed and when I did, somehow I knew we were not alone and that others were around - others, which could not be seen by the normal folk, yet I felt an energy and a presence around me that scared me. My Gran eventually passed to the spirit, and I think it was in the spring as I remember lots of daffodils around.

Anyway, on the day of the funeral I walked into the church and took my seat with my family. Soon enough, the church service started and as the priest was saying the sermon, I saw an image build up to the left of the Altar. It was my gran and she was standing there smiling, no words, just an enigmatic smile. No sooner had I seen her – she disappeared. I thought it was prudent at this time not to mention this to any member of my family, as I feared ridicule – especially from my other family members. I was already ridiculed as someone who was spiritually motivated, and I was often called a Jesus freak and other names like that, you can guess why I remained so inert about my spirituality.

I am sure that my story is reminiscent of some of you who are reading this, and if you have experienced similar traits then it is time for you to wake up and realize whom you are. It is now time to develop these gifts that you have been given in order that you can serve your fellow human being. Service being the order of the day and not the order for yourselves, we will get to the latter later in this book.

As a young boy, I did not have many friends and instead chose solace as my friend. Nevertheless, my inquisition into spiritual matters resulted in gaining an acute understanding of the opposite of good, of what temptations and evil there was in the world, and this seemed to be very creed oriented and did not fit with what I felt in my heart, it scared me.

However, the more I learned about the evil that permeated the world from my discussions with those holy men, the more frightened I became, until it ingrained in me a fear that held me a prisoner of creed and dogma.

I remember reading books like The Calling by Redemptorist Publications, which was about your vocation to the priesthood and what it meant. I did not resonate with this and always knew there was much more to life and through my own experience, there had to be something more. Reading these books was like a light bulb moment, for the content of the books tried to explain how life was and what divinity was. Yet I knew something different. I had always experienced spirit direct and was aware of the angelic forces from a young age. It was through these works and my experiences that I sought answers elsewhere and began to study many more avenues. I always knew that I had a destiny but what it was I could not put my finger on, and so I tried many avenues to find what it was that sat well in my soul. I had to let spirit guide me in whichever way spirit could, though later in life, I repressed my natural gifts, joined the military, and made my own mistakes in life, which taught me valuable lessons. Spirit never left me and when the time was right, and I had experienced enough, I was called to service.

Spirits around me

I have always had a keen awareness of the spirit world, and even though I admit that I perhaps never really understood this until later in life, I have felt energies and seen spirits from an early age. When I was in various public areas, and even during my military years. I would feel and sense or see beings that were not living and to this day, spirits often contact me while I am in town or when I am having a coffee in my favorite haunt – pardon the pun. Well, I know that now, but a long time ago the feelings that I would be receiving would be unknown, I suppose at the time I would not have recognized it.

Case 1: You Must Be Going Mad

One evening while down the local pub with some of the guys, I got very drunk, and as is the normal modus operandi of soldiers, I became rather hungry but did not have enough money to buy anything from the kebab house on the way home.

I remembered that I had left some sandwiches in the fridge back in the office where I was working at the headquarters. As I knew the codes to get in, I decided that a night operation was in order.

I convinced my mate to come with me to stand watch, to alert me of any of the guards doing their rounds. Stumbling and singing along the path, we began to shh! each other as we got closer to the back entrance of the camp.

We made our way – rather drunkenly of course – to the rear of the HQ, and I entered the code for the door and walked in. Inside, the corridor was incredibly long and dark except for the light that cascaded in from security lamps outside. I had one thing on my mind – sandwiches.

I began to make my way down the corridor moving silently to ensure that no one caught any movement or saw me from the outside if they were passing. I am sure I got halfway down, when I looked up and saw a man standing at the bottom of the corridor, just looking at me, but not from a window or door. I had the fright of my life, waited for him to shout and heard nothing, and turned so quickly I forgot about my sandwiches and ran out toward my friend at the rear of the building.

"We're caught," I said, "there's someone in there, and he saw me, I am sure he will call the guards." Looking back, he was gone. Bazza, my mate, said to me that I must be going mad as no-one was in, all the lights were out and there were no doors or entrances to offices where he had been. I knew what I saw, and said nothing - just waited for the call from the Regimental Sergeant Major the next day.

The call never came, though I did bump into RSM Brown, "Heard you guys had a bit of a night last night." My heart was racing, I waited for the bollocking, and it never came. Knowing what I know now about the spirit world, it had to be a visiting spirit, though I have no proof.

Spirits have often made themselves known to me at the most inopportune moments. I have often felt a hand on me, or a vibration surrounding me, and wondered what it was. It was never frightening, I would consider it more of a curiosity, though at the time, I had no idea that I was able to communicate with them so easily. My mother and certain priests would tell me that it would be the devil playing tricks on me, and so a fear grew in me that still persists to this day, though now I understand it better due to my spiritual growth and understanding our divine connection.

Not all spirits are good; they cannot be, so it is prudent to assume there are bad spirits. Inevitably, my interest grew and when I was on holiday in the monastery in Perth, I would feel safe enough to study this side of things on a deeper level. How could I have known this would be a preparation for my life's path? So, my years of study have culminated at this point, to alert you to the realities and the dangers of accepting your path as a medium.

A Few Words on Religion

Religion is a positive thing when understood and properly practiced with truth, love, compassion, humility and justice prevailing. There is, however, a negative aspect to this, and the existence of evil is there to deny us all our birth right or awakening to our divinity, and this evil will try and stop you every time from doing good. It causes man to fight man and religion to fight religion and to cause hate. Even so, the basis of religion is truth and eventually when you peel away all the man-made layers, you do get to truth in the end. I suppose this is why my early psychic experiences were thought to be evil and terrified me so much. I then held back my gifts myself from lack of understanding, which surfaced later in life.

I studied many religions and found good and bad in every one of them, yet all tried to maintain three principles of love, compassion and forgiveness. I learned that prayer and meditative experience were a basis of all, which was inherently divine communication. Psychics and Mediums are labeled as evil just as most prophets such as Jesus and his apostles, Mohammad, Buddha were in their time.

Look around on the Internet and you will find many organizations ready to help you develop spiritually, learn mediumship and expand your psychic potential -- and at the same time separate you from your hard-earned cash. They will tell you that being a psychic or a medium is a wonderful thing, and they will pander to your ego and your ego's desire. Everything in the garden does indeed look rosy and after all, what is there to worry about? It is a wonderful thing to do and to develop, no matter what drives you – there is nothing to fear. How many books can you read that tell you how to develop, or books that intimate the dangers are minimal except for a few associated emotional hurdles, or how many experts in the afterlife are there, who really don't have the experience? A true life afterlife expert is on the otherside, that's when they know the reality and mechanics of the afterlife. We are mere explorers. Now STOP! LISTEN; the reality is different and developing those wonderful gifts that you desire so badly is fraught with danger if you do not know what you are doing. You had better become aware of this now before its too late.

In our modern day world, science is moving at tremendous speeds, and its development is changing the world we live in vastly. Again, some good things and some bad things have of course come from science. Splitting the atom, was it a good event or a bad one? Who knows, we have to remain content in the knowledge that we are developing at a great rate and to damnation with the consequences, and with every new breakthrough in science is a new breakthrough in destruction.

It is in man's inquisitive nature to continue to challenge the boundaries of science, though we are perhaps only one-track minded. For when we come against a concept that has no material proof or no scientific basis for explanation, we tend to mock that which we fail to understand, because we cannot perceive it. In many religions throughout the world, you will hear them talk of faith. Perhaps a concept only understood in this context yet it is a feeling, belief, or emotion. It is a concept that is born of the spirit and soul and has no physical conception because there is no tangible evidence.

Everything in our world has to be tangible in order for us to believe in it, from the food we eat to the money we can hold in our hands. With this tangibility, we conclude that physical perception of things gives credence to our beliefs – we see, so we believe, yet faith is not seen, nor is it perceived - yet it is believed.

You have a hidden gem of the universe in your grasp; within these pages are the secrets and the realities of what it means to become a professional spiritual medium. It will enlighten you and teach you that you have a tremendous amount of responsibility on your shoulders, which at times is not an easy burden. This book will shock you, it may even scare you, but the result is that you will be empowered more than you ever have before. I aim to help you release that innate potential that you have within you and to show you how not to fall into the dark pitfalls that others do, and how to truly protect your mind, body and soul.

So why am I the best person to take you on this journey? I am a professional and highly evidential spiritual medium. I have experience in all forms of mediumship and I am under continual development, my mediumship is always in a state of development and that will continue well into the next life. I do not claim to be an expert primarily because we are always developing and the understanding of the spirit world is forever developing and changing – no one can really claim expert status. However, I have experience and the knowledge of my years of development and study and share this with you in this book that you may learn and understand all aspects of the afterlife both good and potentially negative, and have included knowledge from friends and colleagues in the field of paranormal and afterlife research.

Writing this book, I have been mentally attacked, suffered from lack of sleep and negative voices, and I know that they do not want this information out there. Who are they? Well, simply put, everything that is in polar opposite to God or the Universal consciousness or whatever you believe – need I say more? Why would I? – So let us call it the Dark Side, which sounds like a Star Wars science fiction movie, but this is no movie. Why would the dark side want you to learn how to protect yourself from them or to be able to discern between good and evil? Of course, this is a reality of development of your gifts, and there is so much conjecture surrounding this. Have you wondered why most development information refutes the existence of evil? Yet every light worker in the world is a target - you need to know the truth and you need forearming with this information to protect you. Mediums who deny this existence are foolhardy and at times can cause more damage than good. Again, this book is your protective talisman if you will. It holds the keys to your spiritual power. I want you to harness this power and use it in service and to better humanity. First comes development.

Why Develop?

The greatest gift that you can give humanity - or anyone for that matter - is service. To be able to ease the suffering of those who have lost loved ones or to put someone back on the path to recovery is surely the greatest service that you can give. This is as good as any reason to develop your gifts. If you study the lives of those enlightened individuals such as Jesus, Buddha, Mohammad and others, you will immediately arrive at the conclusion that their whole lives and ministries were about spreading truth and being of service to their fellow man. Spirit calls us to service and it is your free will if you answer the call.

Therefore, there are many ways we are called to service and one of these ways is to develop the psychic gifts, which can be used in service to humanity and yourself. These gifts enable you to make wiser life choices and to develop your spirit on the path to enlightenment. Psyche means soul and in this case, we are developing the gifts of the soul, which is the divinity that we hold internally. The most important reason that we develop is to be of service to others, no matter whether a medium, psychic or as a healer. By developing your spiritual power, you can learn to listen to that inner voice that will keep us on our true vocational path – the voice that will protect us and guide us in our time of need. You have heard the statement that "all answers are within." This is a truth of life, for in developing our soul gifts – we can have the answers that we need. All we need to do is ask. Try this; the next time you have a particular problem that you are facing. Hold the thought in your mind and say a little prayer to God or your higher self to be enlightened about what path you should take to deal with the issues. You can guarantee the answer will come to you in a dream or as a flash of inspiration the next day or advancing days after the question. You may also receive subtle little signs around you, which will give you the answer.

Now I know that some of you want to know what these signs are or how you will notice them. If so, continue reading through the book, for within this book are the answers you seek, to help you find the answers that always lay within to develop your life to the highest possible standards.

Developing our psychic abilities can help us in our daily life. It can aid us in making correct business decisions or with our relationships. We can keep our family and ourselves safe by recognizing our intuitive feelings. In my last book, *Powers of the Sixth Sense* (O-Books, 2008), I discuss at length how we can listen and recognize those subtle intuitive signs around us. Your intuition is like your early warning and guidance system. It will help you to navigate the waters of life, but you must understand that every vast ocean has its inherent dangers, and it is these dangers that many do not understand.

An example of using your intuition would be as follows; suppose you are offered an amazing job, and it needs you to leave your own employment now, and suppose that offer promises you vast fortune and successful direction, what would you do? The boss before you is a nice enough person. On the surface he or she seems to be honest, but what is that gut-wrenching feeling you have at the pit of your stomach? What is it that stirs when he or she offers you these gifts on a plate? It's your intuition warning you that something is not right, and that may cause you to question further, thus finding out that it isn't all it's cracked up to be. You make the decision to pass and obviously, that is the right one.

Yes! The path to development is beautiful and through it, we can learn to manifest what our hearts desire. I recently did a reading for an individual who had lost all hope of finding their soul mate or partner with whom they could share their life. I recounted my own experience of how I would never marry again after having a difficult marriage in the past. Then one day I wrote to my guardian angel of what I wanted in a partner and as I wrote I could feel all the emotion and feeling that my desire was manifesting. I then put that notebook away. I found it again four weeks before my marriage to the most perfect woman in the world. I had met my soul mate and I got everything on my list and more. The truth is that your divine power is there to help you manifest your desires and wishes and another truth is that lack does not exist. The Great Spirit has provided everything that you need and therefore learning to harness your divine power really does empower you to beyond the material and physical realities of life.

People do not realize that desperation to get somewhere or something pushes away what it is you desire, therefore we have a phenomena if you will called divine timing. I am sure you have heard of this; everything comes to you at the right time of your need, so do not push too hard. Imagine walking through a door, you have to push it open. More often than not the door pushes away from you – so the more that you push for your desires, the more you create distance. Wanting, needing, and desiring are different altogether and sometimes one is not in line with the needs of your soul or matches your vibration under the law of vibrational attraction. By developing your psychic gifts, you will learn to create that bridge to the spirit that joins the emotion, feeling and desire that is the secret to manifesting your own destiny and successes in life. In short, you are psychic and the sooner you learn that, the easier life will become. Nevertheless, the more you want it and try to force it – you push it away. Most of us that are successful mediums have never asked for it – spirit decides - not we who want it for wrong reasons.

If you really have a desire to raise your vibration and to develop your innate psychic gifts and with the right intention – this book is your compass to navigate the psychic wilderness safely and to help you deal with the many negative aspects that you will face in your lifetime as a professional medium. If you are willing and you can take that step towards truth and enlightenment, then join me on a journey that will forever change your life and will test your very faith and existence. I have taught scores of individuals to develop their innate spiritual gifts and now I want you to learn and develop them too. Moreover, I want you to develop safely and be secure in your own spirituality. When you have the coordinates to navigate safely, you can get through those murky waters. This book is your spiritual compass to help you achieve all you should be, and help you to live a blessed and abundant life.

About This Book: It's Not Dark!

I have written this book in order that I may awaken individuals to the real dangers of the spirit world and the inherent risks that you will have to take on a daily basis as a medium or professional psychic. For students, my aim is not to frighten you, but to arm you as you take up the burden of what we do as professionals. I hope you will use this information wisely and see the lessons that exist between the words. Moreover, for everyone who stands accused, I have felt your pain and the best advice I can offer is – TRUST IN SPIRIT ALWAYS for spirit will never let you down.

In this book, you will be guided through a bewildering labyrinth of emotions and quandaries facing not only those who are currently developing (or considering developing) their psychic and mediumistic gifts, but also those who are already practicing as professional mediums and psychics.

Throughout, there are practical solutions to (and many personal examples of) the many unexpected pitfalls that are likely to face all mediums at some time in their professional careers.

Included in the wide spectrum of advice, is the fact that the decision by potential spiritual mediums and psychics to de- velop their mediumship is not to be taken lightly; professional mediums must be fully aware of their responsibilities and obligations towards their clients. It is important for professional mediums to have the right motivation for pursuing their craft. They must be dedicated in their endeavors, and have an overwhelming desire to serve both Spirit and Mankind in their work. They must be prepared to undergo a long period of hard work during their time of development, which can often seem tedious, and not allow their ego to take over from their spirit guides, so that their messages are clear, concise, and evidential. Good mediums must possess a high reserve of humility, compassion, and honesty while giving readings; delivering only the messages spirit communicators need to give - not just what the client wants to hear!

Truly spiritual mediums and psychics should aim to keep their fees to a fair level so that, while they deserve a reasonable lifestyle in their chosen career, their first motivation to do the work should not be financial, but spiritual.

This book addresses the negative and dark forces that most mediums may come across at some time in their spiritual careers. You are given the ammunition to deal with this aspect of psychic work and overcome any problems that might arise within your mediumship, and allow yourself to achieve total balance and positivity in life - and in the lives of your clients. But one word of warning, there will come a time when you must know your boundaries. There are forces beyond you that are dark and highly developed and intelligent beyond your understanding.

A Word from Another Expert:

"Though Jock and I approach our subject matter from very differing spiritual perspectives, I can recognize the breadth of his experience and knowledge. I especially give him credit for his willingness not to deny the "dark side" of the realm of spiritualism and mediumship. Given his personal journey he is unusually well aware of the role of less benign spiritual elements in the world of the various phenomena he explores. My own perspective, as set forth in my upcoming book Demonic Foes, is more traditional than Jock's heterodox views, but I acknowledge he sets forth his alternative theories in a manner much more cognizant of the role of the dangers involved than most traditional mediums allow." – Richard E. Gallagher, M.D.[2]

---

2 Richard Gallagher, M.D. is an American board-certified psychiatrist. He is a Phi Beta Kappa graduate from Princeton University in Classical Latin and Greek. He trained at Yale in psychiatry and in psychoanalysis at Columbia, where he remains a faculty member. He is now also a Professor of Psychiatry at New York Medical College. He served for a time as scientific adviser to the International Association of Exorcists. For the last twenty-five years he has consulted and lectured widely about the subject of demonic possession and the need to carefully differentiate such states from psychiatric disorders; he

PART 1:

"DO" Understand Your Psychic Abilities

How do you know you are psychic? The truth is that we all are, to a degree, yet the individual that has more power will display the traits of psychics more readily than the average Joe. For instance, one may be overly sensitive and will also be a creative individual or will usually not wish to be in the company of five-sensory individuals, finding themselves sometimes alone or seeking some kind of solace. These five-sensory people are the ones who live according to material values in the world surrounding them. Conversely, they drive themselves further from spiritual reality.

Even from a young age, you can identify traits such as playing with spirit friends who cannot be seen by those around you. You may see and hear things that are beyond the senses of the

has probably seen more of the former cases than any other physician in the world and reports upon his findings in his upcoming book *Demonic Foes*.

29

'normal person,' which can be disconcerting to the loved ones who do not display this character traits. Have you ever had a funny thought about someone, only to have him or her contact you suddenly and out of the blue? Sometimes the individual will sense things that may be wrong with loved ones and friends and so can prophesize events that are already in motion. These are only some small examples that show you the expression of the psyche.

I can bet this book is not the only development book you will ever read. Perhaps you have read many already because your desire to develop is so strong. When we choose the path to psychic or mediumship development, we choose a new life, and as it would seem, a life of harmony, of wiser choices, of seeing the future to enable you to make these choices.

It is a life of endless possibility and limitless potential when expressed properly. In the realm we live, we are tested, and we learn through experiences and feelings to achieve a greater prize of recognizing exactly who we are in this life. Therefore, one must expect to be tested and for the psychic or medium, these tests can be a more difficult path to tread. But, after all, how can you help someone end their suffering if you have no idea what it feels like to suffer?

These tests will depend on your weaknesses, your fears, and your experience. When you successfully pass these tests through the gauntlet of life, spirit entrusts you to help others that need guidance and so will guide others to you? Do not be disheartened for one thing that I can tell you is that all struggles and tests are temporary, and if you keep this in mind, you will not allow your emotions to get to you the way they have gotten to me. I learned the hard way, and I want your path to be slightly easier with this example from my own experience of how you can be tested before you are able to empathize with others.

Case 2: Learning Empathy

My father and I had a very strained relationship when I was younger. I remember issues with my father and my mother, which was primarily down to the way he lived his life and how selfish he could be. My father's underlying trait, however, was a very caring man whose heart was as soft as mallow covered by a solid exterior.

Nevertheless, dad led a hard life, and this usually affected my mother and myself in many negative ways. I think that dad and I were very alike and just like our similar traits we clashed sometimes and instead of learning from our issues, we allowed them to remain and create negativity between us.

My father's negative living soon took a toll on his life, and he became very ill. His drinking and smoking habits affected his physical body, and I am sure that he was emotionally very unhappy as my father used to be an incredibly fit man. My dad hid his emotions well and unfortunately only ever showed emotion when he was blind drunk.

Now I do not want to portray my father in a negative light, as he was an incredibly kind man to those that were less fortunate than him, though he was not averse to playing the system to get ahead, and he had a terrible hate for government control. I digress for a moment.

The years of abuse had eventually taken its toll on my father, and he became seriously ill. I remember a time when he was in the hospital and my father and I were not really on speaking terms. We had fallen out a while before, and the truth is that I don't remember what it was. I decided that life was too short, and that I would like to make amends with my father. I took some time away and traveled a few hours to go and visit him in the hospital. I had some concerns about meeting my father and seeing him in the hospital, these concerns were soon to be realized. Astonishingly, *my father turned away from me when I tried to make up with him.*

I tried to set our differences aside, and he turned from me, which deeply hurt me and haunted my thoughts for a very long time.

I returned home the next day absolutely devastated at my dad's behavior and believing that was that - maybe someday we would make up. Never in my wildest dreams did I even consider that might be the last time that I would see him.

Time passed and my father was still in the hospital. I had a call from my mother one day to say that dad was very ill again, and I should see him as soon as possible. My exact words to her was "Screw him - He turned his back on me, the bastard's got nine lives and will be back to his old ways in no time."

Later that night, I had a dreadful feeling and put it down to the anger that was raging inside of me. I kept receiving flashes in my mind of my father, and I could not sleep. I sat up in bed and decided that I should calm myself - have a cup of tea and just relax. I sat in my living room on my own, feeling awful and at three-thirty in the morning my phone rang.

I knew immediately that my father had gone as in my mind his presence raced. I was right, my cousin Brian called to give me the news and in tears, he mumbled that dad had passed. I was devastated but incredibly numb and sat motionless in my chair.

I never said good-bye, I never said I loved him, and now it was too late. The guilt began to consume my soul.

Time slowed down for me, and it was the longest night in my life. I drove down towards my childhood home, and the journey felt like it was taking days rather than hours. Imagine if you can, what was going through my mind at the time. I felt so guilty, what had I done? My dad was gone and I would no longer hear his singing in the morning or his whistling while he worked outside – something I hated but now yearned for.

Big Al, as we all called him, had left this world and I could not say I loved him or that I was sorry for the way we both behaved. As I write this, the tears are still streaming down my face, as I loved my father very much. The last memory that I had was not a good one, and it was confounded by the vision of seeing my father in his coffin. He did not look like himself and when I kissed his forehead, he seemed so cold, lifeless yet somehow I knew that he was watching me and was still around. My grief clouded me in so many ways, and I could not for one minute consider that I would see him again.

I have experienced this tragic loss, and this is only one of the ways that I, myself, was tested. Why? Simply, because my job as a medium is to provide evidence of life after death – to show that our consciousness survives the state that we call death, and that our lives continue in the world of spirit. How could I possibly understand the pain of loss and how emotionally binding it is not to say goodbye, or that you love your loved one.

I know the realities of this, and this is why my work is so rewarding in its own way, somehow I am able to bridge that gap and help to bring closure to those who are suffering through their own grief. I also know that my father watches with great interest when I work for spirit. Sometimes I hear him say "Good job, son" after a particular piece of spirit work.

It is not just for evidence of life after death that we use our psychic gifts. It is all about listening to our inner voice to make the correct business decisions, too, or indeed decisions that affect our lives in the present moment. In the following example, a "test" turned out well for the client as he managed to use his own innate abilities to make the right decision based on his sixth sensory feelings.

Case 3: It's Not Always About Life After Death

When I was still living in Scotland, a client contacted me from America wanting advice and help with issues surrounding his business. Even though I gave him plenty of evidence of the spirit world and his own life, I wanted to show him how he could use his own vibes to make the right decision. I asked him to sit with me a while, even though we were thousands of miles apart, and took him on a visualization and showed him how to distinguish from his vibes and rational thought. After a while, he made a life changing decision based on his feelings, and I am happy to report that since that reading, his dreams have flourished.

CHAPTER 1:

A Call to Higher Service

M ost individuals that wish to develop their gifts are guided there by spirit to be able to make sense of what they perhaps experienced when they were young – a calling to a higher service.

Case 4: Surprise!

A male client came to me for a reading and just before he arrived, I had an immense feeling that he had many questions which he needed answered, and that he was a spiritual person. Although he had members of his family in spirit, he found himself at a quandary and stood before two paths going in opposite directions.

As I tuned into the spirit world, I began to communicate with many of his discarnate relatives – giving evidence of life after death and help with the problems he faced in his personal life. During the reading, another figure of foreign descent appeared in my vision and told me that she was his guide - that she had spoken to him clearly, which is something he was denying because of his confused feelings.

When I passed this information, he nearly col-lapsed with shock and continued to tell me the story of how he heard someone call his name while he was relaxing. This obviously startled him, but from that day, he began to research the psyche and spirit. His main reason for coming to have a reading was to make sense of the spiritual experience he had and this was spirit's way of calling him to develop his innate gifts. I was honored that spirit chose me to be a part of his awakening.

Obviously, in my day, we were told these psychic experi-ences were bad, that nothing good could come of them, and that they came from Satan himself – what a load of crap that was. I remember seeing spirits of old priests and monks in the mon-astery and could not accept these were evil. Besides, whenever I would bring the subject up, I was told not to "play with fire." That was until I met an old priest called Joe, who was the head of a youth ministry within the religious order that my uncle was a member of and where I had literally grown up.

Joe was, as far as I knew, also an exorcist and was happy to discuss these and other paranormal subjects while we were in our nightly discussion after prayer. The discussions fascinated me and although it terrified the other lads, it made me want to know more - to learn how to protect oneself from these.

I was a practical joker and reveled in winding up some of the other lads. One evening after Joe had scared us half to death, I retired early with a friend of mine. We had acquired some fish-ing line, which I tied to the chair in one of the boys' room. I led the line under the carpet and to the room where my friend and I were. When the other lad went to bed, we started to bang on the pipe gently and could hear him stirring – getting scared. When we felt the time was right, we pulled on the gut and yanked the chair halfway across the room, to hear the terrifying screams from the boy in that room. How funny that was, and yet I did not recognize how real it could be until later in life.

I was warned the Devil could appear as a cloak of light and from then on was wary of everyone. I learned how to protect myself, and I learned the reality of the darker side of the paranormal through Father Joe and his real stories. This was to be my area of study and contemplation for many years.

Of course, as I grew, I learned more, and I studied more and more of spirituality and religion. I soon learned that man manufactured religion, though it is a good thing when the underlying truth is realized. I found that it was man himself that created his misconceptions of religion and its truth. I learned that individuals that fear damnation and destruction if they do not follow a set of rules written by another human followed most religions. Later in life the experiences that I had dwindled, why, I do not know, but I feel that was because of material values that were instilled by learned behaviors from family and friends.

When I was in the army, you did not talk about these experiences; you had to lead a tough masculine skeptical life. I had seen spirits of soldiers that passed on and when I got a chance to speak to our padre during our "Padre Sessions", I would be the only one there and the only person asking questions. It seemed the only time individuals in the military turned to any thing remotely religious was out of fear when they were in trouble. Soon, I forgot all about these experiences, and although I remained spiritual, I fell away from that path until later in life. This is when spirit decided it was time for me to get off my ass and work for them, and not as we would call it, 'work for the Man.' Therefore, my path to development began.

Many of you would have been in a similar position, and your own path would be similar, in essence. Others develop through trauma, such as the soldier in Vietnam who banged his head and started to have paranormal experiences. Alternatively, there is the individual that has an out-of-body experience and comes back to this earth plane - experiencing newfound powers that he or she seems to have acquired on his or her travels. There are the other individuals that begin to develop through another phenomenon I call the "Gucci Handbag Syndrome." This is when an individual witnesses what a medium or a psychic can do, and does not see the reality of it. Instead, they see it as the new cool thing to do, and their ego is fueled – Oh if only they knew how dangerous it could be without the proper guidance and knowledge! Would they rethink? They develop for one reason and one only – to impress others, and give no thought to the suffering that people feel through bereavement or other events.

Some individuals will develop to feed their own ego and make money. There is nothing nicer than having someone like you and recognize your work, but it is important to ensure the ego remains in check. To accept the compliment when done with the right feeling and reverence is good. Others wish these gifts for fame and fortune, with the latter of the two being the main motivation. They do not even need to have well developed gifts, but will prey on the needs and grief of individuals that may be suffering or perhaps scared of the unknown because of personal experiences. We will go into this subject in detail within the continuing chapters. You must be aware that spirit is watching, and you must have the right motivations for doing the work you are called to do. I would personally prefer to turn people away for readings if I feel there is no need, and have done on many occasions, because for me the work is not financial but in-service to spirit and humanity. To those that have the wrong motivations, I have this to say - "KARMA is a bitch."

We are All Vulnerable

I have been asked some strange questions in the past because of what we do and why we charge for services. A woman once asked me, not knowing that I was a medium, if I thought that mediums and psychics all prey on vulnerable people. I went quiet inside and asked my own guide - TC. The words that were put in my mind instantly were, "You are all Vulnerable." This got me to think about our natural vulnerability. The truth is that we are all vulnerable in some way. You cannot go through this life feeling that you are invincible; from the moment that we leave the womb, we are vulnerable. The word vulnerable (adjective) comes from the Latin word vulnerabilis, which means *to wound*. The dictionary terms explain that vulnerable means susceptible to physical or emotional attack or harm, i.e. *"We were in a vulnerable position"* or *"an animal is vulnerable to predators."* It suggests that a person may be open to some form of attack, which suggests a pre-determined act against a potential victim, whether this is physical or emotional. Predator suggests that a person or animal stalks their prey to a point that a successful assault can be made.

Anyone who is seeking help from a medium or psychic is coming to them of their own free will. Therefore, one cannot claim and prove that we prey on vulnerable individuals. Instead through divine intervention and gifts, we offer solace and comfort to the recently bereaved by offering evidence of the world of the spirit.

Let me go back to the reality of our vulnerability. I mentioned that in some way, we are all vulnerable and that is a truism of life. We all have weaknesses that make us vulnerable; it could be from a failed business, a relationship or even injury. Even so, does that vulnerability measure more or less than someone who may be suffering the pain of a lost loved one? If you have problems in your life, you may turn to a doctor, surgeon, or perhaps a counselor if you suffer from depression. No matter what, you will obviously turn to someone who may be able to ease your burden in some small way - to offer you that missing comfort or to ease the suffering you are experiencing. No one is correct one hundred percent of the time and this is down to understanding and communication. We even turn to religion to ease the vulnerability and yet one man's under- standing can be misjudgment and so the real meaning becomes lost, yet we rarely condemn our religion or our physicians. Instead, *we choose to condemn that which we fail to understand* through immutable ignorance. Our vulnerability is what keeps us searching for inner truths and comforts. Furthermore, we will cling on to someone else's ideals and beliefs without real evidence.

Free will cannot be taken likely and so one who will seek out a professional in our field is not being taken advantage of because they seek the help from the divine gifts that may be bestowed on that chosen person. If the medium or psychic then uses their free will to extrapolate financial rewards or to cause hurt - they have then exploited the situation. This does not make the person any more or less vulnerable. Nevertheless, we believe that spirit will guide those that most need help to the right conduit, and that may not be a medium or psychic, it could be a physician, friend or third party.

Mediums and psychics are only another doorway to the spirit or to comfort and understanding - merely a catalyst to begin the healing process. There are unscrupulous individuals that will cause suffering from ignorance and there are always those that will prey on the weak, but to tar the spiritual community is tantamount to ignorance of the highest degree. This is some kind of paradox, for we do the same thing with religion, politics and in our daily lives. Man truly is inhumane to man, and it seems the in thing is to revel in someone's misfortune and suffering, then cloak our guilt by helping financially. Perhaps it is time to wake up to where the vulnerabilities lay and who truly is predator and prey. We exist to be of service, and that is why we develop.

Being Called

There is another contrast of development for the student to be aware of. There are some who are told by a spirit in a message to develop, and that is normally from the platform of the spiritualist church. For those of you who do not know what a spiritualist church is, it is a non-denominational place where a divine service is held. Evidence of life after death is given to the congregation by the medium. Of course, like in any organization, you have your good and your bad, and I can tell you this from direct experience, which I will go into later.

Case 5: I am Called

Again in my own case, I woke up – a calling from spirit – why I do not know – to see a man standing at the foot of my bed in Aberdeen. For some reason, I had no fear. He smiled and then disappeared. My dog saw him too but did not bother much about it. Next day was Sunday and all day I could not get the ghostly vision out of my head and decided that I should perhaps visit the spiritualist church down the road. Now I used to pass this church on the way to work at the nightclub that I was head bouncer in, and every time I passed, I would get a shiver down my spine and think, "Bunch of nutters." However, on this particular day I was a little apprehensive, but knew that these spooks as I called them would maybe make sense of what I saw.

*I approached the door apprehensively and no-
ticed that it was locked and no sound was to be
heard. Something was controlling me and, whatever it was, would not let me leave. I knocked
as hard as I could and heard movement from the
other side and mutterings of a negative nature.
They must have been none too pleased at me in-
terrupting them.*

*Suddenly, the door opened and standing before
me was a displeased elderly and portly woman
whose eyes bored right through me. The instant
she laid eyes on me, she said, "Ah, there you
are, you're late. We have been waiting for you."
As you can imagine, this frightened me even more,
and I made my way into the building and through
the doors, to walk right into a church service,
and not at the beginning either. I saw a seat on
the back row, and I made my way there – trying
not to catch the eye of someone in the audience
or anyone who seemed important.*

*I noticed one woman on the stage, and she stared
right at me as I sat down and tried to make myself comfortable in the awkward position I found
myself in. "Can I come to the gentleman who has
just come in and sat down, hiding himself up the
back of the church?" Oh no, that's me, I thought,
and she must be the medium.*

*The medium then said, "You have been brought
here for a reason. There is a gentleman here who
belongs to you, you're a fitness trainer of some
kind and use weights, and you fight, I am being
told, as a job." That was spot on; I remember
feeling uneasy that she should know this. "There
is an angel beside you, and you stand at a doorway with beautiful lights all around. These are
spirit lights and you are here for the next journey in your life. The door of spirit will now
be opened to you." That is how I was called to
service for spirit and from then on. I have not*

looked back, and oh boy what a journey, and some-
times terrifying.

Case 6: I Deliver the Call

I also remember giving my own message like
this from the platform. I was in church in Wales
and one of the church presidents and I was doing
the service. I stood on the platform and noticed
that my eyes were fixated on a particular woman
in the congregation. "Can I come to you," I said,
"I have a gentleman here who comes with the name
Charles or Charlie. He tells me that he has been
trying to talk with you, and that he passed in
his garden with a heart attack a few months ago.
There is a female name connected to him like Mary
or Margaret and May the 7th is an anniversary."
This turned out to be the name of the woman I was
talking to and her birth date. Her husband who
passed was the communicator. "He reminds me that
you have been cutting down a tree lately. He says
that you should be doing the same job I am doing
now, you have heard a spirit call you when you
were cutting the tree and have ignored it – this
is your nudge once again."

The truth is that spirit can call us to service in many ways, from dream state visions, spirit messages and events that awaken us. I have to add that when spirit calls you, it is the most wonderful and challenging call that you can ever have in your life. It will change you in many ways, and you will throw away the shackles of materialism.

PART 2:

"DO" Learn the Basics FIRST!

believe that everyone who decides to take up the burden
of becoming a medium should learn the basics first, and
I am not talking about the basic psychic skills. There are
many who begin to study and throw themselves into learning
the psychic skills first, take a test and voilà! – a professional
psychic is born. These ones are so out of balance; they will find
themselves treading the murky waters of the lower astral seas –
deeply in trouble without knowing why. They should first learn
about spirituality, what spiritual authority actually means, and
the power of discernment. It is important to recognize that you
have been given this authority for a higher purpose and you
must allow the Great Spirit to guide you.

This spiritual authority is the divinity that is in you. The God
in you; that spark of the ever-flowing love and compassion that
is life itself. In knowing that you have the innate power within
you, and can express this in the material realm, you have a spiritual command over all that would seek to harm you.

There have been spiritual masters in this world who have
expressed the true level of spiritual authority – Jesus showed

this in his life, Buddha expressed this authority, and in the modern day there is an individual who I believe is the epitome of this authority – Sri Sri Shankar[3] (The Guru of Joy), who has displayed this spiritual authority, Mother Theresa, Padre Pio, St. Benedict and countless others.

You need have no fear when you have managed this marriage of spirit and the material realm, because it is then you realize that you have an innate power of spirit over all earthly conditions, and so have nothing to fear. So having an awareness of spiritual authority is not enough, it is in understanding the power of your awareness of this authority. This is not easy to comprehend and no explanation will suffice. Spirit will let you know when you have awoken to this truth.

---

3 Gurudev Sri Sri Ravi Shankar is a humanitarian leader, a spiritual teacher, and an ambassador of peace. His vision of a stress-free, violence-free society has united millions of people the world over through service projects and the courses of The Art of Living.

Numerous honors have been bestowed upon Gurudev, including the highest civilian awards of Colombia, Mongolia and Paraguay. He is the recipient of the Padma Vibhushan, India's second highest civilian award and has also been conferred with 15 honorary doctorates from around the world.

(Shankar, n.d.)

CHAPTER 2:

Understand Your Spiritual Authority

W hether you are looking to further develop your gifts for your personal benefit or wish to dedicate your life to mediumship as a service and profession you need to understand the do's and don'ts of safe successful mediumship. You must know that dangers exist within the unseen world and that a higher level of intelligence exists that are far more intelligent than an under-prepared individual with a modicum of ability.

If you were a marine biologist, it is unlikely you would enter shark infested waters without an escape plan or protective cage. If you were a firefighter, it would not be prudent to run into a burning building without protective gear and training in how to fight the flames.

Mediumship is as serious as swimming in dangerous dark waters or running into a burning building. There is much we don't know about what exists beyond the veil. We need to treat all such exploration with the respect it deserves.

Afterlife communication has been popularized in the media so much so that many potentially gifted but underdeveloped individuals hang their shingles without fully understanding the ramifications of careless afterlife communication. They continue with the perception that there is nothing you should fear on the other side of life that and that everything regarding the spirit world is acceptable. The reality of course is very different and is evident in many cases throughout history. The popularity of the afterlife has increased over recent years and now more and more people who believe they have a natural ability for communication delve into the unseen world, emblazoned in false perception, ignorance and driven by materiality and the need for adulation through a narcissistic personality. No wonder there are increased cases of paranormal activity.

I have asked my friend Kai Muegge[4] to answer a few questions regarding the dangers of development, and what he considers as spirit obsession.

What are the dangers that you would associate with untrained and ill-prepared mediums? What are the dangers of mediumship? Kai had this to say:

"Let us start with the obvious and with the certainly most determinable! In the seventies, Prof. Hans Bender, a world-renowned parapsychology professor in Germany, applied for the first time, the term 'Mediumistic Psychosis.' The term describes a psychiatric or dissociative condition, in which the patient feels disturbed and stalked by unseen entities. The classic progression is that mediumistic activities stand at the beginning. Meanwhile in the beginning, the communication doesn't seem to be different from others that follow communicative practices with unseen forces, a practice which can be counted as an inherent human ritual in the oldest civilized and pre-civilized cultures: the communication with unseen forces, mostly dead relatives or supernatural powers of every color – these cases turn bad.

---

4 Kai Muegge is one of the few current professional mediums demonstrating physical mediumship. His development circle, The Felix Experiment Group, welcomes you to learn more about the developing phenomena at their website: http://felixcircle.blogspot.com

"If, for example, the patient had ongoing strong Ouija-board experiences, he suddenly recognizes at first at home unexplainable things. Maybe he finds written messages addressed to him, or he sees or feels the presence of spirit around him – that sooner or later start to talk to him – and at this stage this patient is at the edge of a severe dissociative state.

"As far as we apply higher grades of a mystical, a magical – i.e. the vitalist's – worldview, we reveal additionally different negative potentials that are active on this spiritual level, into which mediums dive when they open themselves to trance and channeling – to mediumistic – techniques.

"More spiritual seekers than one might think have - unprepared - opened their mental systems to outside influences of a negative kind, and are affected now to different degrees, without being, right from the start, a case for the Asylum. No, such processes can evolve subtly, but at last influence active social areas of the obsessed. The obsessed himself loses many personal attributes that have once characterized him, and besides a permanent apparent energy loss, there is a long list of symptoms in connection with this condition.

"Several therapeutic activities are able to decrease the influence. Modern Psychiatry has developed since the eighties in the use of spiritual practices – at least in addition to classic applications."

The Importance of Balance

Like everything in life, you have your positive and your negative, a balance of nature if you will, and so it is the same with yin and yang, one needs the other to exist. Without the yin, the yang would not exist, and so without a north pole you could not have a south pole. These opposite polarities are needed in order that one can balance the other, and one can learn from both. If there was no evil in the world, nothing would need to be learned and we could not grow spiritually. We are all supposed to learn from our mistakes.

Notice also that there is another aspect of yin and yang: its colors, one is in the opposite to the other. The white color is indicative of everything good and everything of a higher vibration, and the black holds a heavier, more negative vibration that is representative of the opposite - bad or negative. Of course, this is simple and it can have many individual meanings such as feminine and masculine, but the important point is that one is in contrast to the other, and without it would cease to be yin or yang. The two shapes fit together and complete a whole circle. Without one of the shapes, there would be no circle and all would be imbalanced.

When nature is out of balance, it is man who causes the imbalance - and we suffer because of our lack of understanding.

Remember at the beginning I told you there had to be balance, this is so we learn the lessons we need to in order to return to Source (or God, All There Is, the Creator, et. al.). To understand that we are spirits having a human experience, and not the other way around, is to recognize the divinity within ourselves as sentient beings. Understanding this truth of life will lead you to real development of your innate spiritual gifts in order to serve humanity for the highest good. This book will teach you all that you need to know in the world of professional mediumship and psychic work to make you the professional that you can be in all areas of your life.

CHAPTER 3:

Historical Mediums' Gifts of the Spirit

I t's helpful to know you're in good company as you learn the basics.

Interesting to note within Christianity is the fact that after the persecution of Paul and the other apostles, the Christian church put itself up as the only medium. This was because the many addresses given by the entranced mediums were deemed to be of the Holy Spirit, and therefore, the church took power and became the medium for its own gain. Accordingly, the truth is that our first churches were conducted by Trance Mediumship, which was deemed to be of the Holy Spirit. In the fourth century, it was not the priests who led the ceremony of the church service, but the medium who was the bridge between the Holy Spirit and the material world. Therefore, it is safe to assume that early Christianity started with mediumship. Ah, I hear a gasp from your challenged minds. This of course was the same in many other religious traditions.

Mediums in today's world demonstrate the gifts of the spirit regularly in spiritualist churches, on stage at public demonstrations, and in homes on a one-to-one basis. Through trance addresses, we convey teachings from the spirit world, and through mental mediumship we pass on messages of hope, the continuance of life after death, and messages to intervene when necessary to guide and protect. Physical mediumship offers the world a deeper and realistic view of the afterlife, and we now have a new science emerging. Pioneers, such as my colleagues in spiritual science, Robin Foy, Dale Graaf, Russel Targ, and Bob Olson, are continuing to challenge modern beliefs and challenge professional skeptics of all creeds and beliefs.

Sometimes we are persecuted for the gifts that we use, due to the lack of understanding from humanity, but it is not our job to change a skeptic's belief but to offer a new perspective. It will always be true that lack of understanding can cause contempt.

Let's break with tradition for a minute and analyze some of the saints about whom we know. Forget the divinity of the sainthood for a moment and look at them as being mortal, which granted, they were. Furthermore, remember that I am using examples that are appropriate to Christian understanding as I was brought up a Catholic. However, I am spiritual and do not believe in religions and doctrine; I know there are many other examples from other traditions, yet these are the examples I use from my own experience. I will mention various spiritual gifts that I will discuss in depth in a later chapter.

Padre Pio

Let us first examine a saint by the name of Padre Pio[5] who was a Catholic capuchin priest of Pietrelcina, Italy. He was most famous for displaying the existence of stigmata that resembled

---

5 St. Padre Pio was born Francesco Forgione, on May 25, 1887, in Pietrelcina, Italy. Died September 23, 1968.

the wounds of Christ. This could be presumed as another form of physical phenomena. Take into account that millions of people gave witness to his stigmata, and the incredible miraculous healings and teachings of the great priest. Is this not an indication once more of the Messiahship of Jesus Christ or merely an expression of physical phenomena due to inherent divinity? Now it was evident - even from his colleagues - that he was having conversations with someone in his chambers. Many times, doctors and other professionals could not label him with insanity even though they tried. It could only be understood that the other priests were overhearing conversations of a paranormal nature.

It is claimed by his mother that Francesco was able to see and speak with Jesus, the Virgin Mary and his Guardian Angel, and that as a child he assumed that all people could do so.[6] This is another obvious trait and signs of psychic and spiritual ability. As a child, I myself displayed these abilities but religious dogma from the Catholic Church taught me that it was wrong. Of course, Francesco (Padre Pio) developed these gifts to a tremendous extent and became an amazing spiritual medium. The young man had constant heavenly visions in his youth, thus identifying with the gift of clairvoyance of an objective and subjective nature. He became spiritual director of the monastery that he resided in and had five rules for spiritual growth, namely - weekly confession, daily Communion, spiritual reading, meditation, and examination of conscience.

Padre Pio wrote of five rules for spiritual growth: (1) confession, (2) communion, (3) spiritual reading (study), (4) meditation, and (5) examination of conscience. These are a reflection of the prerequisites for developing the gifts of the Holy Spirit, or what you perceive as divine. The most interesting of these is that of meditation, and if we examine all spiritual directions in

---

6 "St. Padre Pio," Catholic Online, accessed 22 October, 2016, http://www.catholic.org/saints/saint.php?saint_id=311

all faiths and denominations, we see that the only constant is, in fact, the meditative state and the change in consciousness.

Due to Padre Pio's internal divinity and the physical reflection of Christ himself, he was tormented spiritually and physically by diabolical spirits. It is no wonder then that Padre Pio should develop extraordinary gifts of the spirit through his dedication and subjective analysis of true divinity. He recommended the performance of meditation and self-examination twice daily: once in the morning, as preparation to face the day, and once again in the evening, as retrospection. He advised on the practical application of theology, which was summed up in his now famous quote, "Pray, Hope, and Don't Worry." He asked that we should recognize God in all things. To desire above all things to do the will of God, and to become the best we can be in the eyes of God - to live the life that we were born to live. This may seem like a profound request but is also the recipe to be able to conquer evil in any form, by developing the ability of discernment through the realization of the spiritual self, the real self - that is constant and a facet of the Great Spirit. Read on and find out what happened with the padre and his own battle with Evil.

The Devil appeared before Padre Pio in many deceptive forms: as young girls that danced naked, as a crucifix, as a young friend of the monks, as the Spiritual Father or as the Provincial Father, as Pope Pius X, a Guardian Angel, as St. Francis and as Our Lady.

In a letter to Padre Agostino dated February 13, 1913, Padre Pio writes:

> "Now, twenty-two days have passed, since Jesus allowed the devils to vent their anger on me. My Father, my whole body is bruised from the beatings that I have received to the present time by our enemies. Several times, they have even torn off my shirt so that they could strike my exposed flesh." (Ruffin, 1982)

Fr. Gabriele Amorth, senior exorcist of Vatican City, stated in an interview that Padre Pio was able to distinguish between real apparitions of Jesus, Mary and the Saints and the illusions created by the Devil by carefully analyzing the state of his mind and the feelings produced in him during the apparitions. This is perhaps one of the best examples of the gift of spiritual discernment, which we will discuss later. In one of his letters, Padre Pio stated that he remained patient in the midst of his trials because of his firm belief that Jesus, Mary, his Guardian Angel, St. Joseph and St. Francis were always with him and helped him always. Perhaps we are able to learn from his experiences and his faith; he himself was a great teacher of discernment, and of being earnest in all your life.

Again this gives credence to the fact that there is a polar opposite to good and that exorcists are required in some form, though my belief is they do not have to be ordained. It also shows that demons exist, and evidential questions must be asked as to the reality of possession and exorcism. Further, it is important to note that anything of an evil disposition is controlled by God and in his name can be commanded.

Therefore, God is the only one that can allow diabolical possession to take place for a higher purpose. I will go into this in more detail later as it is much misunderstood. It is also incredibly strong evidence for clairvoyance, clairaudience and claircognizance due to the fact that there were witnesses who experienced this phenomena.

You must remember that evil can show itself personified in a cloak of light, but through discernment, we can break through the illusion. Discernment can only come from a true heart and the highest of intentions; moreover, with the spiritual knowledge given by a higher power comes this form of enlightenment. There is a clear distinction between negative thoughts brought on by fears and true spiritual intention that comes from the innate divinity within. Thoughts can pollute you and cause turmoil through your own weaknesses and self-sabotage. Padre Pio exhibited signs of and experiences of Transverberation, which is an altered state of consciousness – a heightened spiritual awareness and ecstasy that one could achieve only through enlightenment, and a state that we will very rarely ever get to experience in this lifetime. This was evident in other spiritual beings such as Buddha and Gandhi or the Guru of Joy (Sri. Sri Shankhar - who is still alive).

The Transverberation state is characterized by reduced physical awareness, and greater spiritual awareness giving rise to visions and ecstasies not associated with physical existence. It can also be thought of as experiences of an objective nature. Perhaps for all you Star Trek fans out there, this could be like the HoloDeck on the starship Enterprise. On one particular occasion, Pio admits how one vision occurs and the way in which he saw a vision:

In a letter to Padre Benedetto, dated August 21, 1918, Padre Pio writes of his experiences during the Transverberation:

> "While I was hearing the boys' confessions on the evening of 5 August, I was suddenly terrorized by the sight of a celestial person who presented himself to my mind's eye. He had in his hand a sort of weapon like a very long sharp-pointed steel blade, which seemed to emit fire. At the very instant that I saw all this, I saw that person hurl the weapon into my soul with all his might. I cried out with difficulty and felt I was dying. I asked the boy to leave because I felt ill and no longer had the strength to continue. This agony lasted uninterruptedly until the morning of the seventh. I cannot tell you how much I suffered during this period of anguish. Even my entrails were torn and ruptured by the weapon, and nothing was spared. From that day on, I have been mortally wounded. I feel in the depths of my soul a wound that is always open and which causes me continual agony." (Ruffin, 1982)

This statement certainly gives some acceptance of the fact that Pio was seeing visions in his mind's eye (subjective clairvoyance), and was experiencing clairsentient feelings that were manifesting in physical injury to the body (transverberation).

This is another indication of Pio's mediumistic gifts and spiritual advancement. Through this spiritual advancement, Pio received further gifts of a divine nature and those closest to him attested that he manifested several spiritual gifts including the gifts of healing, bilocation, levitation, prophecy, miracles, and extraordinary abstinence from both sleep and nourishment. He had the ability to read hearts, the gift of tongues, the gift of conversions, and emit fragrance from his wounds.

Perhaps Padre Pio brought this upon himself by believing that his soul was in tatters, and that he had to suffer to be able to receive the love of God and Jesus. This could be because of the dogmatic belief system he followed. Within such a belief system, we can create what we believe if it is so strong, and as with anything in the world - here and in the next - it is created by the thought. However, there is a stark contrast as to the types of thoughts as not all thoughts have their own power. I do, however, challenge the belief that thoughts create material reality; instead, I can concur that it becomes a constituent of a greater recipe. Could another hypothesis be, that he induced these states through the power of his own mind? Quite possibly! Nevertheless, the fact remains that there was also so much more evidence that gave credence to the paranormal events that occurred regularly.

Padre Pio is only one of the saints who displayed gifts of Spirit; there are of course others, such as:

St Francis of Assisi

St. Francis is probably more known for his connection with animals and nature; however, St Francis was the first individual to receive the three wounds of Christ, and interestingly, also received visions of a clairvoyant nature. In the church of San Damiano, it is said that he had a vision of Christ on the cross which came alive and spoke to him, saying "Francis, Francis, go and repair my house which, as you can see, is falling into ruins". It is evident from the statement that as well as Francis seeing visions utilizing clairvoyance, he also heard Jesus speak to him clearly, which suggests that Francis was also a clairaudient medium.

On another occasion, just before he received the wounds of Christ, he had a vision which was witnessed by one of his holy brothers (Brother Leo) – accounted as follows:

> *"While he was praying on the mountain of Verna, during a forty day fast in preparation for Michaelmas, he had a vision on or about 14 September 1224, the Feast of the Exaltation of the Cross and as a result of this vision - he received the stigmata.*

> *"Suddenly he saw a vision of a seraph, a six-winged angel on a cross. This angel gave him the gift of the five wounds of Christ." (Chesterton, 1924)*

This is of course the first true account of stigmata. However, it also reveals that as well as Francis being clairvoyant, his brother Leo also had this gift but to a lesser degree, due to him witnessing the account of the stigmata and the angelic vision. Perhaps a higher divine authority allowed this to ensure that the claims had some structure to them, and no one could blatantly refute the words of two holy men, saying they orchestrated all this.

St Bernadette

She is known worldwide for her visions of a lady, which were at first denied by many skeptics until a canonical investigation gave support to her statements. She was also known for her prophetic visions and the miraculous healings that still take place in Lourdes (France) to this day. The woman whom Bernadette was seeing objectively was, in fact, the mother of Christ. Interestingly, the young girl experienced eighteen visions (divisible by three) but did not know who the woman was until the 17th vision, in which she identified herself as the 'Immaculate Conception'.

Now, during Bernadette's visions, onlookers witnessed inexplicable events, including that of a lit flame on a candle the young girl held. It had burned down to the end yet the flame remained intact on the skin for over 15 minutes, and those that witnessed the phenomena were astounded at the sight, some of course being rather skeptical had no explanation at all. Physicians were aghast as Bernadette showed no sign of pain and showed no physical signs of burning. She continued to have the clairvoyant experiences and the clairaudient experiences whereby the Lady spoke to her clearly.

What you may find astounding, and in direct relation to today's world, is the fact that skeptics taunted her and gave her no quarter. Many scientific tests had to take place -- even her own family at some point did not believe the revelations of the little girl -- sound familiar? Consequently, the Vatican also denied these claims from Bernadette and, through jealousy, could not accept that such a child would be given favor by a religious deity — let alone the mother of the savior Jesus Christ. Though this does seem to be a parallel to the choosing of the disciples, perhaps even paradoxical, one might conclude.

The Children of Fatima

Perhaps the most influential of all visionaries who utilized the gifts of mediumship were the children of Fatima. Further study would conclude that prophecies from Fatima are proven in our modern times, due to the events that have happened since. However, one would say that the visions could be made to fit but the symbolism itself is irrefutable and at certain junctures in time cannot be placed elsewhere – only where described and interpreted. They have stood the test of time. The three visionaries were young children, Jacinta Marco, Francisco Marco, and Lucia dos Santos. Two of the children passed to spirit in their younger years, yet Lucia still lives to this day, I believe. However, I cannot be entirely sure, as events change in life just as those same changes occur with every tide.

Three secrets were passed from 'Our Lady' to the children, and these secrets were revealed over the years. The first two secrets dealt with clairvoyant visions of Hell (though we know through trance teachings that hell does not exist, and is what we create within the world and in ourselves), war and destruction and the third secret is considered apocalyptic. However, only in recent years has the third secret been revealed by Pope John Paul II and is transmitted in imagery of symbols and visions. We will look at each secret and show the gifts of the spirit within each.

The First Secret

"Our Lady showed us a great sea of fire which seemed to be under the earth. Plunged in this fire were demons and souls in human form. Like transparent burning embers, all blackened or burnished bronze, floating about in the conflagration. Now raised into the air by the flames that issued from within themselves together with great clouds of smoke, now falling back on every side like sparks in a huge fire, without weight or equilibrium, and amid shrieks and groans of pain and despair, which horrified us and made us tremble with fear. The demons could be distinguished by their terrifying and repulsive likeness to frightful and unknown animals, all black and transparent. This vision lasted but an instant. How can we ever be grateful enough to our kind heavenly Mother, who had already prepared us by promising, in the first Apparition, to take us to heaven? Otherwise, I think we would have died of fear and terror."

It is evident that the three children witnessed at the same time, the same vision, and that vision above came clearly in clairvoyant imagery of an objective nature. Though the vision was terrifying, it gave evidence of a lower astral realm of spirit, which may be understood as hell, and what may be interesting is that Mother Mary did not label or tell the children what they were seeing. That is not to say that hell is real or fake. The children would have recognized the image due to their own teachings in a country steeped in Catholicism. Even so, we must also assume the vision had a deeper meaning, perhaps a correlation to suffering and despair with a soupcon of hope. Therefore, Mary would show, by symbolism, the images that appertained to their belief system, or indeed, that had depth to the symbolic meaning to be identified at a later juncture in time.

Mediumship symbolism is given according to your understanding, which allows you to decipher the message. The paradox is thus: there exists a place where the souls of the tormented dwell -- not necessarily a hell -- known as the lower astral planes. It is important to note that no one is damned for everyone has the will to turn to the light, and the light within can never extinguish.

We judge only ourselves by our actions and intentions from a soul point of view. Credence is also given to the fact that demonic entities are real and exist in some form or another but are under the control of God, as I have mentioned before. They do not roam around looking for unaware individuals - after all. God and Michael cast them from the higher realms of heaven. Nevertheless, a serious word of caution: if you dabble or are involved in some form of black magic or even in their domain, you are unfortunately an open target because you are willingly inviting through your intention and that is all that is needed, more about that later on. You also create your own hell within, and this is by your own will and thoughts.

An interesting point to note, is that Lucia maintains that had 'Our Lady' not previously have promised that they would go to heaven, their fear would have consumed them further. This also suggests that 'Our Lady' was in direct communication with the children through the gift of clairaudient Mediumship. In addition, it is suggested that the children heard the pain and suffering of the lost souls, and this was heard clearly, again giving further support to Mediumship of a clairaudient nature.

The Second Secret

"You have seen hell where the souls of poor sinners go. To save them, God wishes to establish in the world devotion to my Immaculate Heart. If what I say to you is done, many souls will be saved and there will be peace. The war is going to end: but if people do not cease offending God, a worse one will break out during the Pontificate of Pius XI. When you see a night illumined by an unknown light, know that this is the great sign given you by God that he is about to punish the world for its crimes, by means of war, famine, and persecutions of the Church and of the Holy Father. To prevent this, I shall come to ask for the consecration of Russia to my Immaculate Heart; and the Communion of reparation on the First Saturdays. If my requests are heeded, Russia will be converted, and there will be peace; if not, she will spread her errors throughout the world, causing wars and persecutions of the Church. The good will be martyred; the Holy Father will have much to suffer; various nations will be annihilated. In the end, my Immaculate Heart will triumph. The Holy Father will consecrate Russia to me, and she shall be converted, and a period of peace will be granted to the world." (Marie, 1917)

This secret is perhaps the most prophetic, but within the words are hidden proofs of the gifts of the spirit and the spiritual lessons for the world. We have seen that the children displayed the gifts of the spirit, just as Jesus did. Within the visions are hidden meanings, and perhaps one of the original codes of universal truths. The opening two sentences suggest much more about destiny and truth:

"You have seen hell where the souls of poor sinners go. To save them, God wishes to establish in the world devotion to my Immaculate Heart. If what I say to you is done, many souls will be saved, and there will be peace."

The first sentence intimates the path of those who turn away from God and the second suggests that your path in life is not a

DEADLY DEPARTED | 63

written law, as some would think, and that even from the fires of hell or the lower astral – souls will be saved. Mary at this point tells the girls this is Hell, but as I believe, only from their own understanding; for instance, if they considered the word cloud to be of the same consciousness, then that word would have been the understanding of the lower realms of the world of spirit. This perhaps will upset many theologians, and the words of 'Our Lady,' *"To save them, God wishes to establish in the world, devotion to my Immaculate Heart."* This is proof from the very words of our Immaculate Mother, that your destiny is not written; that free will is there, to be as one with God or turn from God. It also gives proof that God is not a God of destruction as depicted in the Old Testament but rather one who shows compassion and forgiveness through the opportunity to save souls from the clutches of darkness and man's created Evil.

Therefore, what is the Immaculate Heart? It is the essence of divinity, for Mary had to become as Jesus and God-like in every way, reaching a state of enlightenment that was one with the divine essence. The goal of every spiritual individual is to accept this as a truth and a destiny of everyone, no matter creed or dogmatic belief.

"If what I say to you is done, many souls will be saved, and there will be peace." Again, this part of the statement suggests that we have the free will to choose what is right and wrong for ourselves. Our Lady clearly gives us the choice to accept her offer or not. However, at the end of the secret, she tells us that inevitably there will be a state of peace after the intercession of God and the Holy Mother. How long must we destroy ourselves before that intercession? This is recognition of our weakness and of our divine right. The awareness of the duality of our human nature, for one is physical and the other is divine, yet the veil that separates is very thin indeed and one cannot survive without our innate divinity and birthright. Is this perhaps the

main weapon against all that is evil? It is this awareness that we call upon when needed.

> *"The war is going to end: but if people do not cease offending God, a worse one will break out during the Pontificate of Pius XI. When you see a night illumined by an unknown light, know that this is the great sign given you by God that he is about to punish the world for its crimes, by means of war, famine, and persecutions of the Church and of the Holy Father (Family, n.d.)"*

This statement from Our Lady is a clear prophecy that was transmitted to the Fatima seers/Mediums, and this prophecy happened. Interestingly, she declares the First World War was about to end, and yet another, more volatile war would take place if humanity did not awake to the path it was on, a path, which was undeniably different to one that would lead to divinity. In the next part of the secret, God shows himself as a being to be feared and prophesizes the Second World War. The lights in the sky are akin to the bombings in London, which of course is transmitted through the aforementioned symbolism. This act was apparently in response to the denial of the acceptance of the righteous, and God himself punishes humanity for its misgivings. Surely, God will not punish us, and the wars that escalate are brought on by humanity itself; man's inhumanity to man and the innate need for power and control is the cause. Conversely, Lucia may have misinterpreted this part of the prophecy. With the case of Mediumship in question, clearly the medium has to be able to interpret the messages as they see them and hear them, and perhaps some of the message would have been misinterpreted. In contrast, the essence of the message was not misrepresented.

Offending God, what does that mean? Well, as we are all a divine spark of God and his divinity, we are offending ourselves, and we are the only ones that judge ourselves, for our God is not one who will judge. This is alluded to in the trance teachings of Silver Birch, who was the Native American guide who spoke through the medium Maurice Barbanel.

The Third Secret

"I write in obedience to you, my God, who commands me to do so through his Excellency the Bishop of Leiria and through your Most Holy Mother and mine. After the two parts which I have already explained. At the left of Our Lady and a little above, we saw an Angel with a flaming sword in his left hand; flashing, it gave out flames that looked as though they would set the world on fire. However, they died out in contact with the splendor that Our Lady radiated towards him from her right hand. Pointing to the earth with his right hand, the Angel cried out in a loud voice: 'Penance, Penance, Penance!' And we saw in an immense light that is God: 'something similar to how people appear in a mirror when they pass in front of it' a Bishop dressed in White 'we had the impression that it was the Holy Father'. Other Bishops, Priests, men and women Religious going up a steep mountain, at the top of which there was a big Cross of rough-hewn trunks as of a cork-tree with the bark; before reaching there the Holy Father passed through a big city half in ruins and half trembling with halting step. Afflicted with pain and sorrow, he prayed for the souls of the corpses he met on his way. Having reached the top of the mountain, on his knees at the foot of the big Cross he was killed by a group of soldiers who fired bullets and arrows at him, and in the same way there died one after another the other Bishops, Priests, men and women Religious, and various lay people of different ranks and positions. Beneath the two arms of the Cross there were two Angels each with a crystal aspersorium in his hand, in which they gathered up the blood of the Martyrs and with it sprinkled the souls that were making their way to God." (Family, n.d.)

Pope John Paul II revealed this secret in the year 2000, even though Lucia had admitted that the secret could have been revealed earlier, and was refused by the pontificate. The third secret lay at the heart of controversy throughout the world and with the church, and many thought that the third secret revealed the revelation of the third world war. Possibly even the end of the world.

It is evident from studying the direct transmission. The Mediumship in this instance was symbolical, and the real meaning will only be revealed to those that would understand the symbolism. Of course, within the third secret was another prophecy that came to pass, which was the assassination attempt on Pope John Paul II, and as some others suggest, the assassination of Bishop Oscar Romero of San Salvador, who was gunned down as he said mass. One important point that you should all think about is the Mediumship of the first two secrets, which literally were translated word for word as our Lady spoke it. The third secret is clairvoyance and symbolism only, and at no time on the published literature is there any evidence of Our Lady speaking or being heard through the Mediumship of Lucia. Could this suggest then that another part of the third secret is not revealed yet nor will it ever be? This perhaps suggests that something more sinister may be withheld from the people of the world.

Misinterpretation

I have mentioned this in passing before, but you must all think about this and contemplate this truth. Each Mediumship message is delivered in many ways utilizing the gifts of spirit, and each Medium's gifts are stronger in one area more than the other. Nevertheless, the importance of the medium's ability to discern can mean the difference between failure and success. The most important facet of this is that of the ability to interpret the message correctly.

As a medium myself, I know very well the pitfalls in being able to transmit information to the individual when you receive the message in a multitude of ways. As you may hear or see it in symbolic form, or just words, it is rather like a jigsaw puzzle that you must put together to make sense of the meaning of the message in its entirety. None of us has any scientific evidence of how the messages at Fatima were transmitted, and we must all have a certain amount of faith in the medium.

Therefore, it is of fundamental importance that we do not take a translation as a literal meaning or truth, when, in reality, the essence would become more important than the message itself. This is true for all Mediumship messages and all transmissions from the heavenly realm; all are open to interpretation and, in contrast – manipulation.

There are many truths and many paths, and one symbol could mean something completely different, but the symbol has to be given according to the medium's belief and understanding. Perhaps if those seers had been of a Buddhist origin or Shamanistic, would the secrets have been passed using completely different symbolism? It is important to note that one path is not the only path to enlightenment, and there are many to choose.

Look at the world today and you will reveal to yourself the mysteries of Fatima that are happening. We have disregarded the message of the Holy Mother, and humanity is making great strides towards its own destruction. Perhaps the greatest change in consciousness is to come, and as we wait for the next shift, we can perceive new spiritual sciences that are contributing to the understanding of our true nature. With this free will level of destruction, we have built a new playing field – Evil is on one side, and we are on the other. It is our choice to release our spiritual authority in order to deal with the fight quickly and fearlessly. Our weapons of choice are our innate gifts and spiritual union with the divine.

PART 3:

"DON'T" Underestimate the Need for Protection

U nderstanding the nature of evil and your inner power - given to you by the Divine – is the first step in learning the Gift of Discernment. This is not anything that your psychic development teacher or I can teach you. This is a process and a quest that you must partake in yourself. The way you live your life, your spiritual growth, and your level of compassion and forgiveness is what will open your awareness and Gift of Discernment. It is not just the ability to ascertain that you are dealing with something negative or good; it is a yardstick in your spiritual development. Many mediums think they have the ability to discern, and I have known of some, who - thinking they understood - caused their own issues and imbalances to be exacerbated.

So, discernment is a heightened awareness of the power of the soul, of becoming aware of movements in emotions, thoughts, imagination, clairvoyance, clairsentience and clairaudience at its highest expression; a knowing coming direct from the holy spirit. It is recognizing desire and need - being aware of attractions, and what repulses you, an awareness of the state of your aura and the sensitivities surrounding you. All of these create awareness of the outcome and of the direction. You travel in duality – of the soul and the physical self. Amalgamation of all these forces into one, as symbolically similar to a trinity, is the power of discernment. This, of course, is not something you can learn on a course and is not something that can be taught - it has to be found from within, the other aspect of course is that it is given with love from the great spirit when one is ready. One who says they understand discernment or knows discernment – knows nothing of discernment.

You, as a developing or professional medium, have a duty to the divine to serve at the highest level, and this means putting in the required work needed to reach this stage of enlightenment. Face it - you will be a target. The way you live, and try to act in accordance with the will of the divine, could be the fine line that you walk between the two realms. You may never come across anything of a negative disposition, or at worst – very evil -- and you may be content with carrying out other mediumistic duties. You must accept that, however small a chance there may be, you will be called to service, and you should be ready, for if one day you are fighting the war of your life. You may as well fight from a place of advantage instead of disadvantage.

CHAPTER 4:

Dealing with the Nature of Evil

So we have now touched on the nature of evil and what it really means including its discernment, though I understand this is from a Christian point of view, and which is a very simple principle of polar opposition. It would be prudent to examine the same nature in other religious writings, and one would be able to draw the conclusion that there are similar parallels and contrasts. Furthermore; we must also accept that God (also known as the Great Spirit), who created everything, also created this evil. This is of course for a higher purpose. Nothing can happen that God won't allow, and those who deny him, stand against him and are easy pickings for evil spirits.

It would be wrong to assume that the Catholic Church is the only one sufficiently capable of dealing with evil. In every religion, are those who are adequately armed for this battle, and of course many mediums are also called to this service, either by default or by the church, but always guided by the Great Spirit. Remember that you as a medium, if called to this service by the Great Spirit, will be made a target. It would seem prudent to prepare yourself for this and acquaint yourself with procedures and rituals that will help. I do not mean that you should remember and know how to carry out the Rituale Rominum (Catholic Right Of Exorcism)- this is best left to clergy who have studied and practiced this. The greatest power you have at your disposal is to assert your innate spiritual authority that is your direct divinity and power over all.

It is probable that when you begin to develop your spiritual gifts, or if you are already a seasoned professional, you will at some point come across something of a negative nature. As I have said, your best weapon is the recognition of your reality, though the chink in your armor can be a weakened mind, for this is giving an opening through which an evil entity can launch an attack. I have spoken about living as clean a life as possible by remaining in balance and keeping your mind strong. I will investigate this in more depth, but for now. I would like to discuss a little about exorcism rituals.

CHAPTER 5

Exorcisms

The truth is that exorcisms are not driving out evil, but commanding the entities under spiritual authority and binding them into oath. You must remember that even all evil is controlled by divine law, and fears the divine authority, which is God or The Great Spirit. I am not going to go into the ins and outs of the Rituale Rominum as I am neither ordained in the Catholic Church, nor suitably qualified to question its authority and validity. However, it works, and I have studied the ritual. The one conclusion that I have reached is that it involves calling on spiritual power, which is innate to everyone, but a deep understanding of the spirit is necessary. Have a look at this yourself and see beyond the words. There are many ways to carry out an exorcism and one must not be tunnel-visioned into thinking that the rite of exorcism as compiled and taught by the Catholic Church is the only way, though it is a very powerful way. There are many ways in all spiritual paths, yet the basis of these is the fact that one who is chosen to deal with this evil must be adequately prepared. Don't think you can just run into a blazing fire and put it out because you have a little knowledge and a fire extinguisher.

I make it a priority that if ever I am asked to deal with something of a negative nature, including menial investigations into what I know are merely grounded entities. I will take some time to prepare myself - this is a prerequisite for all mediums. There are many who would dive into the murky waters of the psyche, only to find themselves out of depth and in torrential currents. One of the ways in which one must prepare, is to meditate regularly with the intent on strengthening your spiritual power through calling on your divine authority. This is not, by nature an easy form of meditative practice. By this, I do not mean chatting or communication with guides and other entities; I am talking about going within and connecting with the God-Self – the essence of your soul, if you like. A period of abstinence is necessary in order that you are not affected physically by anything, which may be there, and ensures that you do not ingest any negative energy. When I feel sufficiently energized, then I call upon my guides and Michael to aid me by releasing the spiritual power I need to deal with the situation. If it is a grounded spirit, I will call upon my guides and angels to help me communicate and offer solace and safety to the entity. If it is something more sinister, then I have other modus operandi and leave much of the work to my main spirit consort.

I will then prepare certain tools of the trade that I would use, which I know is merely that act of increasing the power of the intent by employing the action of using the tools; the tools are useless without the authority. When one is adequately spiritually in marriage with the divine, there is no need for these tools whatsoever. I will use virgin olive oil, sea salt, a crucifix, holy water, a Benedictine medal and the Rosary of Our Lady. Some of you may laugh, but when you know of the realities, you will want to 'be prepared' as the old boy scouts would say. I have only had to do this a couple of times, and I am glad of it, for if anything is out of my ability or beyond me, I will gladly hand it over. Over the years, I have relied less and less on tools as the important aspect is the reality of your spiritual authority and power of your inner divinity.

Before you go around chanting rites and commanding by the name of Jesus, you need to have a deep understanding of what you are doing. I will take each of these tools and explain them, according to my own understanding.

VIRGIN OLIVE OIL: The use of the oil dates back to the time of Christ when he allowed a prostitute to anoint his feet. He was accepting of this woman and saw no evil in her as others had seen or believed they had seen. Allowing her to anoint the feet showed his messiahship, power of forgiveness and of course spiritual authority. The olive oil is blessed and the prayer of exorcism is said over this. I would then sprinkle the oil around all entrances to the home and use the tip of my finger dipped in the oil to make the sign of the cross on all doors and windows. To my mind, this ensures the intention and direction of the spiritual power is incredibly strong. This of course is similar in all religious or spiritual practices.

SEA SALT: By its very nature, it attracts moisture. No one really knows how or why it works, but my thoughts are that as spirit requires an environment with moisture in which to conduct itself, it would seem probable that denying it such conditions would aid in the carrying out of the ritual. In ancient times, salt was thought of to be purifying and this is another reason why it is hated by evil entities so much. Sprinkle the salt in the home and around doorways and entrances.

THE CRUCIFIX: This is a symbol of Christ's passing and again of his power over all natural law by rising again, showing that he could not be destroyed, and would be triumphant over all evil that would seek to destroy man's nature. Use a crucifix in the area you are cleansing and on the person who may be affected.

HOLY WATER: Holy water can be made by anyone, and asking with the correct intent for a divine blessing is all that is needed. The secret, however, is in how it is done; and also sea salt that is added to purify the water. Sprinkle the water on clothes, and around the home. Throughout, remember it is all intent.

THE HOLY ROSARY: Our Lady, who appeared to many individuals throughout the world, has always maintained the rosary is a powerful weapon against evil. This is epitomized in the following statement:

> *Concerning the Holy Rosary, once while the priest placed a rosary around the neck of the person who was being exorcised, all of a sudden the demon began crying out, "It is crushing me, it weighs on me, and it is crushing me, this chain with the Cross on the end of it." The exorcist exclaimed, "From this day forward this sister of ours will pray the Rosary every day."*

> *Immediately the demon replied, "But you are so few who say it (the Rosary), compared to the whole world! It is just as well for me that it should be so, because it (the Rosary) harms me. You invoke That One (referring to our Lady), you make me remember the life of That One." (Referring to the life of Jesus meditated in the mysteries of the Rosary).*

> *Another day, while exorcising the demon, the exorcist pulled a rosary out of his pocket; immediately the demon cried out: "Take away that chain, take away that chain!" "What chain?" "The one with the Cross on the end. She whips us with that chain." This, of course is metaphorical language; it makes us understand, all the same, in very concrete terms, the power of the Rosary and how much the devil fears it. -- Translated from (Bamonte, 2006)*

THE BENEDICTINE MEDAL: I wear this medal every day more or less. St Benedict was particularly adept and known for casting out demons. The medal itself has the rite of exorcism on the back of it and is used and noted throughout the world for its power against evil.

What all of these tools do is foster and cement the devotion and relationship we have to God. It makes us aware of our own powerful spiritual authority and gives us nudges to apply it in our lives. The rosary not only solidifies our devotion and relationship, but also teaches us the value of a meditative practice, aligning the mind and body with divinity from within. It is also important to note that the intention is the fundamental part of the recipe, which gives not only the act of tasting, but also the essence of its flavor. Catholicism does not have all the answers, and even messages that are passed by medium-to-medium and then to the people are distilled; therefore, it is important to look deeper into the very nature of the message and see the essence. You do not have to be Catholic to utilize the rosary, for Mary (Mother of Christ) does not judge, and will not judge who should devote to her intercession and thus the Christ consciousness. Furthermore, remember that if the individual reacts violently to any of the religious artifacts or rituals, you can be sure that you are about to deal with an entity not of this world, and I would advise you to call in the professionals.

Now Pray

Now it is important to pray and call upon your innate spiritual authority. You can use your own incantation or utilize approved prayers of exorcism. If I had to recommend anything, I would use the Rosary and the prayer of invocation to Archangel Michael, which is a powerful exorcism that can be used as a layperson – it can be found in Apendix A at the end of this book. Your prayer must come from the heart, and you must fully believe in the power of what you say.

I am going to give you the keys to learning how to spiritually protect yourself from the unseen. No matter what you do in life, you should always take certain precautions to ensure that you do not fall foul to other people's mistakes or your own decisions. If you go out in terrible weather, you would ultimately take the right precautions, and choose the appropriate attire to protect you. This is what I am going to teach you now, for you are on the ship in a torrent, and I am giving you a spiritual compass to guide you through the dark waters.

Like everything in life, there are negative and positive sides to all, and as I discussed previously, there is a need for balance in every part of your life. Spiritual teachers would have you believe there are no demons or negative spirits, and there are no real dangers to development apart from the obvious imbalance within your energy field. My hypothesis is that these teachers fear this, and that forcing them to believe that it does not exist is tantamount to a false sense of spiritual safety and of truth.

Ignorance is no protection. There have been many cases where individuals have succumbed to the control of negative spiritual influences. Havoc has resumed not only in their lives but in others', too. Many mediums and psychics that go to help someone deal with a potential problem can cause a more severe problem to manifest through their own ignorance and lack of understanding. Perhaps the murderer who carries out the odious act after hearing voices; can it be a brain imbalance with scientific explanation – perhaps? However, another theory may be that the individual was influenced spiritually; therefore, it is not the human that has committed the crime, but is the negative spirit, which remains attached.

I will not deal here with statistics and medical theory about assumed hypothesis on psychosis, depression, and schizophrenia. That is well-covered elsewhere.

Developing your psychic gifts is a wonderful experience but it also automatically puts you in danger, and the chances of coming across different aspects of the netherworlds are very high indeed. Allow me to take you back to a blockbuster movie and one of the most famous fantasy novels ever written – Lord of the Rings by JR Tolkien. You will remember from this that Mr. Frodo (the main character) had come across a ring that was fashioned by mystical leaders using magic and wizardry. When Frodo would put on the ring, he would break the veil between the two worlds and would find himself in a dangerous position whereby he could be seen by the evil creatures in the netherworld. He would have disappeared from the material plane making him a target. This is perhaps a good correlation to the reality of what potential dangers you may find yourself in while developing your psychic gifts. In following chapters, we will look at this in far greater detail, as well as teaching you how to develop safely.

CHAPTER 6

Protecting Yourself When Opening Up

I cannot stress the importance of learning to protect oneself from an outside influence, especially when you open yourself up to spiritual energies. In my mind, this should be the first law of Mediumship. My life has always revolved around the elements of protection, and in my younger days, I worked on security details for business executives, the wealthy and famous, and diplomats from other countries. However, I was spiritually asleep myself at the time, I believe. After many years of making my own mistakes (missed opportunities) and learning from each one, I teach people how to protect their mind, body and soul through my study of the afterlife and Spirituality. Furthermore, now that I am more progressed along my spiritual path, I am teaching them how to protect their souls from the unseen. This is my journey and the reason I had to experience the physical before awakening the spiritual.

Now we are going to look at the methods of protecting yourself and how, just by using your intent, you will be able to do this. This is an incredibly important discipline to employ in your life, and it certainly will not hurt to do it regularly. It is easy and does not involve weird rituals. A clear mind and intent are the main tools that you require, with a large dollop of belief, faith and understanding, and that is it.

A point to note for all you professionals out there who think you may know it all. Did you know that the method of infestation and obsession is not through your aura but through a weakened chakra, where the catalyst can be a weak mind? The aura is just a point of attraction and attachment for feeding reasons if you will, but a weakened chakra is the point of entry, especially at the solar plexus. Edgar Cayce (the sleeping prophet) was once asked why, when he lay on his couch, did he cross his hands over his solar plexus? And the above was the reason he gave. He made it known this was the most likely point of entry for a negative entity.

I am often asked, "What are the keys to psychic protection? What are the secrets?" Normally when I am asked this question, I smile and reply, *"It is the reality of your nature and the amalgamation of mind, body, and soul as one spiritual force."* Then I am usually asked how we can achieve this, and for me, I have found it in the way of the spiritual warrior and through years of dedication, study and service. A word of warning, spiritual warfare is not for everyone and it's not another Gucci handbag syndrome, it can be a greivous and dangerous task to take. Many who do this, often come to a point where safety means more than anything else and they will retire and stop.

CHAPTER 7:

The Way

There are many ways to achieve enlightenment in life, and there are many ways that we can adjoin the facets of our spiritual reality as one unit. All too often, in this life, individuals wander like lost souls trying to develop one facet above another, and refusing to recognize the spirituality within them. Anyone who is weak in the mind is called crazy and normally sectioned in a psychiatric unit, yet the truth, my friends, is that many of you are weak in mind and refuse to see the very nature of your own reality for you are divine in nature and have all the power of the universe at your finger tips.

If you fail to recognize your innate divinity you open yourself to the evil that pervades the world. How can you judge what is wrong, when you are on the point of the fulcrum yourself? Moreover, to you mediums that think you are balanced. You may be playing poker with the devil, and you have the losing hand if one part of you is weaker. This is why you attract to you all those things that you call negative experiences.

Complaining that nothing goes right in your life and falling into the trap of a five-sensory existence weakens your mind and your resolve of your inner potential. You cannot develop as a psychic or medium without having to face your fears and exposing your weaknesses, in order to develop to your full spiritual potential. Living in an airy-fairy existence removes you from reality, and does not afford you instant protective wings.

Sooner or later you will have to face up to your trials. This is why you are navigating your awareness from the moment that you decided to read this book, you hold in your hands the keys to the innate power that you hold within yourself.

Therefore, many must find a way to understand the secrets of nature and their place in the universe. As an example, I would like to offer you my own experience, in order that you will be able to make comparisons to your own particular way. You might find this in hill walking, mountaineering, or achieving something through joining your mind and body as one. For me, it was the study of traditional Budo - not a way of combat, but the way of becoming a warrior in mind, body, and soul. Allow me to explain what I mean.

We all have the desire to protect what we have or what we achieve, normally by extending the material security that enhances our material existence. However, what of protecting the very nature of who we are – spirit in a human form? What of learning to protect our soul from the discordance of negativity and possible evil in the material realm operating under a cloak of spirituality? It does not follow that we should put our faith in trinkets and such like. We should recognize the spiritual authority we have within us, tools are mere focus. Knowledge does not give wisdom, and wisdom alone cannot protect you on all levels. Our mind, body, and soul must be one. We must not consider these as three separate aspects of our reality, but instead bring all together in one unit. This of course is the secret of psychic protection.

By studying other avenues that allow you to disassociate from the material realm, that short space in time allows you to bring these three aspects together as one unit, while concentrating on the task. Therefore, for me the study of the martial way is disciplining the mind and body to draw closer to the unity of the soul. This, of course, can be experienced through expressing this unity in other ways, such as outdoor pursuits, or hobbies that require similar discipline to a meditative principle. Aligning these meditative aspects draws the three together to work as one unit, and this is the basis of the protection of the self on all levels, and I find the study of Budo to have all the elements of a perfect recipe to achieve this goal. I also find the study of landscape photography or taking part in such pursuits and hobbies blends the three aspects as one. There will always be a pursuit suitable to everyone. Success is therefore inevitable.

Success is measured in the positive changes that you see in your life - your heightened awareness and understanding of the truth of nature. Your mind and body are strong, and therefore, you are only one step away from releasing the spiritual power and intent that will ensure your safety. No matter how many crystals or amulets you wear, a weak disposition makes you an easy target. When your mind is strong, your intention and belief becomes immovable; this is why it is said *"faith can move mountains."* A strong disposition, belief, and intent are the required elements to ensure the success of your psychic protective practices.

CHAPTER 8:

Mind Control

A s I have maintained, a strong mind is the basis of your protection, it is so easy to fall into the trap of being obsessed by a spirit or attacking yourself and causing much distress. I want to discuss this aspect of attacking yourself, as this is more prevalent than you would imagine – especially when you are developing as a medium or psychic. As mediums or psychics, you will be prone to negative thinking, and as you develop, your ego will question that which you are trying to achieve, and you will find yourself thinking the darkest of thoughts. I have thought negative things, especially if I am dealing with something of a dark disposition, and I know that many of you reading this will have too. I have woken up thinking that I had contracted myself to be evil because of the thoughts I was having, and have scared myself half to death. I have had others, such as developing students and professional mediums, experience the same and ask me for help. I am here now to put your minds at rest and to draw that peace that seems so elusive closer to you.

Many have stopped service to spirit due to their fear. I have a little comfort for you, my friends, please realize these thoughts come from the ego self and not the true self. It is your own fears becoming exacerbated in a manifestation of discursive thoughts, which terrify you or cause you distress. These are illusionary and cannot harm you, though they may provoke unease and discomfort. You are not evil, and the real you harbors a strong innate spirituality that cannot be destroyed – how much of an amazing comfort is that? You just have to have this realization, and you will find the thoughts will become less and less each time as you become the master of your mind. You are training your subconscious rather than allowing your conscious thoughts to be captain of your ship.

Some of you will also have the same thoughts recurring all the time, and the fact this obsessive thought is happening is your feeding it with your own fear. Thich Nhat Hanh maintains the first step to transmuting anything is awareness, and so to awaken this awareness puts you in control once more. When you understand this strength of mind, and you are able to control your thoughts, your protective practices, rituals, meditations, and visualizations will be impenetrable to anything of an evil disposition.

CHAPTER 9

Psychic Attack

B efore we learn to cleanse our areas and cleanse the aura, we need to understand what a psychic attack is. I have already discussed how a negative energy or an entity may try to affect your aura, gain entry through a weakened chakra or influence your mind, but there are many other forms of psychic attack. An attack can leave you open to a plethora of problems on all levels of mind, body and spirit. It can be the cause of physical attack, rape, violence, and even terrorism of a sort.

So what is a psychic attack? A psychic attack can be described as a negative thought, which may be compulsive -- an urge or compulsion that is not in keeping with the natural nature of the individual – it is not you. The cause is normally telepathic in nature, or an emotional signal within the aura, or coming from the mind of another entity. It can be a suffocation of negative energy on the individual at all levels. The more a person suc-cumbs to a psychic influence, the stronger the influence will be as it gains strength. As it gathers momentum, it gets stronger, faster, and more ferocious. A negative spirit can focus this en-ergy upon you.

A person who is angry, and exuding that emotion, can cause a psychic attack without consciously knowing that they are doing it or being aware of the effects it may have on an individual. Violent encounters and other forms of criminality can then ensue.

There can, of course, be deliberate negative attacks, and these would be encompassed under the umbrella of negative voodoo and other curses, or perhaps black witchcraft or satanic practices. Be aware! It is the intention behind these emotions that cause the spell or curse to manifest – not the actual carrying out of the pomp and circumstance of such a spell. In most cases of a precipitated intentional attack, a negative entity will be attracted to the evil intent. Psychic attacks can be short-term with effects that cause psychological damage, or long-term that can destroy the person's life. The attack can go beyond more than one person; it can affect a genealogic line or group. The stronger a negative influence becomes, the more of an effect it can have on the family unit or environmental conditions.

Case 7: A Curse Removed

A woman brought her husband to see us, worried because he was displaying behavior that was out of keeping with his normal behavioral patterns. He had become increasingly aggressive, involved in altercations at his work-place, very tired and having problems with his wife.

A skeptical man, he expected the fortune-teller stereotype - when he arrived, he was very disappointed on that. Imagine his relief when he realized I was a man's man dressed in combat bottoms, a vest top and displaying my two tattoos – not the sort of person he thought he would meet - and he agreed to try anything that would help him.

His father came through immediately from the spirit world and told us that he had had a bad run-in with a man in Africa, who used a hex on him, which is a sort of spell conjured through the elements of witchcraft and dark magic. The *intention behind the hex is all that is needed to affect the energy of the individual, and so my client was suffering from a severe form of psychic attack.*

We managed to identify the negative energy that surrounded him and the curse that caused the problems. We asked angels and guides to join us and help his spirit to remove the hex. This was done using prayer, intention, and belief that the divine powers would remove the curse for his highest good. After the session, he claimed that he felt as if an amazing problem had been lifted from him. We balanced his chakras and taught him how to strengthen his protection by cleansing these areas of energy.

CHAPTER 10

The Chakras

This leads me on to discuss our chakras as I mentioned previously, which are the psychic vortices that run from the top of the auric field at various points through the physical body. These energy vortices are different in color, and correlate to a particular frequency that is suitable to the auric field and its essential layers. These are the energy areas that you need to be concerned about and learn to cleanse and protect. There is a mnemonic, which will help you to remember the set up of these chakras. Chakra is a Sanskrit word that means *spinning wheel*. The mnemonic is:

'Richard Of York Gave Battle In Vain.'

This represents each color of the chakra:

Red (base chakra),

Orange (sacral plexus chakra),

Yellow (solar plexus chakra),

Green (heart chakra),

Blue (throat chakra),

Indigo (third eye chakra) and

Violet (crown chakra).

I will not explain each chakra or what the imbalances are, because this is available in thousands of other books. If I did, I would digress from the truth behind this work.

Vibrations of Chakras

Each chakra has a different frequency of vibration, symbol, color, and sound that it is attuned to, and is affected by contrasting vibrations and sounds. When the chakra is balanced, clear and energized, it would be in tune and play the most wonderful vibrational tune of its own, emitting the proper vibration for that chakra. This is parallel to the vibrancy and color of the chakra. Have you ever wondered why, when hearing a particularly emotional piece of music, you get the shivers and the hairs stand on end? – It is the dance of the chakra.

Each chakra needs to be able to function at the correct frequency and independently of the others. Each needs balance, to be clear, energized, and properly spinning; if not, they are out of balance and cause various problems. Each time all the chakras spin and reach a level of unison, the entire physical vibration of the human body is raised, and a spiritual connection can be made. This is what we mean when we raise our vibration with meditative practice and intention.

There are many other issues connected to the chakras. The aura and chakras are of course the gateways to the other worlds and hold the sum total of everything you have ever done in deed, emotion and speech. It is evident that from the many readings I have done, the colors and the energy associated with these psychic centers come up repeatedly as the imbalances show within these energy fields and vortices. It is important to recognize that these will not be appropriate to everyone and one must use intuitive feelings to separate the meaning and imbalance associated with the individual and the chakra. This can be an accurate method of reading someone before delving into the other aspects of intuitive readings and indeed healings.

CHAPTER 11:

Strengthen Your Aura and Cleanse Your Area

There are many ways to ensure that your aura remains strong and impenetrable from outside forces. These range from crystals, meditation and connecting with nature or invoking high vibrational spirit beings to help. Use your natural ability to commune with spirit; after all, you are spirit having a human experience, and you have this power at your disposal. You can invoke the help of the universe to strengthen your aura and cleanse or bless your own homes. Remember tools only help focus, the real spiritual authority is the power.

I am a great believer in simplicity. There is no need to sit around humming or waving feathers in the air or holding hands and chanting.

Case 8: Ground Yourself

I went on an angel course once, and to be honest, it was more like an AA (Alcoholics Anonymous) meeting. Individuals on the course were in need of a lesson in balance of life and reality.

These people claim they are on some mission to change the mass consciousness of the world and do not know they are alive themselves in the present moment.

The teacher looked like a throwback from hippie days and spent more time dancing and listening to problems than teaching a course on angels, which included spells, incantations, and waving around feathers. The students were no more grounded than a flock of geese. One participant got up in the middle of a meditation and walked out of the house crying. When he came back, he said that my energy was overpowering him. This person had endured suffering in the past, though in essence, we all have our crosses to bear but there is a line that we should draw, and have a boundary – a cry for help is just that, a cry for help. It is important to remain grounded while developing your gifts. Living too much in your head can cause you to miss information and vital signs from the universe.

So how do you cleanse your aura or an area? There are a number of primary methods that I will support here, and with each method, I will try to teach you the easiest way to use it. Remember: **the stronger the energy surrounding you, the stronger you will be in securing your environment** – helping you to heighten your awareness, to protect all that you have in mind, body, and spirit.

CHAPTER 12

Intention, and Believe to Conceive

I believe these are the first two fundamental keys to life and success and to strengthening your energy centers. I have been in many tight spaces in my life, and the belief I hold within my heart has kept me safe in the face of danger, and warned me of events that may harm me. It brought me the most wonderful things in life – one being my wife. By believing in my abilities and myself, I have to realize that my belief will come into my awareness in physical form. If I believe that I am strong and impenetrable to harm, then inevitably I complete that cycle by conceiving the belief and making it real.

Secondly, I have to work within my own intent – my will to make it happen. Everything you do in life is done with intention. If I have intent on something, then that intent will happen no matter what. Good or bad, the universe will respond to my intention and cause the intent to manifest. This is also why individuals who dabble in the occult without knowing the power of intention, can inevitably co-create their own hell on earth. Moreover, this is tantamount to creating a gateway where evil entities may enter.

Believe in Your Spirit

One important facet that we all need, is that of belief. No matter what we believe in, whether it be a powerful external guiding force or just your inner voice, belief is something we all need, an emotion to allow success in all our endeavors. It is an energy that helps forge our bond with our environment, and the place you are in within the universe at this moment in time. Belief is also a catalyst to feeling comfort in a time of need, without belief, we would never question and would not strive to make our future better. I implore you all to expand your inner sight and open yourself to a world of belief. This belief has no doctrine, no religion binds it with rules that stunt the growth of human evolution to the point that you cannot explore the universe for yourself; belief that is all-knowing, all-forgiving energy which is unconditional, no matter of creed or color. Knowing that everything is impermanent (it's not a permanent state that we do not die and forever evolve) and believing in this, creates within the belief its own protection, for impermanence means no destruction and no barriers, the spirit is free and can express itself through any energy or medium.

It's not enough that you learn how to drive a car or fly a plane, you need to believe in yourself and the knowledge you have learned to enable you to drive safely or fly. If you do not believe that you can fly the plane, no matter how much knowledge you have of it, you will never achieve it. Thus the catalyst for success is belief. Therefore, the catalyst for developing your sixth sense and putting into practice all that I teach within this book is indeed belief. If you believe that you can achieve everything in this book, then you can, and that unfaltering belief in yourself will open you to a world beyond what you only physically percieve with your physical eyes - a world that exists within every individual, a world that exists to protect and serve.

Your belief is borne from your intent. Now here's the paradox, its beyond belief, it is knowing, which is its highest form.

Intention

Allow me to explain what I mean by intention as I have referred to this time and time again, therefore I had better explain it, and it's very simple.

If I am sitting on a chair and I decide to stand up and move into the kitchen, I use my intention. Firstly, my thought is conceived in my mind – the feeling of wanting to move from the chair to the kitchen. I see this visually, and then make the intent manifest to move. This is the same with any intent that you have in your life, day in and day out.

Many years ago, I studied another martial form called Taekwondo. Part of learning this art is learning how to break blocks of wood; the first time I tried, I failed. The instructor recognized that I had not visualized breaking the wood and my intention was not focused on that. After a long lecture and a bit of training on visualization, I took my place and did it again – this time, with success.

You have to have belief in your ability and in yourself. Believe that you can make yourself safe, and you will.

CHAPTER 13:

Meditation for Protection

M editation is by far the easiest way to increase or decrease your aura by your intention only, but a strong mind is important to have awareness and control of what happens in meditative practice. By visualizing and believing in what you are doing, you will succeed in strengthening all levels of your auric field. Visualize yourself inside a bubble of white light. To increase this light, you must breathe in deeply, asking for the universe to cleanse your aura. As you breathe out, use your intention to release any negativity that is within you or surrounds you, and send it back to the universe for transmuting to positive energy. As you breathe out, you will note the white energy filling your aura and making it strong and impenetrable. You must learn to visualize this in picture form and believe in what you see - "to believe is to conceive."

Golden Rays

One of the ways that you can protect yourself is to imagine that you are engulfed in a beautiful golden ray. See it surrounding you and entering every part of your being, imagine that ray going through all your chakras and cleansing them and protecting them with a golden shield. Believe that you have achieved this and know it is done. This is a very quick and easy visualization to do and one that can be employed while going about your everyday business. The importance here is that you see yourself being surrounded in these golden rays, rather like creating pictures with your imagination, and then your intention will do the rest.

The Bodyguards

This is one of my particular favorites, and is an exercise that, although incredibly powerful, is quite fun to do. In this exercise, you will be employing the use of Angelic beings and creating your own team of Bodyguards by request and by your intention. Ask in your mind to be surrounded by the Archangels of the four directions, and visualize four of your favorite angelic presences surrounding you at all four points of the compass, North, South, East, and West. I always ensure that Michael is at the front of me, but you can choose any Angels that you wish. Feel the energy of the angelic presences surrounding you, and note that you will feel a change in the energy if you are using your intent, visualization skills and your inner belief. These angels will now follow you wherever you go and will protect you from any oncoming energy onslaughts.

Mirror Energy Field

Another method that I often employ is to imagine that you have a mirror energy field that follows the contours of your auric field around your body or the perispirit, which I have mentioned before. Know that should anyone unconsciously or deliberately try to drain your life force energy or launch a psychic attack on you, it is reflected out to the universe to be used as positive energy. This works with your visualization and your intent working together, and should be employed the minute you feel you are being drained or the victim of a psychic attack.

Linking

I adopted this exercise from my background in Budo. I know the intention and bringing the forces of nature together as one is enough to repel any energy attack.

The first thing you need to do, when you immediately feel that you are being drained, is to bring your index finger and thumb to interlock in a circle. Then with your fingers extended, you will point them to the heavens. The first linking is the earth, and water (chi, sui), the rest are the elements of fire, wind and the void (ka, fu, ku), which will be pointing upwards to the heavens. This will be the act of sending the energy to a place where it can be transmuted. You must have the full belief and intent that this exercise will work immediately and without question. You should feel an immediate change within your energy field.

Etheric Cords

Building on the etheric elements in order to learn how to harness spiritual power is the understanding of spiritual chords. For those who can clairvoyantly see spirit or auras, you can train your psychic vision to see cords of negativity that may be attached to someone. When someone psychically drains you, or sends out negative emotions to you, they create an etheric cord with that emotional intent. The cord attaches itself to your auric field and then drains any life-force energy from you. That is why you may feel tired and listless just after you have been in the company of someone in emotional need.

Case 9: Cutting the Cords

Here is an amusing little story that happened to my wife and me. Before we were due to marry, a certain individual was doing everything in her power to split us up. She caused as much trouble as possible, and spread as much gossip as possible, she tried to manipulate my wife-to-be. She had been on one of Jo's courses and became a friend, though more of a stalker in the end. She was jealous of my abilities and my love for Jo.

We decided to do a cord-cutting session with her, as we had not heard anything and the gossip had quieted down, and this was the opportunity we needed to cut cords. We took time to meditate and continued with our cord cutting. After the session, we felt an amazing relief and went to make dinner. We had not heard anything for a few months, but only five minutes after the cutting, the phone rang and it was her. She obviously did not want to lose the attachment and tried once more.

You must keep carrying out your exercise regularly to ensure that the individual creating the cords does not re-create them.

CHAPTER 14:

Call on Your Angels

A s a medium I have a strong belief in angels, and their existence in all religions is written in the religious texts of each individual faith. I have a particularly strong relationship with Archangel Michael, and through him, I ask for protection and guidance in my daily life. I always see Michael vividly and he never fails to help. By just asking for help – especially with cutting cords of negativity to anyone or anything, he will respond to you with love and in the name of God. You can ask him to increase the strength in your auric field and to cleanse and repair it wherever it is needed.

Angels can help you on many occasions, though I have a bit of difficulty in believing that I should ask them for a car parking space and such like. I invoke the power of angels in my life privately, and usually when I need them for a protective measure - to guide me in endeavors where I may be a bit lost and for help when I need it. To be honest if you are happy to ask for a car space - then do it. They never judge.

Try this little exercise to increase the level of protection around you. This does not matter where you are and you need not get yourself into a sitting or lotus position. It is a simple case of belief in your visualization that you create within your own consciousness. No matter what scenario you find yourself in, if you feel down or are in need of some extra protection, imagine Archangel Michael standing by your side or in front of you. If you have difficulty with this just say it quietly to yourself. See in your mind's eye, Michael removing his golden sword of truth. Witness this majestic angel encircling you with the sword of truth and creating a beautiful ball of golden energy around you. Know that Michael protects you and that you have nothing to fear. Remain strong in your belief and it will be done. This very quick visualization can be used anywhere and at anytime. It will help you to reduce your fear and you may actually feel the energy of Michael surrounding you.

Case 9: What happened on 'The Hilly Rose Show'

In September 2007, I was asked to be a guest on the Hilly Rose Show in the USA.. The Hilly Rose Show is an American institution and he is famed for having experts in the field of the unknown and the paranormal. However, I do not consider myself an expert – more a student of Universal Love and wisdom.

The subject of the show was about the dark side of the paranormal, and in response to incidents of a negative nature that happened within the USA. The day and the time had been arranged and the talk was going to be about protecting yourself from evil influences.

On the day of the show and before we were due to go on, I had a terrible feeling and my wife had said to me, "Jock, please be careful, something or someone does not want this to happen and you must protect yourself."

I confirmed that I felt the same way, and in that instant the phone rang - it was Hilly saying *that something unusual happened and his equipment had blown.*

He said, "Jock, this is strange but I think someone evil, and you know who I am talking about, does not want this show out there."

We both laughed, but recognized the possibility of what we both experienced. We agreed that we should try to get the interview done, but may have to cancel due to the events. I took some time and prayed to my angels and asked that Michael help us to get this important information out there, then Hilly called back and said that he had gotten hold of some new equipment and that we should get this done soonest. We did and the show was a success, but what a strange set of events.

After you have invoked Michael's help, you will feel an amazing sense of freedom or you will particularly feel an amazing tingling sensation all over your body. This is mainly how I feel Michael, and then I see him clairvoyantly in my mind. Sometimes you will feel a surge of heat rising in your body and of course, there is the highest awareness of all – just knowing that he is there tending to your needs.

CHAPTER 15:

Using Crystals for Protection

Another favorite of mine is using crystals to strengthen or repair your aura. They work exceptionally well in providing positive energy within your home and transmuting negative energy.

I know that some of you will start to think, "Hang on, he's going all New-Age." Let me assure you that I am far from that. Consider the small crystal that powers your watch or the crystal that is used in medical lasers. What about Harry Oldfield's crystal[7] that works within his invented scanning equipment? This shows images of the aura and the imbalances within it (electro crystal therapy).

There is no doubt about it, crystals have been used for eons, and every crystal resonates at a particular frequency. They have their own inherent energy. If you hold a crystal in your hand and meditate on it for a short time, you will feel some kind of sensation from it – be it heat or tingling or just an inner knowing. Just holding a crystal can have a profound effect on you

---

7 www.electrocrystals.com

emotionally and psychologically. It can increase your aura and repair it.

Case 10: Crystal Healing

One time, I was in a shop in the north of Scotland and I happened to be wearing a large piece of Celestite, a crystal that is known to resonate with higher angelic frequencies.

The assistant behind the counter asked if she could hold the crystal. When I placed the crystal in her hand, she began to cry.

Her father from the spirit world joined us and told me that she was suffering from depression; I passed information to her, which was validated was in order for her to begin the healing process. After several minutes of holding the crystal and crying, she gave it back to me and told me that she felt an amazing sense of relief.

She needed to heal and by holding the crystal, the energy held within it helped her to release blocked emotion. I gave her that crystal because it was better that she have it than myself.

Certain crystals are particularly useful for protection of mind, body, and spirit. They help to create a barrier that will protect you from negative vibrations. Below I have listed a few that are readily available and will help to keep your aura strong and your area clear from negativity. I could write a whole book on psychic protection and the use of crystals, but for now I will just stick to basic facts.

TIGER'S EYE: This crystal is known to help with getting through difficult times in life, inducing courage within the person that uses it. It helps to distance you from external negative influences and mitigates moods and stressful situations. This is an excellent crystal to use when in a relationship that is particularly stressed or abusive. Never wear this for more than a week as it has a profound effect on the flow of energy within the body. Meditation is preferable.

BLACK TOURMALINE: This is one of my favorite crystals for psychic protection and neutralizing negative vibrations. It is especially potent when placed in a glass of water in your home or hotel room. Using this crystal can stop any unwanted visits from lower astral entities and prevent any form of infestation. By preventing this type of barrage from a negative source, no problem can manifest to bring about harm, so you feel safe in mind and spirit.

AGATE: From Nepal and India to other areas of the world, agate has a reputation for being a protective crystal, with lucky qualities into the bargain. It is one of the founding components of protective amulets. Agate promotes security and safety on all emotional levels by dissolving tensions and resisting external influences. The energy that exudes from this amulet does not resonate with a lower vibration and repels that energy. Anyone intent on causing harm is repelled by the potency of its vibration.

SMOKEY QUARTZ: In my last home, I used to keep many very large pieces of this crystal. It is tremendously useful in protecting your immediate area, transmuting negative energy into positive energy. It has an amazing relaxing effect in any household and when worn, it works in a more profoundly spiritual way.

BLOOD STONE: There are many misconceptions regarding this stone, however, it is a hidden gem amongst the crystal world. Its main property is for protection from undesirable influences spiritually and physically. It works on the emotional body by calming irritability, aggressiveness, and impatience. It truly is a little gem and can work wonders personally or within the home.

ROSE QUARTZ: My wife and I use rose quartz when we meditate or whenever we have a headache or are feeling stress. Rose quartz has a profound effect by calming the emotions and promoting a feeling of love; it works on the heart chakra and releases us from worry.

SALT: Salt is used in many, if not all, rites of protection. Even in exorcisms, salt is a main ingredient for protecting against negativity as I previously explained. We know that salt has the ability to absorb negativity. Imagine the process of osmosis, where water-soluble particles are attracted and absorbed. Salt is a basic crystalline product, and crystals have always been recognized as being able to absorb atmospheric conditions. Salt is used prior to exorcisms to make pure the water when blessed. Spirits require moisture in the air to manifest and this is denied by the use of the salt.

Sprinkling salt at the entrance of doorways or entrances to your home is an excellent preventative measure. It denies entry to any negative entity and absorbs any negative energy moving into your cleansed atmosphere. Another method is to place salt in a bowl of water with the intent that it will absorb any negativity within the atmosphere. You can if you wish, add the presence of black tourmaline into the equation just as an added measure.

Salt baths are an excellent way to cleanse your auric field; the salt acts by absorbing all negative energy from your auric field. Ensure that when you make a salt bath, you only put in two tablespoons of natural salt crystals. Too much salt in your bath can be dangerous. Have you ever looked at dried fruit? It has very little shape and no moisture within it – so it looks rather wrinkled.

Case 11: Salt Bath Blues

My wife and I had suffered from a serious psy-chic attack and so we needed to cleanse our-

selves. I chose to meditate and call in help, and Jo decided she would try a salt bath.

She had her bath and felt immediate release from the negative entrenchment. Jo likes to soak in the bath for an incredibly long time and this time was no different.

Later, we left our house to travel to another location and on the way; my wife became incredibly ill. She was feeling sick and getting weaker by the minute. I was so worried and could not find any reason for this sudden illness. I turned to spirit and asked my guide to tell me what was wrong. Immediately I heard Ellie tell me that Jo needed water and she needed it fast.

I then saw a clairvoyant image of a bag of salt and I asked Jo how much she put in the water – a full measure close to a cup of salt went into the bath, instead of 2 tablespoons.

Her body was shutting down due to not having healthy levels of water, and her levels of salt were far too high, causing blood pressure problems and putting a severe strain on the heart.

I stopped and put the requisite water and minerals back into her system and slowly but surely, she came back. So please use only 2 tablespoons of salt in the bath. We both learned what should be used that day, from what was just a simple case of using too much because she believed the water volume in the bath warranted that amount.

CHAPTER 16:

Sacramentals

S acramentals are in all religions and in all spiritual disciplines. Catholicism, Hinduism, Judaism, Pagan, White Witchcraft, Buddhism, New Age and Shamanism all utilize some form of sacramental as protection. A sacramental can be a medal of some description, depicting a religious iconic figure. In the Catholic discipline or Buddhism, the use of prayer beads is more common. In the Philippines, talismans are used as a form of protection. It does not matter if the sacramental is considered the protector, or the fact that the belief has some form of placebo effect within the subconscious – as long as it works. Again it's more about the intention.

CHAPTER 17

Sage Ceremony

The Native Americans were an incredibly spiritual people; they understood the universe and nature perhaps better than anyone did. They were closer to natural spiritual law and so were unaffected by the material world until much later in their earthly development. One thing that remained constant with them was the faith and belief they had in Mother Nature, and so they turned to her for aid in many of the problems they encountered. They were particularly adept at spirit communication and understood the realm of spirit more than anyone. This is why, to my belief, these individuals are sent back from spirit to be guides within our time.

Sage is a native plant, that when lit and used in certain ways, is thought to remove negative entities and energies, and the Native Americans used this practice regularly, but merely to cleanse. This belief has continued to this day, and many spiritual teachers will attest to the use of the sage but mainly for cleaning negative energy, not removing demons as thought by some ill informed people.

In many trance addresses that have been brought from the spirit world, these kind and loving spirits have confirmed the use of the sacred sage for cleansing energy.

The sage ceremony is used to drive out negative energy, to cleanse and purify areas and auric fields. Traditionally white sage is used with cedar, normally in a wand formation, and wafted with a white feather.

To begin a sage ceremony, it is important that your mind and body energies are aligned and have the purest of intentions. You must light the sage and put this in an abalone shell or hold it in your hand. Start from the farthest eastern part of your home and wave a white feather over the smoke that is created.

Traditionally it is said that you should start at all four directions. This is said to bring in the winged beings (which you and I will understand as the angelic realm) to help purify. As the smoke permeates through the atmosphere, it binds the negative energies and it is believed - spirits and carries them up through the atmosphere to be transmuted to positive energy. It is important that you also open windows and entrances, in order that you create a space through which the smoke can escape. Ensure you clear all areas and walk slowly, ensuring the smoke is abundant and cleanses and purifies.

As I have said previously, your intent and belief is the secret to making any ceremony like this work. Any single piece of doubt will cause you to block yourself and therefore hinder the process. I am not a fan of ceremonial acts like this and prefer the power of my divine authority.

Remember there are no absolutes. You have your own free will, and you are here to exercise that right. Sometimes your decisions may be wrong, but then you must learn from them and accept the consequences. There are occasions when your rituals and protective measures will not work and it's not because of the Sacramentals or the crystals or the rituals - it is you. It is your emotional point of attraction and the belief in yourself that will cause it not to work. It may also be what you are dealing with. Let's understand our gifts of the spirit before we move to the heavier stuff.

PART 4

"DO" Know Your Psychic Gifts

I have been talking about our psychic gifts or faculties time and time again, and I do not presume that you the reader will understand what they all are and how they work – for there are more than you think. I will go into each gift in detail, for now all you need to know is that these gifts are the basics of our soul abilities.

Here is the scoop – we all have them, no matter whether you are a natural psychic medium or not. Little Johnny has it and your mates have it. They just do not know it or, like a skeptic, choose to refute it.

Firstly, I do not give much credence to the Bible in its current form, but I do believe it is the greatest spiritual and psychic book ever written. I wholeheartedly believe that many books and much information has been omitted by religious decree, from those running the religions at the time, which of course suited the politics of the time too. Even so, I do believe in the Nazarene as I know him – a spiritual man of spirit and as far as the Bible is concerned, it is the greatest book of psychic and mediumship evidence that ever was.

Jesus Christ was a Man, who was brought up as an Essene. The Essenes were very spiritual people and lived according to the laws of spirit rather than doctrine in the time of Christ.

There is a great deal of conjecture surrounding the Essenes, and it has been suggested that they are indeed fable. Those who suggest this are at the head of other religious organizations and, one would indeed have to deduce this, it suited the leaders at the time. The Essenes meditated and practiced spiritual law. One of the main subjects which preoccupied the Essenes was the protection from evil spirits. This was in order to protect the purity of their divinity. It would seem fitting then to mention these individuals that, by–and–by, taught Christ. They considered themselves guardians of divine teaching (Who Were the Essenes?, n.d.) and had in their possession many old manuscripts, which only they could decode (Manitara).

Like Jesus, Buddha, Mohammed and other prophets, our task is a divine order from spirit. Why? Because we as mediums are charged with the teachings of the gifts of spirit, just as Jesus and the other prophets displayed in their time - to be of service to mankind. Mediums regularly display the gifts of clairvoyance, clairaudience, clairsentience, claircognizance and the gift of Healing. Through these gifts of the spirit, we keep these spiritual teachings alive as well as the other prophets' teachings, of which many still live on in the modern world. However, that does not detract from the fact that everyone has these abilities inherent within them and these gifts are not exclusively for the divinely endowed. This is the only constant, but because of religious doctrine, these gifts have been forgotten through time, and our material lives have taken over from our spiritual selves. Therefore, it takes the demonstration of these gifts of the spirit to act as a catalyst for awakening the spiritual self.

Once you are awake and the new awareness has arrived, you cannot go back to sleep for the divinity within has now awakened and is rising. It brings with it challenges that make you question old beliefs and search for new truths. The physical self is the vehicle that allows the expression of the spirit, and so we are on this earth plane to develop our spirituality by testing and passing those tests, to recognize who we are – spirits in human form with innate spiritual gifts that give us a direct line to internal spiritual power. The use of these gifts came with a high price tag, and you will be tested – just as Jesus and other prophets were tested. These are different kinds of tests to the one I mentioned before, these are based on the laws of spirit, and only you will know when you are being tested while upon the path to enlightenment.

You will come across situations that will test your faith and your trust; you will enter a war that is waging between good and evil and developing your soul is your ultimate goal. Therefore, one will experience the good and the bad which tests the fortitude of the soul. Unfortunately, this is necessary and all must face these tests and learn the realities. I think a statement given by Silver Birch can sum up a good measure of this:

> "The soul that lives on in its own butterfly happiness and chases always the illusion and the shadow, one day must learn to touch reality. Do not envy those who you think have an easy time. The hardest road in their life is yet before them." (Birch, 1938)

These tests help us to develop our spiritual gifts to the fullest expression that we can handle. Now let us look at these individual gifts.

Each gift of the spirit has a particular function and through the evolution of time we have learned of more gifts than the original four that are discussed within the Holy Scriptures and other spiritual works. Most of you that read this book will have a basic understanding of these, so I will not go over the same thing - except to reinforce certain points and particular parts within this work to initiate the uninitiated. The main gifts of the spirit - commonly known as Clairvoyance, Clairaudience,

Clairsentience, and Claircognizance - are discussed in the following chapters.

CHAPTER 18

Clairvoyance

C lairvoyance is the gift of spiritual sight and is often endowed in different strengths to individuals, though this
gift is one which, with the right intention and cultivation,
can be trained to a high degree of sensitivity. This gift is the
ability to see the world of spirit and to receive images from the
void.

Subjective or Objective? Know the Difference

There are two methods of clairvoyance. There is subjective
clairvoyance, where the individual perceives the images in the
mind's eye, which is known as the third eye. Most individuals use this form of clairvoyance and everyone has the ability to awaken this dormant gift through training and spiritual
discipline.

There is the second type of clairvoyance, which is objective,
which is the ability to perceive images and the world of spirit
outside yourself by using your physical eyes. I have to say that
many psychic mediums claim this when they are giving readings and it irks me. You know the ones! They tell you that your

father, or someone who has passed to spirit, is standing next to you and then fail to give you accurate information regarding the aesthetic state of the individual. The truth is that they see subjectively. However, there are those who can perceive outside themselves, I am one of those, but I have to admit the times that I do see are rare. It is the spirit world that controls this, besides which, I scare myself every time and my heart feels like it is going to burst from my body, so I mainly use my subjective clairvoyance.

The process of discerning what is real clairvoyance and what is coming from one's own ego can be quite disconcerting as no one can teach you how to do this. One must take this quest on the self.

At the beginning of our development we are bombarded with what I would term as R.I.E.I. (Randomly Induced Egotistical Images), and these can be misconstrued as communication from spirit or psychic guidance. The difference is entirely diverse.

Real guidance and communication will come from outside of oneself (a spirit being) whereby the EGO has had no time to process the request for information. For instance, sometimes I will have the answer before I ask the question; my intention is read by spirit and not the physical or material desire for information.

CHAPTER 19:

Clairaudience

This is probably one of the most misunderstood gifts of the spirit. The ability to hear both objectively and subjectively is the gift of Clairaudience, the normally silent dialogue that goes on in the mind of the medium when working subjectively.

It is the ability to perceive words in the void in your own language that you would understand and in your own head voice. Again, there is the contrasting part of the gift that allows you to hear clearly with your own physical ears and believe me, that when and if this happens to you, it will frighten the proverbial crap out of you. It most certainly had this effect on me. However, it is worthy to note that certain world-renowned mediums developed this ability to a high degree so that they often heard the voice of spirit physically. One such medium was Doris Stokes[8], whose remarkable gift of clairaudience was enjoyed the world over.

If you are reading this in silence, you will hear the words being imprinted in your conscious mind as you follow each word. This imprinting of the words in your mind is what we under-

---

8 Learn more about Ms. Stokes at http://website.lineone. net/~enlightenment/doris_stokes.htm

stand as clairaudience of some sort. When you hear the same dialogue in your mind, but perhaps different words come to you unexpectedly that give you a warning or tell you something when your conscious mind remains focused on something completely different, this is clairaudience of a subjective nature. I refer to a story from a very close friend.

Case 12: A Lesson in Listening

"One day in the summer of 2000 I had departed for this daily ride and had gone about one half mile from my home. I was pedaling up a small hill and beginning to breathe rather heavily when a voice went off in my head. It said, 'Ed, get off this bike or you will fall off'. I pulled over to the side of the road and got off.

"The next words the voice spoke to me were, 'Ed, lay down or you will fall down'. I laid down on the grass and remember popping the strap on my helmet and that is all.

"The next I knew was a couple had parked their car and were walking across the grass to me asking if I was all right. At that point, my mind was crystal clear but my body was too weak to get up. I didn't even know I'd passed out until I realized that my bowels had let loose and I had fouled myself. Well they called both my wife and 911.

"Both arrived very quickly and by then I could stand, so after first going home to clean myself, I went to the hospital. It was found that my aorta valve had closed to six tenths of a centimeter diameter from the normal two. I was receiving only a fraction of the life-giving blood to my body and brain that should have been flowing. I had already gone into oxygen debt and if I had not listened to that 'voice' would have died right there on that street.

"Anyone who has had such an experience no longer questions the existence of such senses; they would be a fool to. For all others, it is much better to keep an attitude of 'suspension of disbelief' then to refuse to accept such a possibility. I urge you to keep such an open mind." -- Ed Martin (taken from the "Book Of Six Rings")

You can clearly deduce from this that he heard the warning subjectively which more than likely saved his life.

CHAPTER 20:

Clairsentience

Clairsentience is the ability to feel spirit or to feel conditions of energy that surround you, which is felt within your body and on a physical level. This can be an unconscious feeling or a direct result of spirit allowing you to feel conditions prior to their passing from the earth plane.

To give you an example of this type of feeling I will recount one of my own experiences.

Case 13: Feeling It

During a Budo class one evening, my eyes were fixated on this particular student in my dojo, and every time I looked at him, I felt physically sick and dizzy.

I asked to see him in the back room, as I knew I was picking up some physical feelings of a psychic nature from him.

When I went inside, I heard a name called to me. I was immediately aware of a spirit person who was the father of the student who stood be-

fore me and I knew that he passed tragically. I felt like I could not breathe and was gasping for breath myself. I then felt a physical rope put around my neck and I knew beyond a shadow of doubt that his dad passed while committing the act of suicide.

I imparted this information to the student in question and it was confirmed through his tears – he had begun the healing process. The student in question felt like a heavy weight was removed.

This is an example of how we, as mediums, are able to perceive feelings and conditions of the spirit world.

Sometimes the barriers that we build are by ourselves; this is because of emotional turmoil that we experience. It feels rather like a pillow suffocating the sound of something. You know it is there but you cannot quite hear it clearly. Because we erect these barriers, there is a strong emanating, pulsing negative energy that attracts lower level or grounded spirits. These spirits will be happy to keep you in the depressive state.

We can also feel the physical conditions of those we meet on a daily basis. A medium or psychic can feel the sickness conditions of someone they may be reading, which is rather unusual. It tells the medium what the person is going through at the time, and can be a good indicator as to which chakras are blocked.

This feeling can come upon the medium by way of a headache that comes and goes, or a feeling of dread, or of sickness, which are normally felt physically then let go very quickly. This is why it is important for highly sensitive individuals to clear themselves regularly. There are certain cases where the spirit will carry on the feeling with the medium, and it is important the medium remains steadfast and direct – commanding the entity to take it away – clear it.

CHAPTER 21

Claircognizance

C laircognizance is probably the main psychic sense that you will use in the employ of your duties as a psychic medium and under the right conditions, it is a phenomenally accurate way of validating and passing information from spirit through spirit to spirit. This higher awareness may go unnoticed for a very long time and you will have no conscious knowledge of where or how you may have perceived this information. In essence, this is the highest form of knowing. It is divine in its very nature and has been a part of spirituality for centuries. Consequently, this is primarily understood as being taken over by the Holy Spirit. It is the bypassing of two minds to go directly to the super consciousness or divine source itself - amalgamations of mind, body and spirit as one complete unit. It will happen and you will not know it.

To explain this on my own terms, it is the ability for a medium to know exactly what to say without the employment of conscious thought. It is also one of the most powerful forces or gifts use in dealing with non human entities.

A Scriptural Perspective

The gift of clairvoyance, which is the gift of clearseeing with the mind's eye, can be seen throughout all of the scriptures. Moses used this gift when he went to Mount Sinai and saw a burning bush. He secondly used the gift of Clairaudience, which is the gift of hearing, when the Lord God spoke to him directly. Even John, one of Christ's disciples (or another John – there are arguments) foresaw clairvoyantly the revelations that were imparted to him during his time of writing the revelations, now included within the Holy Bible.

Jesus, although he was able to use all of the gifts just as efficiently as each other, was particularly adept at claircognizance. This is the highest form of communication - of knowing; the clear natural communication that bypasses the conscious thought and the subconscious as I previously mentioned. It is direct from a divine source, which could be labelled as super-consciousness, though I feel it is even higher than that. We will not know until we pass on to the world of spirit. This suggests that Jesus was indeed in touch with the divine stream of the Holy Spirit.

There is plenty of scientific evidence for the sixth sense. Therefore, I would not like to enter into this debate in this particular section of the book. My previous book, "Powers of The Sixth Sense – How To Remain Safe in a Hostile World", clearly discusses and documents some of the scientific research on the subject of the sixth sense. There are other works out there that should be consulted too. It should be enough to know that it has scientifically been proven that the sixth sense exists. However, I know that the most hardened skeptics would continue to deny and refute the evidence, these are Psuedo Skeptics. Even today, there are scientists who are attending circles of a physical nature whereby spirit is proving life after death by individual manifestations of spirit bodies and physical phenomena.

Nevertheless, if you always look for a problem, you will always find one, even if you manifest it from the mind of ignorance. I would, therefore, like to continue and examine the gifts of the spirit from a biblical and spiritual sense. I would like to make it clear that there are other comparisons in other doctrines, but I concentrate on Christian doctrine for the ease of understanding, though my stance is that I follow no dogma and no man-made religion.

You May Be Psychic

So what is the difference between the two, between being a medium and being a psychic? Well, in simple terms, a medium receives communications from a discarnate entity, while a psychic will read energy around animate and inanimate objects or individuals. This means that they will read the energy that permeates all living and non-living objects or individuals. This is known as the aura that surrounds the living body or the inanimate object.

CHAPTER 22:

Healing

ealing is one of the greatest gifts that can be bestowed on a medium and it takes very special individuals to dedicate themselves to this type of Mediumship.

There have been many great healers in history and one such healer was Harry Edwards. Harry was able to channel divine energies that enabled spontaneous healings to take place. The blind would see and the lame would walk, emotional conditions were broken through in order that healing could take place. One of the truths that Harry propounded was that all healing was from the same source and came from Spirit – through Spirit – to Spirit. It is this teaching that is still used today throughout the spiritualist movement.

Another great healer of note that exists in modern times is a man known as "John of God"[9] in Brazil. Thousands flock to see this man in order to be healed. John is a humble man of peasant origin and is a natural trance medium. He is taken over by a spirit control known as the entity and carries out healings

9 Learn more about this healer at http://www.friendsofthecasa.info/index.php?page=joao-teixeira-de-faria

to the sick and lame. Witnesses have watched him carry out psychic surgery -- even by making incisions into fully awake patients. The remarkable thing is this man has no former medical knowledge or training and claims it is not he who does these remarkable things but his spirit team of helpers.

Some mediums are amazingly gifted and have an affinity for healing; one such medium is my wife Joanne Brocas[10] who would rather help heal individuals through teaching and wise counsel than offer predictions for entertainment. Her ability to use her gifts of the spirit to get to the root of problems is astounding, and words of consequence and wisdom are often partaken through her own Mediumship. Jo often travels and teaches her healing workshops throughout the world in order to teach others that the mind, body connection is powerful enough to heal you. If you are interested in the power of your spirit to heal, read Jo's books and get on her workshops.

Healing can come in many forms, from spontaneous healing that has no scientific basis, or words of wisdom that are often the catalyst for self-healing. No matter what, it is important to note that in a world fraught with disease, emotional turmoil, and abuse, healing must be one of the best gifts to share for the betterment of humanity. If we look back at scriptural writings, we can see this same gift used repeatedly from prophets such as Jesus and Buddha.

Now I have only discussed the gifts that I feel pertain to our development. That helps us unify all of our five senses and our sixth sense as one spiritual unit. There are however more of these gifts that are readily available, such as Clairalience (smelling), Clairgustance (tasting). However, I do not believe these abilities are possibly a prerequisite to psychic development but they can be awakened later on.

_____

10 Learn more about this healer at http://www.joannebrocas.com/

CHAPTER 23:

The Auric Field

The aura comprises electromagnetic energy consisting of atoms. These atoms vibrate at various frequencies and speeds, and they bind to create illusionary views within the earth plane. This energy permeates and interpenetrates everything. We understand this as the makeup of our aura, and those that have a higher vibratory awareness can perceive this aura. This has been going on for thousands of years. You can see it in iconic religious art and figures; you can see the aura around a saint, which is known as the halo around the holy person. What you see is, in fact, the auric field of divinity and the color is normally a representation of higher divinity in nature. The sensed energy is the model and sum total of everything you have done in thought, word and deed. Your past, present, and sometimes your future can be sensed in this energy field, which is the energy the psychic will read. If the psychic is not trained professionally, they will often mistake reading the Aura for spirit communication through Mediumship.

"Our natural states of being are in relationship, a tango, a constant state of one influencing the other. Just as the subatomic particles that compose us, we cannot be separated from the space and particles surrounding them, so living beings cannot be isolated from each other ... By the act of observation and intention, we have the ability to extend a kind of super-radiance to the world." [11]

The Layers of the Auric Field

This field consists of layers that correlate to energy vortices that make up the seven psychic centers of the body known as the chakras. Early experiments have revealed that no two auras are the same and the aura is affected by ill health, fatigue, depression, anxiety, and emotions such as fright and fear. The energy layers are as follows:

1. Etheric
2. Emotional
3. Mental
4. Spiritual

The Etheric Layer

The Etheric layer is known as the double of the physical body or the perispirit, which was first coined in early spiritualism. It is an extension of the human form, and is understood as the perispirit. Further, this spirit body lives on after the death of the physical body and is a direct replica of the human form without material form. It is normally invisible to the human eye but can be seen clearly by gifted clairvoyants. This is not to say that it is out of the reach of visual perception by everyone. You can train your consciousness to perceive this energy field. It lays 1/16th to ½ inches around the body and is normally silvery blue. It is important to note that it is without mental consciousness yet holds powers and faculties that respond to uni-

---

11 Lynne McTaggart, The Field (Updated Edition)(New York: HarperCollins, 2008), 138.

versal laws, which are perfect in operation, and directed mental thought. It is the intermediary between the physical body and the astral body and changes universal energy for vitality and sustenance. It also relays consciousness from the astral to the physical body.

This is also the intermediary for the serpent energy known as the Kundalini. It is responsive to the astral energy within its consciousness. This is not theory, and it has existed over the years - perhaps 7,000 years that we know of. The subject has now become inherent in the practice of Yoga, Zen Knowledge, Budo and other Occult and religious practices. The mastery of this energy through the Etheric can aid in developing strong psychic powers.

However, improper use and control of this energy is also the vehicle to which knowledge of evil is awakened. It is dangerous to release this energy too early if your vibration is not high enough or strong enough to deal with it. For some individuals, it will not be recognized whether Kundalini has been released or not. It is normally only felt in sensitive individuals. The Etheric body is also the substance which forms ectoplasm. This dense Etheric energy helps to manifest spirit bodies from the spirit world. This use of ectoplasm is what is known as physical Mediumship, which we will discuss later.

Case 14: Too Much, Too Soon

Jean's husband Frank came to me and asked me to help with his wife who had been a patient of a psychiatrist for a while, and who could not find any explanation for what she was going through. Instead, he put her experiences down to psychosomatic symptoms.

Jean would see horrible grotesque faces and would hear voices, she was not able to sleep, and often her dreams would be terrifying to her. When she had some quiet times, she would be so *exhausted and her emotions would run away with her, she would cry without reason, and she began to lock herself away from everyone.*

Her husband was beginning to feel the strain and asked if I could do anything. I told him "Frank, I am not a medical professional and do not want to mislead you with information that may not be correct."

As I began speaking to Frank, I felt the energy of his deceased mother come in. I ignored her for a while, telling her that I would not pass any information on since Frank and I were having a coffee in Starbucks. This was neither the time nor the place. Giving any evidence in public is dead against my beliefs in how professionals should conduct themselves.

He continued to plead with me. "There's no one else I can turn to, I have been to doctors, psychiatrists, and another psychic but for some reason, I am drawn to you, and I know you can help."

I replied, "I can't guarantee anything and I do not want to get out of my depth."

The spirit was more insistent now and would not leave me alone - I gave in. I began to tell Frank that I had a woman here who I believed was his mother. I told him how she passed, and gave further evidence, which was confirmed. Then the information given to me was like a light bulb moment. Three times, she said Kundalini Rising, Kundalini Rising, and Kundalini Rising Premature. I knew instantaneously what the issue was and knew the reason his wife's physical health had diminished.

She had been taking part in spiritual rituals and meditative practices without real knowledge, only what she read in books, knowing that she was incredibly sensitive. By mistake, she had released her Kundalini energy far too early and was now suffering because of this. She had a chronic awareness of many new things that she had not bargained for – Good and Bad. Her vibration attracted that which matched her wishes and spiritual growth. Her fears were exacerbated to allow her to grow spiritually and she was not ready for this.

Any spiritual experience that you go through is there for your soul growth – good or bad, as you perceive it, this is how you grow. This was the cause of her problems.

After hearing all of this, a look of shock came over his face and he took out a diary with tears in his eyes. He opened the back page and written on the diary was the words, "If this man is the real deal and can help – mum will come through and tell me."

As much as I would like to take the credit for this, I am afraid that I cannot. The truth is that spirit just guided the man to the right medium who was able to receive the correct information to help him then. It could have been anyone.

The above story is just a small example of how the desire to develop spiritually has its inherent dangers, which can be exacerbated through the auric field. The early release of this energy will make you aware of polar opposites, the yin and yang of your experience if you will. Your fears and your weaknesses will be exacerbated in order that you can grow through these lessons, should your soul choose to do so through your conscious experience. If you are not strong enough mentally to deal with some old and new issues that may be raised, you will cause yourself damage, though perhaps unintentionally. This can manifest mental and physical illness, which in extreme cases can be a cause of death.

The perispirit and the Kundalini is housed within the layers of the aura, and this auric layer which consists of various fields dances atomically and rhythmically according to those particular states which affect it at the time. Let us look at the other layers of the Aura.

The Emotional Layer

Emotional - This layer contains the emotions you are feeling at any moment, so the colors within the aura can change according to how you are feeling, and thus this layer is known as the layer of feeling and emotional experiences. It is also through the etheric and emotional layers that the healer can manipulate the energy to promote inner and outer healing.

How can this emotional state effect the ability to look after your mind, body and spirit? If you are feeling the emotion of fear, then you will exude that emotion, and any sensitive individuals would be able to pick up that emotion. We also exude the emotion that we feel for others outside ourselves. Therefore, if you are feeling anger at someone then that emotion would be easily recognizable, or perhaps you are feeling depressed, that emotion can be picked up readily too.

This can be an early warning sign to you if you learn how to recognize the emotional state of others and can help you to take essential precautions to protect yourself from others. In contrast, however, when we are happy our vibration increases and sparks of pure light can be sensed.

This is perhaps better understood when someone tells you that you have light around you or that you are exuding happiness from your inner being – a glow if you will, or spiritual maturity.

The Mental Layer

Mental - The mental layer contains the information on your beliefs, intellect, and personal power relating to the sum total of who you are in the physical and mental sense. The thought processes are registered in this area, and your decisions in what you think are registered in this field. The color of this field is mainly yellow and thought forms are structured as unshapely blobs of energy. The thought forms that are in our awareness at the time are registered in this field. It is obvious that with training and raising our awareness, we can notice these thoughts through the sixth sense.

The Spiritual Layer

The spiritual, or astral, layer is the bridge to the spirit world and receives all information via channeling the higher vibrations through the crown chakra, which is situated just above the head. It is also the area where spiritual weakness can occur and one of the openings to which spirit may attach itself through your weakened mind or indeed faith.

The crown chakra also works in collaboration with all other chakras. This is the main gateway to spirit communication for the medium and the point at which developed mediums allow spirit to work through them in a state of Trance. The psychic rarely works through this spiritual gateway because of the vibration in which they work.

"All bodies radiate those vibrations with which the body controls itself in mental, in the physical and such radiation is called the aura." Edgar Cayce

Reading the Aura

It is through the auric field that psychics are able to pick up information by tapping into the energy of the first three layers of the aura. Mediums use their vibration and energy to communicate through the higher gateways and meet spirit on a higher level. This is why most psychics will not be able to raise their vibration enough to reach these levels of spirit and remain attached to the lower chakra systems. Mediums have a natural ability to work through all levels of the chakras and the auric field. The aura is primarily what a psychic will read by feeling the subtle nuances and changes within the field. The psychic registers the information by using one of their psychic gifts such as clairvoyance, clairsentience, or indeed clairaudience. I know the medium uses these gifts, but there are some major differences, which we will explore in a moment.

Typical information that can be sensed through the aura includes:

- Emotional point in the present moment
- Blockages in the aura causing a physical health condition
- Emotional blockages in the chakras causing psychological issues
- Potential future events
- Past trauma and past conditions
- Information contained within the aura connected to the individual's life history

A psychic will read the aura and will pick up information based on conditions, which is like reading a book in front of you - how you read it will depend on your literacy. Consequently, there will be a difference in the level of success as we have particular phenomena called vibrational attraction, and you will attract to you the level of ability and understanding that mirrors your vibration. This means that I may not be able to relate to an individual on a level that is conducive to the reading and therefore, that individual would be guided to someone more in tune with him or her. This is why many professional psychics read for different people; therefore, one psychic may not overlap the other, unless the sitter is living their own life through psychic guidance and flitting between each psychic.

A medium is different, on the other hand, and will be able to do all of the above and more. You remember that I mentioned that we have, as mediums, the ability to raise our vibrations through our higher chakras, which are the bridge and link to the spirit world. We are therefore, able to communicate on a mind-to-mind connection with the discarnate entity – telepathy if you will. This is how the unheard conversation will go between the medium and spirit.

There are of course deeper meanings to the chakras, though I would advise you to read up on everything you can, but remember that one person's belief will differ from another's. You will have to find what sits right with you. By raising the vibration through the higher chakras, the medium is then able to communicate with the discarnate by using the same gifts. However, the difference is the information perceived is normally of a nature that is evidence-related, and can be validated instantaneously or much later perhaps - even as long as weeks rather than hours. This then can have a scientific basis for evidentially related confirmation.

PART 5:

"Do" Work to Develop your Psychic Abilities

O
k, so what is the secret of developing the Gifts of the spirit? For the most part, the real secret is a meditative and contemplative nature, and living according to the law (Spiritual Law), which is perfect in operation, which is why I do not believe in miracles. Miracles are a perception of what we see as amazing in the earth plane, but the truth is that miracles are a perfect expression of divine law and therefore nothing out of the ordinary.

There are of course many methodologies to developing certain aspects of the gifts, of becoming stronger in one particular gift than the other, but what I must stress is that with everything in life, we must have strong roots to enable true growth. This is likened to the seed that needs to be nurtured with the correct balance of nutrients, light and external energy. So meditation is perhaps the first step to developing your gifts, but also something that is overlooked a great deal, is living as clean a life as possible. What I mean is that you consciously choose to try to live a life that is as spiritually enriched and balanced as possible by living by the three spiritual laws of love, forgiveness and compassion. I have tried to do this for many years - like everyone else of course, we have our good days and our bad days. There was a time when I received validation that I had been doing this. The validation came from Peter at the Edgar Cayce Foundation who had said that, out of all the mediums and psychics he had met, I was probably one of the cleanest; you can imagine how I felt hearing this, it was just the little bit of validation that I needed to keep me on this path.

CHAPTER 24:

Get Ready to Meditate

B efore I begin discussing meditation in this section of the book, I would like to discuss what I suggest about living a clean life. You would be forgiven for thinking that I mean becoming part of a commune or wearing a caftan made of recycled material - becoming the epitome of angelic presence – wrong, so wrong. It is quite simply about awareness, and having that awareness in your life, about becoming grateful and feeding the seeds of positivity rather than those of negativity, which I have mentioned previously. Awareness of something is the beginning of being able to transmute any negativity to positivity, of making something wrong – right, and making the bad – good.

You can envision seeds as the beginning of your spiritual journey in trying to understand life and nature of your reality. Eventually and with the right conditions, your seed will begin to develop its first roots, which will travel down to anchor itself into the earth. You have the beginning, and with the right nutrients and the right natural non-obstructive energy, you will see that the seed begins to grow and reach itself beyond natural limitations as it yearns for the natural energy of the sun and light. Again, on the seed's journey, it needs the right nutrients and commitment to be nurtured not only from mother earth but also from those that tend the garden or the ground.

If we feed those seeds with the right ingredients, and in the right conditions and environment, they will undoubtedly grow into strong roots and will eventually become as strong and as tall as the largest tree in the forest, consequently we live a life that is positive and self-fulfilling.

WARNING

However, we can feed our seeds with the wrong nutrients and the wrong conditions and while you feel like you are making progress in life, you are in fact holding yourself back. You feed your seeds of life with negativity and this negativity can come in many forms. It could be the way you treat another individual. Perhaps by taking part in idle gossip or speaking with a sharpened tongue, this is lack of awareness. It could be reading negative stories in newspapers that are embellished and full of lies that ultimately destroy the self. You could be watering your negative seeds by watching TV programs that contain an inappropriate and negative vibes, or you could be destroying yourself with alcohol, drugs, and self-sabotage, or even taking part in gossip. There are many ways that you will water your seeds of negativity. I know this from personal experience, but you have the choice in how to deal with it. If you want to be a good medium, live clean and that will also help you when and if your greatest battles ensue.

Bonsai Example

Look at the Bonsai; a most beautiful miracle of nature, and yet its life is in the hands of the one who cares for it, who feeds it and gives it the right environmental conditions and energy sometimes this is nature's suicide. This is the epitome of the intricate balance of life. It is no wonder that when we first buy that tree, it dies, and that is because we only perceive the tree with our material vision -- for we have misconceptions of its very nature. You are constantly feeding yourself and your seeds with negativity, and you fail to see that it is as simple as a choice - of making that choice - the choice not only to grow but also to seek happiness through enlightenment. Yet your primordial instinct to destroy and hunt is not the reality of your essence, it is not your real nature and is merely an illusion of material perception.

Words are as sharp as the samurai's blade and can cut as cleanly right through your being; you feed your seeds negatively by your thoughts and your actions, and yet you remain oblivious to your own nature. The true nature of six sensory living is seeing the very nature of reality in the sixth dimension. It is not what you merely touch. The void is within you, and though your ego places you in front of others, you meet or perceive with the eyes of the merchant rather than of the mystic. Seeds of jealousy, anger, and hatred have grown within you; the more you are enticed by the beliefs of others that have already fed the seeds of negativity, the more you are producing a natural forest of negativity.

This is a destroyer of the self; it will at some point show itself as manifested in your life, and you will eventually destroy yourself from the inside out. It is important to understand awareness, and to know that when you are aware of your thoughts, it is better to transform them than to try to deny them or destroy them.

Why always try to win when your winning will only bring suffering to the other person?

Why judge when you have no right to judge anyone other than yourself? In judging others, you are denying the weakness in yourself and you are placing yourself above all. In fact, you may actually be the weed in the garden that, although it has its inner beauty, is destructive in nature because of its greed and desire to take over. The stronger your inner seeds are by feeding them with the right thoughts, actions and conditions, then your true nature and reality cannot be touched. Though you may be the target of those with negative seeds, you receive and give back only positivity, which can help to transform the seeds of negativity - to transform the weed into a beautiful flower worthy of adorning any garden - especially the garden of your mind.

Please be aware of your thoughts and your actions and only feed your seeds with love, acceptance, happiness, and understanding. See that we are all on a path, and that winning or proving yourself above others is the fertilizer that feeds the seeds of negativity within your spirit. You are the essence of life and the divinity within you, so feed your inner being with the purest of thoughts and actions, then, perhaps you may understand your own connectivity to the divinity that is harbored within. By working on these and having an awareness of your thoughts and actions, you are taking the first step to transmuting your negativity into positivity. You do not have to be an angel, and in fact, though I try to live a clean existence, I do tend to swear a great deal and I boil that down to my previous environments; however, life is about constantly working towards your spiritual goals and I am working on this aspect of the self.

This is also one of the first steps at combating that which would seek to destroy your spirit. The stronger that your seeds become on their path, the stronger your mind is to be able to resist evil temptations or manipulation by darker forces. This cleanliness of living will raise your vibration enough to become closer with the spirit and of your own innate divine nature. It increases your protective shields not only against anything negative in nature especially of a spiritual disposition, but also shields the physical body from manifesting disease that is primarily borne through imbalance.

Now that you understand that you have the choice to live a clean existence, and if you are trying to do this, you will find that you will get more from your meditative practice. The importance of meditation is different between individuals, some put a great deal of emphasis on meditation to develop, and others do not. Nevertheless, the power of meditation is phenomenal, and the benefits far outweigh circumnavigating the meditative discipline.

I have asked a good friend of mine and the founder of the Scole Experiment (a physical development circle in Scole, England) to comment on the importance of meditative practice. Robin Foy has been involved in investigating Psychic and Mediumship phenomena for many years and has been the facilitator of many other groups now developing throughout the world. He had this to say:

> "I would say that daily meditation is vital in developing the gifts of the spirit (but I confess I don't always stick to this regimen myself!) The best and most successful mediums of the past such as clairaudient Doris Stokes basically developed her Mediumship using only this tool and stuck to it rigidly.

> "We were all asked to meditate daily by our spirit team at Scole, and rarely missed a day. Our results confirmed the need for this, and showed how it added to our success. We were also asked to link into 'The Universal Harmony' mentally each night before going to sleep, which allowed our spirit team to work with us during our sleep state too.

> "Successful mediums today (some with spectacular results like Kai Muegge of the Felix Circle) also meditate regularly; in Kai's case, he meditates intensely for at least 3 hours before each sitting. Consequently, the results within the Felix Circle have developed with amazing speed."

Meditation is not a secret and is quite simply the art of going within. It is a discipline, which is under great scrutiny and is widely misunderstood. There are of course many methods of meditation. For the individual who is interested in developing, it has to be the most important aspect of developing the spiritual gifts. It has to be understood, however, that we often do forget to meditate as often as we should, and that is primarily down to outside influences.

There is one other important point to make. Most individuals will only identify with a particular form of meditative practice, therefore if they do not sit in silence at the same time every day and for at least an hour they will feel like they have failed. For those of you that have felt this way and including myself, I have some news of comfort. You can initiate meditative practice without conforming to what any other teachings dictate in many ways. Now I am certainly not advocating this as a replacement for the proper method of meditative practice, but as a catch-up method of going within to be at one with the divine source. The good news is that you can enter the meditative state, albeit in varying degrees, by taking some time in a contemplative manner.

For instance, you can achieve this contemplative time in the shower, bath or even if you are waiting in your car for a while, as long as the engine is turned off and you are not driving. Perhaps even just by sitting by a favorite spot, you can enter your light contemplative state. Say, for instance, that you are out walking in the forest; you could take some time to sit in quiet contemplation. Even at work, take just 10 minutes to enter into your meditative state by having quiet time at lunch. I will take you through some various meditative practices that I use in the following passages.

Daily Meditation

Normally I wake up very early in the morning, and more often than not, I will get up and wake up slowly in my living room by watching the birds feeding just outside of my window. This is a way for me to get close to nature so early in the day. After a while, and when I have felt suitably awakened, I will have a short meditation. I will begin by sitting in my chair and carrying out the following steps.

Case 15: A Short Meditation

Sit quietly in your chair and begin to breathe visualizing the white light of the Holy Spirit coming from the heavens above. See the white light permeate every part of your body, cleansing and purifying as it passes through from your head to the bottom, and surrounding you in a bubble of white light. Now see yourself in a dimly lit room basking in the orange glow of a burning candle. At the opposite end of the room is a beautiful wooden door, and the handle glistens from the warm glow. It is a brass handle, walk up to the door, turn the handle, walk through, and ensure that you close the door behind you. This makes sure that you are protected and that nothing can enter through the door.

Find yourself in a beautiful garden, and note that it is a beautiful day in the world of spirit. The sun is shining, nature calls to you, and the animals have no fear of you because you are as one with them as they are with you. Walk through the garden, enjoying the vibrations and energy of all the colors emanating from the flowers that are there. Notice how peaceful everything is, and walk until you come to a beautiful golden gate. Now walk through the gate and down a short path into a stunning and wondrous enchanted forest. You will now find yourself walking down a very peaceful path in the forest and you will note the majesty of the trees that surround you, feel the warmth of the life-giving sun on your body, and feel a gentle breeze comfort you as it passes. You hear a beautiful waterfall in the distance and make your way to the powerful yet peaceful sound. Soon you will find yourself at the side of the waterfall, and here you will sit with your feet dangling in the cool fresh water while you enjoy the heavenly energy from spirit. Know that you are fully protected, and should anyone from the world of spirit wish to join you for your highest good - then allow them. Allow them to teach you and impart wisdom should they so desire, but only if you are ready to receive.

Remain in this ethereal peaceful place until you feel it is time to leave, and when that time comes, say a gentle farewell to your spirit friend - know that you can return to thisplace at any time you wish.

Now begin to make your way back through the enchanted forest. Know that you are safe and take with you any lessons given. Contemplate wisely about the time that you have spent and give thanks to the Great Spirit for allowing you back to touch the void of your spiritual home. Find yourself once more at the golden gate and walk through and into the beautiful tranquil garden - enjoy once more the tranquility of the garden and say a fond farewell. Arriving once more at the wooden door, you turn the brass handle and walk through, en-suring that you have locked the door behind you. Thank God and your guides for being with you and slowly begin to bring your consciousness back to the present moment.

In the above particular meditation, you will have to call yourself back, as normally this meditation is one that I would use while taking students or a circle into meditation.

Walking Meditation

This meditation can be done with a friend or with your partner. It does not involve any particular type of visualization. Moreover, this meditation is perhaps more about gratitude and awareness. However, in the confines of your quiet mind, you will perhaps be touched by spirit or given guidance. Again, this is not difficult to achieve and is more about creating an awareness of your environment and beginning a level of communication with all of nature.

What I am about to tell you may set some of you off and think that I am crazy, but of course, if you met me, you would see that I am probably one of the most grounded mediums you will ever meet. However, I do communicate with nature in its entirety. This is a silent dialogue between whomever, and whatever I am communicating. I cannot take credit for this, for I learned this from Thich Nhat Hanh – one of my favorite authors and spiritual teachers. I am only sharing knowledge that he has taught me through his lessons.

Case 16: Walking Meditation

For example, while walking in the forest I would communicate with the trees and tell them how grateful I was that they were there - offering me protection and shelter. I would ask them to reveal their hidden nature, and at that moment, an answer would come that would show me the continuation of life – their impermanence. I would communicate with the animal kingdom, should I see any, and offer to learn from them the wonder of living on this realm. I remember doing this sort of thing once before and I told my wife that I asked the sun to revitalize my energy and to cleanse my aura whilst I walked. She looked shocked and explained that she did the same thing; consequently, our contemplative state joined as one.

*While you walk, become aware of the earth be-
neath your feet, and recognize how much of a
miracle you are living in this present moment,
feel every step as you walk along your path. Try
to have an awareness of the different feelings
upon your feet as you walk on undulating ground.
Feel the elements that surround you, perhaps the
warmth of the sun, the gentle breeze and become
more aware of life in its connected formlessness.
Know that at this moment you are living a wonderful moment. Clear your mind of your material worries and be grateful for what spirit has brought
you. Enjoy your time and identify with nature as
you watch how the butterfly flutters from flower to flower or the humble bee offers its service. At this moment, you recognize that you are
spirit, you are the flower, you are the bee, the
butterfly, for nothing is different, and everything is as one. As you walk, ask your guides and
your angels to help you on your path and to make
their presence known to you. Perhaps you may see
in your mind – in your clairvoyance, you may hear
the gentle whisper of your guide or have an inner knowing that your Angel is near. Ensure that
you are in no rush to get to your destination for
every wondrous step in your contemplative state
is a heightened awareness of being and of living
in the moment. Answers are within, and in this
state, all is revealed.*

On the Go Meditation

Now in this particular form of meditation, I would like to
make it clear that I have excluded the act of driving or being in
control of machinery etc. This is more for if you are traveling
on other forms of transport, and you have some time to relax
and go within. Even though all around you may be busy with
all the hustle and bustle of material existence, you can shut this

off and once more enter your own contemplative state. I often meditate when I am on the plane traveling somewhere to teach.

Case 17: Meditating on the Go

I begin the meditation after the air flight attendants or stewards have done the obligatory safety brief. During takeoff, I deeply breathe to relax myself. I begin to visualize taking off on angels' wings; and the higher I go towards the sky and the clouds, I visualize dropping my daily baggage of material worries and woes off to make me lighter and in order that I may commune with the higher realm of the spirit. When I have reached the point of leveling out, I take myself into a room on top of the clouds with the Angels and Guides present. It is there that I spend time communing with spirit and often communicate with loved ones. I will normally be in this state of quiet contemplation for at least 30 minutes and often come back feeling invigorated, as if I have learned something of note.

On one particular meditative experience, I was taken to the clouds where I could see the mountains and the vastness of the earth below. The Angel told me of certain earthly conditions that were to befall the earth soon, and that this was necessary to balance and cleanse. Later that year, earthquakes hit, and the volcano in Iceland erupted. Sometimes Mother Nature must cleanse herself of the maladies that man has created and this is often her way of balancing out what we take, and though it may have unfortunate consequences, man manifests these.

When you are ready to return, you must say a fond farewell and thank spirit for allowing you to commune with them. Find yourself becoming more and more aware of your presence on the plane and bring yourself back.

Obviously, you must ensure that you ask for protection before any of these meditative practices. You can use this type of meditation on the bus or even the train, though perhaps these practices are more like you are walking meditation and of more mindful awareness.

Shower or Bath Practice

Here is one of my favorites and an exercise that I love to do before a reading or in the process of my daily ablutions. I normally have a shower, but you can change the process to suit your own daily routine. Before I enter the shower, I let my angels and guides know that I am about to commune with them for a short while, and that I would be honored if they would join me on a mind-to-mind connection. Now at this point, some of you will have that humanistic awareness and embarrassment when you think that spirit could see you in the shower all naked. That is not quite true for they do understand that you have privacy and will not spy on you; even if they did, you have to understand that they are not interested in the physical body as the need for our physical self is only apparent in this realm. Frankly, I do not care if they were there or not, spirit knows when they are not wanted. Because this is on a mind-to-mind connection, you may or may not hear your guides.

Oh, Those Discursive Thoughts

I also wish to give you a little comfort and let you know that we all experience the discursive thought process (discursive means your thoughts bounce uselessly from one thing to another), and we all experience the anger and feeling that we are getting nowhere with our spiritual practice. The trick of all of this is to recognize this is normal and something which you have complete control and power over. You are the master of your own ship and the co-creator of your own life; therefore, you have the wheel of your own thoughts. When these discursive and intrusive thoughts begin to interfere with your meditative process, all you have to do is just breathe deeply and allow the thoughts to come and go. When you are ready, you can return to your normal visualization and carry on from where you left off. This act of deep breath control seems to calm the emotion and allows you to return to that serene meditative state.

CHAPTER 25

Psychic Development Exercises

Now we move on to the developing of your spiritual gifts and at this juncture, I wish to congratulate you on taking the positive step towards changing your life for the better. I wish to ensure that you develop yourself to the highest level that you can achieve. Do not allow your frustrations to take over and when you reach this point take a little time off – remember what I told you about pushing for something too much. Remember that you have your negative aspects and your positive but also be aware that you have an incredible power at your fingertips. It is your free will how you use your gifts and remember that no one escapes Karma. If you ensure that you use your gifts ethically, you will achieve beyond your wildest expectations.

I now want to give you some exercises that will help to develop your clairvoyance, which in turn will also help to develop your other gifts. Take your time and enjoy yourself. Some of these exercises can be done with a partner or can be done on your own. They are developed to give you an immediate measurement of success. Remember though, it is important that you carry out the protective exercise that I have given you before you attempt to open yourself up to any psychic energy.

I realize that most of these exercises will develop your clairvoyance but I assure you the other gifts will be developing alongside. As you begin to become more adept at the subtle imagery that will come to you, other gifts will begin to develop too. For instance, you will begin to hear words; sentences or you may feel emotional trails of energy. This is why there are no hard and fast ways of developing the particular facet of your innate spiritual nature and your gifts of the spirit. Consciously you cannot concentrate on one, as your spirit and your gifts will develop according to your spiritual makeup and advanced understanding or soul development.

Psychometry Excercises

Psychometry is the ability to read energy from objects either animate or inanimate. This information is perceived using any of the spiritual gifts bestowed on the sensitive, such as clairvoyance, clairaudience, clairsentience or clairalience. *Psyche* comes from a Latin term meaning soul and -*metry* meaning measure; therefore, the term psychometry can mean the measurement of the soul. We can also define psychometry as sensory perception, which allows the reader to experience the nature and history of the chosen article when held in the hands of the psychic. If the reader is within its vicinity, it can be read also. Of course, this has to be under the right intention and conditions. Everything has its own emanation of energy and this is what is read. Psychic Mediums can sense these emanations around almost anything, and with proper development can read the past, the present and on rare occasions, the future held within the aura, as well as bridging connections to the spirit world. A person who specializes in only this field of psychic ability is normally known as a psychometrist. It is known that objects receive, store and absorb energy, conditions, and emotions, and hold these within its field of energy. For instance, let us say that you are standing in an area where a particularly violent assault, or even a murder, took place. The emotions of the incident and feelings of the victims will be held in that area and this is often what highly sensitive individuals are able to pick up. This is exactly what psychics do when they work on particular cases for law enforcement.

Now allow me to explain the levels of psychometric reading before I give you a small exercise to help you develop this skill. When you first read or perceive information, it may come to you as an image in your mind. This is something that you should not deny for we often refute psychic impressions as pure imagination. However, the truth is that imagination is also the bridge to your clairvoyance and the developing of it. You may also hear a voice in your mind that will be in the form of your own voice, as if you were reading a passage out of the book, but the difference is that the information will be in response immediately to a searching question or intention without the process of conscious thought. Your clairaudient ability will come to you this way. You may be in a building and hear the word "fire" out of the blue; this would be a great indication. However, if you are a person who is adept at feeling emotions within your own physical being, you may feel the conditions of the person. Say, for instance, the individual has had a terrible time with stomach pains or headaches; you may feel these as physical pains yourself.

The psychic who is reading the object will be able to tune into its history, and if the object is a personal object belonging to the sitter, and will only be able to read its material conditions such as in the here and now. The psychic can offer things such as change of job, car, a new house, boyfriend or girlfriend, money worries and general domestic status. A medium who might read the same object will be able to make a bridge to the spirit and offer far wider and deeper information such as spiritual direction, attitudes, doubts, fears, and will often make a direct connection to loved ones in the spirit realm for information that is validated further. *(Please note: do not read personal objects of a deceased person at the beginning or without proper development, this is not spirit communication as you will only pick up anomalous information attached to the individual's physical conditions on the earth plane.)*

Take a piece of jewelry from someone that you do not know very well. This can be a friend but you must ensure that you do not know too much about the person. You must take time to go through the protective exercises I have discussed and ensure that you are requesting the information for the highest good and to help you develop your psychic ability. Take some time to go within and enter your meditative relaxed state. Answer the following questions (these are the template questions I use in my workshops),

- What did your partner do 3 days ago? (Visualize this)
- What colors did they wear 2 days ago?
- Visualize in your mind and write down where your partner last went on holiday, what did they do there?
- See an important event in their life and what happened -- this must not be generalized like holiday, dentist or a party. This should be something like being given a special gift and what the gift was, a relationship with a favorite pet – what was it?
- Visualize any medical conditions in their life – what are they?
- What car do they drive?
- Give an important first or last name of a close family member including relations.
- Name an important date to the person.
- What is a food they dislike?

- What blockages do they have in their life that stops them from moving forward?

Practice this repeatedly until you begin to score relatively high each time you do this, and do it with different individuals especially those that you do not know. Be aware that when you do these exercises, you will act like a sponge that will also soak up all that emotion and energy. You have to be aware there is good and bad energy, therefore you have a responsibility to protect yourself from bad energy. This is part of your good practices to cleanse yourself with white light, before and after each exercise.

Remote Perception Excercises

Remote perception is a term that I prefer myself to be equally applicable to the phenomena of remote viewing and the perception of information from chosen targets using the gifts of the spirit. I do not claim to be the originator of the term, my friend Dale Graaf tried to have this term accepted by the American military before it was rejected and became remote viewing, much to his chagrin. I will give you a remote perception exercise in a minute that will help you to develop your clairvoyant ability, but first I would like to introduce you to a couple of individuals that I have had the fortune to be involved with in some small way and who have also added to my books by answering questions and providing much needed information in not only this book but my others too.

Dale Graaf – whom I have already named - and Russell Targ are highly respected eminent scientists who were at the forefront of experimentation into psychic phenomena, and along with other colleagues developed the STARGATE program for the American Military. They were both directors of the Stanford Research Institute and continue to investigate and work with ESP, psychic phenomena, and remote viewing to this day.

Both of these scientists have written excellent works on their lives and the work they do, and continue to study the human potential. I wholeheartedly recommend that you read their books too.

Remote Viewing or Remote Perception works primarily in a clairvoyant way. There must be certain scientific protocols in place to prove no fraudulent activity - targets are chosen and given a number, or are unknown to the reader and sometimes the controller of the experiment. The premise is to identify the target by explaining or drawing the target as accurately as possible.

Now what you can do to help you develop this aspect of your clairvoyant nature is to have a target chosen for you and ensure you are blind to the target. Perhaps this may be tuning into someone at a chosen location. Again, you must go within and carry out your protective procedures. Now ask to be shown the details of the target and see what comes to you by way of clairvoyant imagery, emotions, and perhaps what you may hear in your own mind. Do not dismiss anything. This is a way to start to understand your limitations, and how you work. Maybe you will see a bridge in your mind's eye, and the fact that you live near one may cause you to think that you have conjured this from your own conscious thought. Imagine denying this, and finding that your colleague was sitting in a coffee shop that was called The Bridge. You can see how your own Ego may cause you to deny your spiritual influences and what you may perceive from the universe. I am using simple examples, but of course you can make this as hard as you wish, and the harder the better.

Another exercise, which is similar, is to identify a series of contents in a number of chosen envelopes. I teach this particular exercise to students of my development workshops. What I am looking for in this exercise is precise information, and not general information such as a color or shape. I need identification of targets and what exactly is in the envelope.

Take 10 envelopes, five of which will have different photographs or indeed articles in them, and chosen at random. Have an independent person shuffle the envelopes and ensure they are securely sealed. Take some time to meditate and to clear your mind before asking your higher self or your guides and angels to reveal what may be contained. Identify the images within the envelopes and the ones which have no images or nothing inside. Each should be marked as a hit or a miss. Now the important thing is to recognize that you are not looking to get the image accurate by 100% as you are developing that clairvoyant ability. If you see the image and identify several aspects and not just one aspect to it i.e.; colors, shapes, content, emotions, names, places, then this is a correct identification of present ESP and clairvoyant ability. Not general information such as a blue color or it is a round thing. What is the thing that is blue, what is round? Is it a shield on a warrior and is a warrior on the image? This is how strict I am normally. The stricter and more stringent your protocols are - the better you will develop your natural clairvoyance as you strive to reach further and further into your psyche.

Flower Reading Excercise

Flower reading is a wonderful exercise and one that can yield some spectacular results. As I have discussed before, everything has an energy field, which is known and understood as the auric field, which emanates vibrations at particular frequencies. A living thing such as a plant will have a greater vibratory field, due to the nature that it is a living thing and not inanimate. Therefore the stronger its vibration will be, and as it is a pure vibration, it will resonate at a higher level. Now if you have someone take their time and select a flower they are drawn to, then tell them to pick the flower. You can actually give a very accurate reading using the flower by reading the energy the same way that you would have done while doing the psychometry exercise. The energy of both living things dance together and so the patterned vibration can be left upon the flower. Again, this is a tool to activate your clairvoyant nature and I will discuss the use of tools later. The person who has chosen that flower will leave their own personal trail of energy within the flower and you will pick up the vibrations, which emanate from it.

When you hold the individual's flower and with the proper intent, you will begin to visualize images or symbols that will give you personal information of the sitter. However, the flower they have chosen will also give you information, for they have been drawn to that flower for a reason - the color, shape, petals, and leaves have their individual stories to reveal of the person's past, present and future.

Each trainee psychic medium must build their own library of images, words, and associations that mean something to them because the same image may mean something different to someone else. Allow me to give you a quick example. For instance, when mediums perhaps see an image of a rose, it will normally mean love, and the offering of such from the world of spirit, but to me it means something completely different.

I know that when I read a flower, if I see a smaller baby leaf hiding behind the main head of the flower, then I know without a shadow of a doubt, that I am looking at the fertility issues of the person, or perhaps that a little one is about to come into the world. These are just subtle clues that lie within the nature and purpose of the flower, for the universe will know the need and would have guided the individual to selecting that particular flower. It is all a matter of harmonic resonance.

The more you practice the stronger you will become at using these gifts. As well as receiving the imagery within your third eye, you may also hear words and/or sentences that will be guiding you to giving the correct information to the sitter.

Dream State Clairvoyance Excercise

I have tried this exercise a number of times; however, I must stress that you will get varied results, and there needs to be a high level of understanding and degree of development. Therefore, this is better to do when you have been having great successes with other forms of clairvoyant exercises. To explain this better, I will not go into the ins and outs of how to do this but rather use an example of my achievements with the readings using one client case.

Case 18: Dream Reading

I had a reading for a woman named Michelle who had called to have an emergency appointment. Luckily enough, I had a cancellation and decided to fit her in the next day when the previous client was supposed to have the reading. I went to bed that evening with the intent that I wanted to carry out a scientific experiment regarding the reading the next day and before going to sleep, wrote in my journal. I also explained to my wife what I wanted to do, and so prepared myself. I prayed as I normally do each night. I also had a meditation before going to sleep, when I asked my guide Ellie to bring to me the information either from the loved one who was coming through for the client, or from Ellie to my dream state, and allow me to take note of the information prior to the reading.

I then went to sleep and early in the morning, I started to have a vivid dream of people, places, events, imagery that told a story and a man who came to me with the name Michael, who told me that his partner was the one coming to see me. I was then given further information and was di-

rected to take note. I immediately took note of the information using my journal and got my wife to verify it.

Later that day the woman came for her reading at the appropriate time and before I started the reading officially, I asked her to verify the information of which 90% was completely accurate, and the ten that was not accurate probably was not understood by myself as I believe spirit are able to impart the information, we often fail to interpret.

Exercise into the Future

When you have become adept at receiving those clairvoyant images and symbols, and you have worked within your capacity in learning to discern between a higher influence and your own mind, you can move onto the next exercise, which is predominantly the ability to predict future events. This of course can be fun and we have added a timescale to allow you to have a measure of your successes and failures.

You will need your journal or a suitable notebook for this exercise and of course, there is nothing difficult about it.

Take some quiet time to go within by quieting your mind. I must reiterate that you must complete the protective exercises that I have taught previously.

When you have gone to your quiet place, instead of visualizing a particular scene, I want you to concentrate on creating a cinematic space within your mind's eye. When you have done this, create the intention and request from your higher authority to reveal to you things that will happen over the next week. Ask to be shown events that will pass over the next few days. Wait for a short while and take note of anything that you see, hear, or feel. Write these things down on the paper as they enter your mind and do not worry about neatness – you can sort that later.

Perhaps you may see a scene where you are standing by water and feeding the swans. Write down all that you see and feel. You may even hear a name that means something to you, perhaps you hear the name Melissa – write it down. Now after a while, and after you have as much information as you can handle, come out of your meditative state in the same way and thank your guides and your angels for helping you on this occasion. The remarkable thing is this, if you have meditated and entered your quiet space properly, you will be amazed at how accurate the information will be over the proceeding days until the end of the week, and you can witness and score what you have right and wrong. This will give you an immediate measurement of your successes.

Now a word to the wise; you cannot say something like "going shopping", that is far too general and includes 90% of the world's population. However, if you heard or saw that you were going shopping and you were going to buy a particular item that you had not considered or that you were going to meet a particular person such as Melissa - that would be a direct hit.

What's the History Exercise

At this point in the proceedings, you should have become quite good at using your gifts, now it is time to hone them even further. This is something that I did and I want you to try this. Again, instead of me telling you how to do it, I will recount two of my own particular experiences.

Case 19: Get Out of the Way!

Before I met my beautiful wife and soul mate Jo, a medium that I will only name as Helen took me under her wing and tried to help me develop. She took me to an old farmhouse out in the sticks *and took the time to ensure the building and de-tails were kept from me - in fact, this building was not really well known and was not a histori-cal one, but had an incredible history within the area where it was situated. I arrived at this old building in the countryside, which was partially done up and inhabited, and partially in ruins. Helen had asked me to walk around and just to go within myself as I was taught to do, and to de-scribe what I was seeing. At first, this seemed somewhat silly to me, yet I did exactly as I was told.*

I began to see blood and people wandering around in white coats. Then I would hear horses and shouting. The man in the white coat appeared to be carrying an instrument that looked rather horrible. I saw the building as it was and heard a bell toll. I immediately told her what I was seeing and I said, it is an old slaughterhouse. She asked me for a name and I gave what I thought I could hear. Helen told me nothing, continued to walk me around the place then into an old room, and asked again.

I said I saw a disheveled bed and a young man who was in it, dirty and coughing. I could see meat on hooks hanging in the corner. Helen asked me again to explain everything and then tell her what it was; I said, "Ok, it's an old slaughter house," which I thought, given the information and where we are, was accurate. Helen had told me that I was half-right and that I had allowed my own conscious mind into the play. In fact, the old farm was used as a military hospital many years ago and though the information fitted - I had gotten my own mind in the way. That was an important lesson for me.

Because I had some success with what Helen had taught me, I decided to choose another historical place but one that I had never been to or had any prior knowledge of. A friend was coming to visit me and the location was chosen at random. This was a castle in the north of Scotland and yes, the inevitable green lady, and man in white were in the stories, but what I am about to share was perhaps further evidence of spiritual abilities, and is something you can do though perhaps not on the following scale.

Case 20: A Reluctant Tour Guide

My friend and I decided not to go on the tour so that my mind was clear and I had no information fed to me. I began to walk around and explain what I was seeing, hearing and feeling, giving names, dates and other forms of evidence including what I was picking up psychometrically. I am sorry to say that one of the curators heard, approached and asked if they could come along with us, the more I went from room to room, others joined us until I had about six people following me. I was terrified and just did what I did.

Anyway, at the end the curator told me to wait a minute, as she wanted to talk to me and wanted the manager to come along. The two individuals asked me how much knowledge I had, interrogated me and if I had been there before, you know the usual skeptical stuff. However, the manager and the other curator said to me, they had a ghost team up and another medium had walked around with the team. The information they relayed was general and some already on the brochure. The information I gave them was entirely accurate, including events, names, dates and other evidence that was known. It turned out the manager was a family member and owner of the estate, who confirmed the information. After some pleasantries, I was asked if I would return and do this for another group, which I declined as I thought this would be making a farce of my gifts. However, it did give me feedback and evidence of my own abilities.

You can have fun with this exercise yourself and with a friend or someone you trust. Please remember though, this is not about ego, and helps you develop your gifts. It is not for show, and can become a good practice. I have done this in America, Norway, and Japan, some with results and others I am not sure, but it is good to try with the right scientific protocols in place.

The Time is Nigh!

This is an exercise that I do with some regularity, and was imparted to me through trance addresses that I studied. I do it in the mornings, but you may wish to choose another suitable time. What you need is a blindfold and an object such as a clock or something that has a great deal of detail on it.

Sit in a chair opposite your object, which should be situated on a table or shelf on the opposite side of the room from where you are sitting. Now you should blindfold yourself and ensure that no white light enters your eyes at any time. When you do this exercise at first, you may develop some uncomfortable feelings in the area where your third eye is situated and near your pineal gland. You may feel dizzy and will have an amazing amount of pressure on this area. Try to concentrate on visualizing the object that is in front of you.

At first this may sound rather strange as you already know what is there, however you will begin after much patience and practice to perceive the image in your mind's eye clearer than you could ever imagine. Almost like you can see out of your physical eyes too.

Now, if you can remember at the beginning of the exercise, I mentioned that you should place a clock in front of you. The reason is that you will eventually be able to tell the time blindfolded. But, I know that you are thinking that you will already know what time it is at. The way that you get around this is by asking someone to continually keep changing the clock time. If you live on your own and you are practicing yourself, then you should move the clock time every night and then sit first thing in the morning at different junctures. Your clairvoyance will develop to an extremely high degree.

PART 6

"DO" Learn To Use Psychic Development Tools

There is a plethora of psychic tools available at the disposal of everyone, and though the tools themselves are not dangerous, the intent and misuse of them can cause tremendous problems for the developing psychic or medium. Each tool that is used is simply a tool that becomes the catalyst for unlocking the intuitive senses and allows imagery to flow freely through the super-conscious mind to the conscious mind, where the reader will interpret them, according to the reader's experience and knowledge. The problem that you have is that trainee psychics and mediums that become very self-reliant on the tools themselves and get stuck on what they perceive with the tool they use.

This is similar to training a muscle group, for instance. You could train regularly using the same exercise and eventually you will become stuck on that plateau, which will cause you to doubt your progress. Nevertheless, if you challenge yourself and change your modus operandi regularly, you will always develop and should never seem so stuck that you cannot overcome your obstacles.

Now the developing student can cause himself or herself enormous damage when using tools, if they do not take the responsibility to treat them with respect and reverence, while being able to discern the types of intent and energy surrounding them. I will discuss some of the tools here; tools such as the Board, Tarot, Dowsing, Runes, Tea, Scrying, and a little known one called a Psychomanteum are used.

CHAPTER 26:

Tarot and other Cards

Tarot cards, and other divination cards such as angel cards, help you to activate your third eye chakra and unlock that hidden intuitive symbolism. This is known as Cartomancy and dates back to ancient Egypt, and France when it became a popular form of card game in the early 18th century.

Some people are fearful of tarot cards as they associate them with being evil or dark in essence, because of the imagery that some of the cards represent, such as the tower of terror and the death card or the devil card. Some cards do have a questionable birth since they involve necromancy and other forms of black magic as divinatory, however, there are thousands of cards out there today, and most are of a higher vibration and have been designed with the highest of intentions. You will be attracted to the ones that suit your vibration.

These cards are a great way for a developing student to begin to recognize their own intuitive symbolism. This will strengthen the gift of clairvoyance when used correctly and under the right conditions. It is important, though, not to follow what it says about a card in a book, and to develop your own meaning within your own sphere of understanding.

People who believe the cards are evil are those who lack the understanding of the positive benefits of such cards. When a spiritually enlightened person is reading the cards, then they will interpret them from a higher evolved level than that of someone who lacks compassion, understanding, and the wisdom of how the cards can help to guide a person forward in their life in a more beneficial manner. Individuals who are not of a high vibration will, of course, attract entities of a similar vibration, and trouble will often ensue for the reader.

A person who has no training or real knowledge of the workings of the cards can in fact open a portal to the spirit world or be messed with by grounded spirits who would like to have some fun. This often happens and at the low end of the scale, the reading could be inaccurate and send the individual down the wrong path, or in the worse case, can cause a potential spirit attachment to the needy individual.

Someone who is afraid of the tarot cards should not attempt to read them as they will find it difficult to detach from their own fears, and therefore will not conduct an accurate reading, as their own low vibration will get in the way.

CHAPTER 27:

Scrying

S crying is a method which has been used for thousands
of years, and involves staring into something such as a
crystal ball or water to activate deep clairvoyance. The
problem that you have with scrying is that you have no control
of what you are going to see. Some individuals have claimed
they have seen grotesque figures that have undoubtedly been
released through their own fears. The scrying method involves
a process of getting yourself ready and letting your mind go to
have whatever should come in visual form.

Scrying is dangerous if not used with the highest intent and
with protection. As I have mentioned, sometimes one's ego can
cause you to forget to carry out these practices and you will
attract the wrong source of information. Think back to your
childhood, is there a particular time or an event that you saw
scrying without knowing it. You would be shocked if it was
suggested that Walt Disney captivated this mystical art in one
of their most famous productions 'Snow white and the Seven
Dwarfs.' If you can remember there was a part in the animated
film when the evil witch would use a mirror. When she gazed

upon this mirror she would be able to view the present and the future. This is the idea behind scrying; this idea for the movie would have been based on fact. Another well known movie in which scrying was used was in The Lord of the Rings, Galadriel scries in a trough or bowl of water ("The Mirror of Galadriel") she then sees the visions of the enemy and at what position they are at in that regard.

The following is an extract from my book "Everything Guide to Past Life Experience," published by Adams media. The history of scrying dates back thousands of years and was prevalent in ancient civilizations such as the Aztecs and Incas. These ancient civilizations used the art of scrying as a link into the spirit world. The seers of these civilizations used the art of scrying to prophesize events or possible problems or indeed successes for groups and individuals.

Many objects were used for scrying and these ranged from water, mirrors, crystals and oil. Probably the weirdest object that was used for scrying would have to be the blood that the Aztec priests used, the blood would be on a receptacle such as a plate or cup, they would then stare into the blood to gain insights. Furthermore, it must be noted that the culture very much was the catalyst for what one would see while scrying. The visions that were perceived are considered to come from only a few sources; this would obviously be dependent on intention and belief. So, it was asserted that all information came from either God or a religious deity, members of the world of spirit, Satan or whomever their culture personified as evil, the psychic and the subconscious mind.

Religious cultures have also used these ancient forms of scrying and divination. One religion actually is founded on what was gained in this way, and one would have to assert there are many inaccuracies – perhaps the individuals' ego and environmental perceptions have gotten in the way.

Types of Scrying

Below you will now find various methods of scrying.

Mirror Gazing

Mirror gazing is perhaps the widest form of scrying that is understood in the modern day. There are countless tales of mirror gazing. There are many myths concerning mirror gazing and in Victorian England, it was thought that a young lady should hold a mirror in front of her and walk backwards up the stairs in the dark. It was maintained that she would see the future husband for her, though there was a macabre side to it too. If she saw a vision of a skull it was suggested this would be the foretelling of her pending death or that of a loved one. Now obviously this sounds like a bit of an extreme but like most myths and tales, there is some basis of fact within the story line. Another tale exists that involves the story of a young mother whose baby was stolen from her. She was so stricken with grief that she committed suicide – her name was Bloody Mary, though the bloody was added after the event, and there exists some controversy that suggests Mary was in fact Queen Victoria who suffered from severe miscarriages.

The legend eventually turned into a spirit game of sorts. It was said that one should stand before a mirror in the dark and repeat her name three times. This would be the act of carrying out a physical invocation, to force the spirit of the young woman to appear. Of course a multitude of variations in the invocation exists and some with sinister undertones. Another game exists that is a test of courage and this is similar to the Bloody Mary story, this involves other invocations to test the courage of the questioner who will attempt to summon witches and darker entities without showing any fear. The tales of these legends have gone further to suggest that in some cases divination could occur – good and bad and that some of the questioners died mysteriously after carrying out these silly games. Nevertheless the above examples do show the extremities of each individual story.

Crystals

Another method of scrying was of course the use of crystals and shiny crystalline objects. This was especially prevalent in ancient cultures who recognized the high vibrations of these rocks and minerals.

The Aztecs were renowned as were the Egyptians for using Obsidian, which is also used as the wizard's stone or witch's stone in some indigenous cultures. The theory behind this form of Crystallomancy was to put the individual into an altered state of consciousness to make a connection with those in the spirit world. An interesting point is that an Elizabethan alchemist by the name of John Dee used obsidian and a small crystal ball to communicate with the other worlds and to receive images of the past, present and future. The crystal ball and other artifacts used by Dee are on display at the British Museum in London.

Another substance that was used for the art of scrying is oil and this was prevalent with the high priests in Egypt and some areas of Persia. The seer would pour the oil into a suitable receptacle and let it settle. He would then stare at the oil, which would eventually put him into a trance state and he would note what visions he saw. This was mainly used to give information to the gentry of the time (there do not seem to be any cases of the lower classes discussing this). It should also be noted that the ancient Greeks also used this method. Of course this method could also be used in a pool of oil or of water and this was often the case in ancient Egypt.

Candle

This method dates back for many years and is especially prevalent in the modern world. People are encouraged to stare at the candle to invoke angels or to enter an altered state of consciousness. There are a plethora of new age books that support this method of scrying. It is suggested that by staring into this candle, you enter a sphere of birth and death that you are reborn and have access to the realm of the spirit through celestial guidance.

Learning How to Scry & Preparation

Obviously, one has to learn how to do this skill of scrying, yet there are no hidden secrets, and it is not as mystical as it originally seems. As with anything that has been discussed before it follows the same routine and is just another tool to activate your clairvoyant potential. However, there are a few pitfalls that one may fall into rather easy, and this must be taken into consideration. There are obviously dangers that exist, which is similar to any of the dangers that we have discussed before. However, these dangers are purely borne of fear and come from your own self loathing and inner fears, which you have created. Therefore, it is good to follow a regime of preparation before scrying.

This is a personal regime that is used by the author and is offered to you before you carry out any type of scrying. It is of paramount importance that one should cleanse themselves and the area that is to be used before any scrying is attempted and this will involve a period of prayer, fasting and cleansing of the area and the physical body. First of all, you should prepare yourself by eating less and more or less high vibrational foods. It is really important that you cleanse your mind of all impurities, and that may have to include a process of meditation and prayer over a period of time. The reason is you will be activating deeper elements of the subconscious mind and your fears could also be released as a reflection of inner issues. There is no guarantee that you would receive any information that pertains to any past life existence. Nevertheless, with practice you will receive this information, but only when your mind, body and soul is purified. Going through the process of preparation will also release the innate gifts that you have, and what you normally find is that some are more adept than others. Just like anything in life some people are adept at becoming good doctors or pilots or musicians. We all have the same innate gifts, but they are innate at varying degrees of power. With the case of scrying skills, some individuals are more susceptible to the perception and communication of spirits and psychic energy. The mirror seems to act as a powerful conduit but is not restricted to only good things. It can reflect your innermost fears, and you can conjure frightening experiences from this. This then can act as a gateway to emotion and fear and that is why one must prepare adequately.

Scrying Exercise

Again some of these elements will be similar in nature to what you have read before with subtle changes that will allow you to attempt your first basic scrying exercise. Now what to understand is that information you will receive will almost ultimately be clairvoyant in nature and this is concurrent with the intent that is set in place. Now you must choose a large enough mirror that you feel comfortable with and that you can sit just in front of you on a suitable table. Ensure that when you deal with this type of exercise that you do it in pure darkness.

CHAPTER 28

Dowsing

D owsing is by far the easiest of the tools to use, though there is surrounding conjecture which claims that the movements of a crystal pendulum or divining rod are down to subconscious motor movement within the body, rather like the blinking of an eye. The act of dowsing can be very accurate in the right hands, and involves the psychic asking a series of direct questions that will give a yes or no response, depending on the way a crystal pendulum will swing. Now I know from experience that wandering spirits can have their fun with you, and you have to be aware that although there are very little sinister problems with dowsing, a grounded spirit can make the pendulum swing in the wrong direction to fool you, and to them, this is a laugh. Yet again, this will most likely occur when you have not taken the appropriate precautions.

CHAPTER 29:

Guides and Angels

S tudents of psychic development and mediumship are normally so desperate to meet their guides and guardian angels that they will take any opportunity to communicate with anything or anyone from the world of spirit. This opportunity also of- fers those of spirit the chance to communicate too, as they will surely recognize your desire. The problem that you are faced with is ensuring that the communicator is an actual guide or angelic presence, for your desire will overshadow the reality, and you will find yourself being led down the wrong path. When someone thinks they have met their guide, they fail to ask for requisite proof. Silver Birch said that if the information does not sit well with the person receiving the communication, they should dismiss it. This is very important and a necessary factor of discernment. Many mediums forget to ask for proof, and more than just once.

Case 21: A Piece of Evidence

When Ellie, my guide, was contacting me, I asked for three separate proofs of her presence, and in particular, a piece of evidence. I remember that one day while out jogging with my dog, there was a particular place (a log in the forest) where I would stop and have a meditation. Before I went into my meditation, I demanded that if she was really my guide, then I wanted to see a white butterfly land on me when I came back from my meditative state. When I finally came back, I opened my eyes expectantly to find no butterfly near me anywhere. I was disgusted and thought that the communication I had from this person was false. I ran back to my car – my anger building with every step. I got in, and drove away. I could not get this out of my mind, and as I drove down the highway, a white butterfly landed on my windscreen and stayed there, right in my center of vision. As you can imagine, the shock took over, and I was still staring at this white majestic butterfly on my windscreen as I felt a tremendous thump and jolted out of my seat while mounting the roundabout in the wrong direction. I came out of my shock quickly and brought my car to a halt; getting out of the vehicle, shaking in my shoes. I smiled and thought, "Jock, be careful what you ask for." I was on the rostrum that night and recounted the story.

It is important to ensure that you get validation from the spirit that purports to be your guide, and the level of validation must be high indeed. As a student, you will have a desire to communicate with the entity and will begin to rely on the information. Slowly, and surely, this so-called guide will make you become more reliant on them, and you will not be able to do anything without having to turn to the entity claiming to be your spirit guide. One of our students was so into talking with her guide whom she could not do anything without the guide's permission. One day she told me that her guide even told her what toilet tissue to buy. Now, come on, that's a load of crap, if you pardon the pun. It is important to stay rational and grounded.

CHAPTER 30

The Development Circle

The circle is the starting place of any medium who wishes to develop professionally. That is why it is known as the develop- ment circle. A circle is formed by a group of like-minded indi- viduals that wish to investigate the world of spirit and develop the communication between our two worlds. The interesting thing to note is that even though the circle is protected by its nature, it has nothing to do with the act of protection. In es- sence, the circle is where the spirit energies can be magnified and used for the development of the medium and those within the circle. The energies that are harnessed in the circle are con- trolled and worked upon by a spiritual team of helpers, which are chosen to work with the circle itself.

Now another important point is this. You do not choose the members of the circle. It is the spirit team that chooses and brings the right people to the circle. There can literally be hundreds of spirit helpers chosen to work with the circle it- self. A circle may also take a very long time to develop as spirit work with personalities and energies to develop harmony and progress.

You can of course develop on your own but this takes much dedication and will not always have much success, unless you are a natural medium. Doris Stokes was an individual that had a natural gift; she developed largely on her own, but sat every day at the same time in order to develop. Even she admits that it took a very long time to reach a level where she could begin communication and recommends that everyone should sit in a professional circle headed by an experienced medium. In the modern day, there are too many add water and mix courses that manufacture mediums. The communication is not the only aspect of mediumship and dangers can lurk, not to mention the reality of mediumship responsibility.

Members of the circle will include sitters, the medium, a scribe and a circle leader.

An important aspect is the opening and closing prayer, which should be done before any circle, meditation, or séance. Untrained and ill-prepared mediums will often forget this important aspect and will soon find themselves coming unstuck. This sometimes includes professionals.

Helen Duncan was one such professional who, in the beginning of her own development, forgot to do this and suffered. Robin Foy had this to say about Helen and you will note he vouched for her genuine materializations:

"Helen Duncan (Whatever was written about her by so-called researchers, I can vouch for the fact that her mediumship was 100% genuine!). In the early part of her development as a materialization medium, she sat every week in a home circle at her home with her husband and other experienced friends. At that time, the circle did not use an opening prayer when they started their group sitting (which included a request for protection). On one occasion, Helen was in deep trance, and a 'hairy unwelcome beast' of some sort materialized. This was clearly not a friendly entity - and it rampaged around the room, ripping off a piece of the fireplace. The sitters were petrified, and ran out of the house, leaving Helen and her husband behind to face the music. After this dreadful experience, Helen and her husband insisted that in future, an opening prayer, and a request for

protection, was always included at the start of their séances. I believe details of this are included in Alan Crossley's book - Helen Duncan medium - and in the subsequent book by Helen's daughter."

This highlights the importance of protection while sitting for development and I can vouch for the fact that when you do not ask for protection, you can find yourself in deep water – not that it has happened to me. I am so aware of the dangers that I bug spirit, asking for a type of Fort Knox around me, but I have known others that have suffered and have been called in when circles have been very very silly indeed.

You need Harmony!

Harmony is not just a feeling, but also an important requirement that will create the optimum conditions for spirit communication and indeed physical phenomena. Nevertheless, if a negative emotion pervades the harmonious resonance that should exist, this will create discord. It is this jealousy from other members, and sometimes the medium, that may see him or her in need of reproach. It is important that you choose your members very carefully and sit for a while in a meditative practice before moving forward. This allows spirit guides to choose to work with what is available and to choose the medium.

You can join a spiritualist group, but be aware that human ego will play its role. If you are on your own, then begin to meditate regularly – ensuring that you take heed of all the protective procedures I have given you. Contact a suitable professionally developed medium and ask them to guide you to a group that may accept you into their closed circle. Many spiritualist churches will have open circles that you could visit and learn from, but again ego will play its role. Please do not go there and just jump in. Introduce yourself and wait for someone to guide you, before you have a go. You could start your own circle - though if you are going to do that, carry out a great deal of re- search before you begin. The most important advice I can give you is to allow the Great Spirit to guide your endeavors for the benefit of every living being.

How to Develop Your Circle

The first thing that you should do is put the intention and the thought out to the spirit world to let them know that you are going to develop a circle. They will in turn begin their work by sourcing suitable individuals that are of the right vibration and disposition. Circles that are started by individuals without suitable instruction from the spirit team are very transient in nature and often individuals that are not suited will soon depart or spirit will ensure they leave. This may be because of their own spiritual development or the fact they are consumed by ego and not ready for the important work that is about to ensue. The circle will consist of three main personalities; the circle leader, the scribe and the medium. The rest of the members are commonly known as the sitters. The circle leader looks after all the issues of the circle and is responsible for the safety and security of the medium. The spirit team chooses the medium, and it does not always go that the medium has to be one who is already developed. Normally, the medium in the circle will have some experience. The scribe is one who takes down all information that comes from the spirit world through the medium or by direct communication. This information should be kept as records over every séance and archived for future reference. One thing that you must understand is that the circle can take a considerable time to develop and may not receive results for a very long time. Another word of caution that you should take heed, anyone who is hyper critical or skeptical should not become part of this development circle. This is considered to be unfair and even scientists have maintained these conditions would not be conducive to receiving good results. Obviously, when the circle has developed to a high standard, then things can be relaxed, and others can be invited with the express permission of the main spirit guide.

At the beginning of the circle, there should be singing or music and an opening prayer. Furthermore, is also no hard and fast rule as to how long a circle or séance should last, but the general consensus is that a minimum of one hour should be the norm and increase when appropriate. It is also important that the medium especially does not work within the circle with a full tummy, and this is the same with the other sitters too. The reason is that energy will be used for digestion and disturbs the blood stream. It is also important to realize that spirit energies could make the medium vomit the contents. This is why I never get results on a full stomach myself, and I ensure that I do not eat before a reading or a séance. Everyone at séance is just as important as the medium, for without the sitters the medium could not achieve the results that are desired.

Each sitter should also take their allocated seat and remain in this same seat during all future gatherings. The only time this may change is when directed by the spirit control. Now that you have the basis of setting up a circle. Set the intention and allow spirit to bring you the right individuals to join you.

A final thought once more, sensitives - and this is not just the medium whom I am talking about - are all too ready to accept all and any information from an outside source such as a spirit entity. This means they are too eager to respond to any passing influence. They also are too ready to attribute anything and everything to spirit influence to include emotions, feelings and phenomena.

This is not only highly dangerous because of the possibility of negative spirit influence but is also a sure sign that they are imbalanced within their understanding of spiritual matters.

Please remain grounded and do not accept anything as gospel. As Silver Birch (the spirit guide of Maurice Barbanel) once said, test the information by how it feels, and if it is obviously high in nature or offers evidence. This also means that you should examine and look for all possible and normal probable causes that have a materially placed scientific explanation. When these have all been exhausted, you may then attribute the phenomena to spirit influence.

Séances

A Séance is a group of people – headed by a professional medium, circle leader, and a scribe (who takes notes) – that meet with the sole intention of speaking with the dead, (though we do not consider them dead, its just a turn of phrase) or passing on spiritual lessons and proving the existence of the afterlife. In the correct circumstances and with the right professionally trained people, this can be an effective way of experiencing trance communication and physical phenomena. However, in most instances, untrained and unstable individuals or mediums that are deluded - do the séance through sheer inquisitiveness. This is another method of 'calling on spirits' and can be more bother than it is worth. By calling on a spirit, you are sending out an invitation for any spirit to contact you, and, even if you think it is good and from the light, you can be the victim of deception, and deception that could cost your life.

Now the séance is somewhat different from the developing circle as the séance already has a well-developed physical or trance medium. Development circles do not have to sit with rigidity in conditions but with a séance it is different. The reason is that certain conditions are required to conduct séances. One of these is that it must be held in complete darkness in order to achieve good results and then, with sufficient development of the medium and the spirit team, can be brought into the light.

"The only compromise that we have here during a darkened séance is that the spirit team may allow you to utilize the use of a red or blue bulb."

Out Through the Darkness

Ok, I want to explain a little about the reasons behind the requirement of darkness, though I do know that results can be obtained in white light with the right conditions and medium. I know that gives the pseudo skeptics much ammunition to claim that some kind of fraudulent activity is going on because of the lack of light. This means that certain things cannot be perceived in the séance room and that someone could be manipulating the events – I agree. However, one has to applaud those mediums and circle leaders who go to great lengths to ensure that every avenue of potential fraud is covered and proven negative under rigorous test conditions. The medium has been restrained, gagged and searched. The room has been searched for all possible items of trickery. The medium also has someone holding them at all times, and other practices to negate the possibility of fraud are introduced. How then can a skeptic still claim it is false under these conditions when the evidence points in the complete opposite direction? Photographs and film have been taken of ectoplasm and spirit people, and voices have originated at a great distance from the medium – sometimes 3-4 conversations going on at the same time.

The requirement of darkness, therefore, is a prerequisite, and if you consider the reasons behind this, you may then have a better appreciation for the subject. Scientific experiments almost always need darkened conditions with which to work, and in days past, the photographer needed a dark room to develop the images on his film – this is still the same with digital chips today. When you plant a seed in the ground it needs the darkness to germinate and grow to the light, and when you are in the womb, you are cloaked in darkness until you are ready to be born into the light. Now does this all not sound somewhat familiar? We also know that white light destroys some of the cellular structure of ectoplasm, and this is the reason the dark-conditions are required. However, spirit is aware of our frustrations and is working toward phenomena in light. Sir William Crookes actually witnessed the spirit form of Katie King in broad daylight through the mediumship of Florence Cook, but these are few and far between and conditions obviously have to be perfect for this to occur. The aim of course is to bring it into the light, and this is entirely possible.

How fitting to end with a quote from a Great Spirit:

"There is no joy and no service that can match helping others. In a world so full of darkness, where millions have lost their way, where there are countless numbers troubled and perplexed with sorrow in their hearts, who awake each morning in fear and apprehension of what the day brings - if you can help one soul to find some serenity and to realize that he/she is not neglected, but surrounded by arms of infinite love, that is a great work. It is more important than anything else." (Birch, 1938)

PART 7

"DON'T" Risk Possession And Obsession

Now we are going to go further into the realms of the afterlife and get to the dangers within. In the following chapters, you will learn the truth about possession and obsession. I want to displace the myths that are associated with it and take away your fear while giving you a healthy respect for the phenomena. I also wish to show you how certain tools are used, and the many skills that are needed to be able to use the various psychic tools. Yes, some of this will scare you but at the same time will empower you as I give you the right path to take to navigate the psychic wilderness. One note, tools only focus intent and don't think after this book, you will have the discernment and ability to go up against a spirit entity far more intelligent than you. You could lose your life or you could be haunted the rest of your physical life, don't dance with the Devil. Whether or not you believe in bad spirits or demons, they are real and exist in every form of spiritual text known to man. There is always a kernel of truth in all folklore and of course in religious text. Just because you can't see gravity, does not mean it does not exist.

There is a dread fascination with the occult and a plethora of individuals have an unhealthy relationship with the desire to dabble in the occult. The interest in séances, Ouija boards, and spirit communication has risen, thanks to popular TV shows that feature paranormal investigations or hauntings, and our children are in even more danger now than they were before. Their interest piques, and they want to dabble in the paranormal. These shows have also given birth to ignorance, and the problems that have arisen from these foolhardy attempts to dabble in occult practices have turned lives upside down. Consequently, they have destroyed whole families, turned friend against friend and brother against brother.

Walk into most spiritualist churches or new age organizations, and they will tell you that there is no entity such as Satan, and demons do not exist; it is merely a wandering or grounded spirit looking for help. The truth is different, and ignorance does not afford your safety. Demons do exist. The darker side of the paranormal is very dangerous indeed, though there are of course governing laws that control this aspect, and when one understands those spiritual laws, there is no reason to fear but a reason to have a healthy understanding and be able to make wise decisions. Even so, anyone who has a little knowledge and no understanding, places himself or herself in the line of fire. I want to take you out of the line of fire, and I would advise you that you acquaint yourself with as much knowledge as possible. A simple quasi-attempt to communicate with a discarnate entity, or dabble in aspects of the occult without the proper protection, will undoubtedly open a Pandora's Box of problems. If you have a fear of this, then I advise you to study and learn as much as you can from real professionals. You can't become an expert from a book.

If you do not understand the laws that govern our spiritual nature, or understand how spirit communication works and the power of divine discernment, you can be lured into a false sense of security that will undoubtedly cause you a mountain of heartache and sorrow. Look at the examples in this book and cases from the past and even the present and learn from them. Those individuals caused a great deal of sorrow in their own lives that could have been avoided. Many who are so desperate to communicate will therefore accept anything and everything and I would reiterate that you should test the information and of course the evidence. Even within real séances, there should be more testing and questioning. Personally, I am at odds with some of the spirits coming through and consider them to be of a lower level.

Though I have opened with a stark warning, I first must let you know a little of the upside and of the reality of things. Do not think for one minute that demons are prowling and waiting to possess you, just because of negative thoughts or an interest in the paranormal, or because you are a light worker. What you must understand is that everything is controlled by God, and angels do not have free will due to them carrying the will of God, therefore fallen angels have no free will either, unless divinely bestowed for a higher purpose, and are controlled by the heavenly power of divine law, which is perfect in its operation. Anything that would normally happen - will be because of a series of events or conditions that exist because of will. God has given them a job to do and they do it very well. They do, however, still have their heavenly powers, and it is obvious these were left in order to take part in a divine plan. The reality of their hatred for anything from the light is so strong, they will do anything to try and control, but still there is divine law which can't be broken. There have been very few documented cases of true possession in the world and many who think they have toiled with a demon are ignorant and do not know the reality of this fool-hardy spiritual battle. Believe me, what you think you know, you don't and if you really had to have a face off, you would be scarred for life. Those of you that think you have battled demons, think again, your ego is playing a fool with little knowledge.

Most possessions can have a scientific basis of explanation such as mental illness, and very often, as with misdiagnosing a patient, the same can occur within a spiritual understanding. This normally occurs when the individual concerned follows creed and legislation that has no divine innate spiritual authority or knowledge of it, and is created by ego or human perception. The only way that one can be possessed is through the will of God for a higher purpose. Typical scenarios include dabbling in black magic and occult practices, entering an area where demonic presences are prevalent with the intent to control, or conjured by taking part in rituals such as blood rites, or through a grounded negative evil entity that obsesses an individual through lack of faith, or turning from the light.

For the most part, these so-called demonic possessions are merely spirit obsession through the lack of understanding and discernment. There are, of course, threats, especially to the medium, though this is incredibly rare. I will explain the modern understanding of demonic activity later, but be aware this is rare, but does not mean the threat is not there. There are very real cases of demonic possession.

More often than not, you will certainly not recognize the signs and symptoms of a possession or of a darker force until it is too late. By then, the gateway is open and your simple attempts to cleanse and clear could be little more effective than trying to blow out a trick candle – THE FLAME ALWAYS RETURNS.

The problem that we face is that by our very nature, we are an inquisitive species, and we will study what we do not understand attempting to gain some kind of reason for knowledge. Often, we will try to control the outcome of something in any way possible – even to the detriment of ourselves – believing that we have achieved the unachievable. This is rather like a child who, because of their inquisitiveness, will continue to poke and prod and explore until something unnatural or the feeling of pain occurs – they then stop. In the spiritual sense, this could be too late. Let us look at a few of these examples of how this desire for communication can cause harm and how the misunderstanding of certain phenomena causes a misinterpreted imbalance.

CHAPTER 31:

Automatic Writing

One method of communication is that of automatic writing. Many individuals attempt this form of mediumship without any real training or any understanding of the dangers.

Case 22: Automatic Writing Gone Wrong

A woman called Martha contacted me a few years ago and stated that she had done a terrible thing. She was a developing medium but had been rather carried away and let her ego run riot. She was a member of a Spiritualist organization in the UK and implored me not to tell anyone of her problem. She thought she knew more than her teachers knew and loved the idea of automatic writing and channeling.

She began to meditate and when she was ready, she would invite the spirit to draw close and communicate through her by controlling her hand to write messages from the spirit world. For the first few months, the messages were good, and she believed they came from her grandmother, but over time, the messages took a sinister undertone, until one day the words on the paper were evil in nature and claimed that it was demoniacal - in fact said it was the Devil (which I don't believe, but negative spirits can feed on your inherent fear).

I communicated with my guide; I was assured this was not the case. I was told Martha was doing this without protection and had attracted a mischievous spirit, which would be easy to get rid of. This was not evil but the spirit was masking as evil in order to scare her. It was easier to deal with after that.

CHAPTER 32:

Ouija Boards

The Ouija board is perhaps the simplest and most misunderstood method of spirit communication. According to some sources, the first historical mention of something resembling an Ouija board is found in China around 1200 B.C., a divination method known as Fu Chi (or Fuji) planchette writing. Other sources claim that, according to a French historical account of the philosopher Pythagoras, in 540 B.C. that he himself and his colleagues would conduct séances at "a mystic table."

The first use of the modern Ouija board came with the spiritualist movement in the mid-19th century. Divination at that time was used to gain messages in many ways, such as using a planchette that would be controlled by the spirit and used to spell out messages to the sitting individuals. Other forms of divinatory tools were also used in conjunction with the Board including the use of scrying and psychomanteums.

During the late 1800s, planchettes were widely sold as a novelty. The parlor game that was patented by the executive Elijah Bond and Charles Kennard is still sold today in the millions.

The spiritual aspect

It is widely known and accepted that the board is used for occult practices. Nevertheless, it must be understood that the board is not the problem. It is merely a tool, upon which the user has to focus his or her intent. The intention behind the use of the board is the problem, as well as the vibration of the person concerned. The user will normally sit with the intention of contacting discarnate entities. Now this is all very well, but what if you do not understand how to discern between good and bad spirits. How do you know who is contacting you?

Discernment, as I have discussed previously is one of the first spiritual gifts that you should develop and possibly the most important. It is no easy task, and perhaps this is why it takes many years of study and spiritual practice to develop. It is not enough to be able to utilize your psychic faculties, without understanding the internal power of discernment. It is said that a demon can come in the form of light, so how can the trusting individual tell the difference?

Using a Ouija board is like setting light to an explosive charge, it is your decision. You create what your thoughts dictate and if you have the pure intent that you wish to contact spirit – you will. The trouble is this, which ones are you contacting, what is your fear offering or indeed your vibration? Even with the pure intentions that you think you have, your vibration may tell a different story. The way you live your life will determine the rate at which you vibrate. It is therefore important that you live as cleanly as you possibly can in thought and deed. If you harbor negativity in any way then you will replicate that same vibration in your auric emanation.

The important factor is your emotional/mental state. Keep a close watch on how you feel and what emotions you are experiencing. If you harbor pure thoughts and live cleanly, your vibration will be that much higher.

Case 23: Ouija Opens the Door

A mother in the north of England, who had stupidly decided to use an Ouija board with her daughter and her daughter's boyfriend, once contacted me. Nothing much actually happened, or so it seemed, but over a short period, paranormal events started to occur in their home.

The troubling aspect was that the target of the events was the young daughter. She was the easiest target for whatever they conjured, and they were all drinking at the time while using the board. She experienced the episodes, including voices, seeing spirits, having nightmares and a general upset throughout her life. All the signs of oppression!

Slowly, and surely, the mood in the home changed and life seemed out of control. Electricity would blow and objects would disappear. Eventually, the mother admitted that one evening, they decided to play spirit games and used a makeshift board – a simple piece of paper and a glass as a planchette. They had seen this repeatedly on TV and thought nothing of it.

The mother's desire to become psychic was so strong that she used her own family to get there. Blinded by her own desires, she created a portal in the home which invited spirits to communicate – any spirits - and that is when things went disastrously wrong.

Before she came to me, she had requested the help of other mediums, and the mediums that came in fact could not deal with the problem, due to their misunderstanding of the darker aspects of the paranormal.

After much counsel, she learned how to deal with the issue and soon after, peace flooded back into their lives. We still watch carefully.

Using the Board

As I have mentioned, the board works by intention only and is not the harbinger of some mysterious power. Through this intention, you create a portal with which unseen entities can communicate or visit. These entities will more often than not be grounded spirits or darker entities with malice on their mind. Very few times you will reach the light or high vibrational beings.

Why someone feels contact can be made with a loved one who has crossed over to the spiritual plane (heaven), using a board, I do not know. Nevertheless, suffice to say that if I were in Heaven; I would not want to return to this dark energy we call earth. The only spirits that can be contacted through the utilization of the board are spirits that have not crossed and often these are lower vibratory entities on the first level of the astral plane.

Piggy Backs

A lower spirit entity may attach itself to a grounded spirit and thus get a piggyback ride – right to your playground. Think about this, do you really want that happening? There are numerous examples of this happening.

Individuals which have some development of mediumship faculties or indeed the medium himself or herself claim they have some great results with the board. However, I am told this is mainly because of their own natural mediumistic tendencies. Therefore, the expression is via the medium and not really the board. The following is an example of exactly what I have warned you about. I have changed names for the protection of the individuals, but the essence remains intact in its entirety.

Case 24: Ouija Board Nightmare

I received a letter from a woman who was so happy that I got in touch with her. I have to say though, this was mainly because of the message I received from my own guide to help her. I asked her if she had used an Ouija board, and she claimed that she did not. However, after some investigation and the fact that my guide insisted that she did, in fact, use a board – she admitted, she used a glass with a piece of paper, which had numbers and letters upon it. Just because this was not an original board – what they did was make their own make-shift board.

Four members took part in the séance as it were, herself (Katarina), two gentlemen by the name of Arnold and Donny, and her daughter Christine. She explained that when they were in the beginnings of attempting the communication, they got movement from the glass. The important thing was the glass stopped moving when Christine took her finger off.

Katarina then made it clear the reason they decided to attempt communication with the Ouija board was because she had a strong belief in the afterlife. She maintained that she knew there was a spirit in the home, and so she was keen on developing any psychic abilities that anyone of them may have.

What Katarina then told me next started to make my own psychic antennae stand up. She claimed that after using the board, she began to see dark shadows out of the corner of her eye. This fueled her interest even further as she maintained the house had a history of paranormal occurrences witnessed by others who stayed there. Her son also had experiences and often told her about a man that he continually saw at the bottom of the stairs and that the boy could often be heard talking to the spirit telling him to be quiet as his sister was scared.

Her daughter Christine often felt a presence in her room, and she always had trouble sleeping – often feeling sick. Katarina also claimed these occurrences frightened her too. I started to think that all this was just a simple case of grounded spirit trying to be noticed and needing help to cross over to the light of the spirit world.

This was until she told me that she began to smell putrid odors. Things were now taking more of a sinister turn.

She then stated that she received a communication while using her made up board on another occasion that stated to "find my body." Katarina then carried out the wishes of the spirit as she went from place to place and even tore up her home. There was nothing so the spirit entity told them to concentrate on her son's room – there was nothing. The spirit then claimed to be a close family member that passed over, he also maintained there were other spirits with him, and that he could not allow them through until he got Christine. On yet another occasion, the spirit claimed there was going to be a fire at Christine's boyfriends house and that the spirit hated Donny and wanted to attack him. The spirit then gave his name, but it was nothing they knew or heard of – they asked again and the spirit became violent. The young boy became a target and had marks appear on his body.

Katarina told me that she had been to many psychics and mediums and that when she was a great deal younger her parents would use the Ouija board and that her pet dog would display strange behavior when they did it. She then told me that relationships in the house had become strained, and her daughter was displaying very strange be-

havior. Her dreams were becoming more and more violent and frightening.

Katherine then stated the following: "The room I recently moved out of is very active and I have experienced something with my own eyes, I saw a white feather above me and I went to grab it and it disappeared. I have been told that this is spiritual. I also saw what seemed to be a young child as I woke up one evening, which seemed very close to me as I thought it was my child awakening, but as I went to touch, it was like a watery affect and disappeared.

"This room is now my daughter Christine's room and she is scared of seeing things in her room. There have been noises of tapping but I am not sure whether it is household noises." This is not the end of the story and the phenomena continued.

The family was becoming more worried of what they might have caused and had no idea what to do. The spirit now decided to make physical contact. Christine was at home alone one particular day and heard someone whistling to her from the other end of the house. There were times when both her and her mother were physically touched when bathing and this physical contact terrified the pair of them.

They stopped using the board but still felt the presence of the entity. They noticed the house had a continual mist around the inside of the house and the spirit was continually saying nasty things that could be heard by Christine.

Katarina then implored me to help them remove the evil from their lives and she admitted that she believed they opened some kind of portal. They did and this case was not easy.

The above, which explains the events within the family household, is a perfect example of what may happen when 'curiosity kills the cat' – so to speak. It has the recipe for a perfect disaster, including all the elements of a potential obsession. However, a distinct pattern that emerges tells you the spirit is malignant, or grounded and mischievous, and it is the content and essence of the message. Spirits with an extremely high vibration and from the light cannot impart information with any negative intent. Therefore, anything that comes with a negative intent is from a darker source or grounded spirit.

The medium should be able to discern in an instant the vibration of the entity through the medium's auric field, and secondly, by the historical accounts of the imparted knowledge or information. I am happy to say the above was dealt with effectively and the family returned to some normality.

CHAPTER 33:

Working with Paranormal Investigation Groups

U sing Ouija boards is not the only way that problems can occur. In this day and age, we can see more and more 'ghost hunters' turning up, and anyone with an interest in the paranormal can start researching ghosts or spirits – untrained, and "more fool them." The problem we have here is that it needs some form of interaction between the investigator and the spirit entity. We are seeing repeatedly, investigators and mediums alike, calling on spirits or even challenging them, which is like playing Russian roulette with a loaded gun.

Professional researchers will always use a professionally trained medium because they know that they need someone who can control and discern spirits. Other non-professional investigators rely on themselves and do not have the luxury of using professional mediums. This is candy to the entity, and the games can begin and be played over many years.

Very often though, I have witnessed psychics and mediums claiming that the entities are non-human, which causes an exorbitant amount of fear, when actually it is merely a grounded spirit. However, this can be out of ignorance or for material gain from the medium or psychic. Nevertheless, it is so easy to fall into the trap of ignorance – with good intent, yet not finding any way out when it may be too late.

If you are going to investigate this kind of activity, try and join a respectable scientific group that will also use professional mediums. You can then learn the ins and outs, rights and wrongs of investigating paranormal activity.

One thing you must realize is that we are all energy in motion; we are spirits in a human form, not the other way around. Therefore, it makes sense that these spirits already have a handle on the manipulation of energy, and know exactly your thoughts and your fears. Never challenge the spirit - for you cannot fight what you cannot see or feel. Your fear will mask any chance of discernment. A darker spirit is far more intelligent than you and can easily remove itself till it returns. This dance can happen over years.

CHAPTER 34:

Electronic Voice Phenomenon (EVP)

How shall we start?

With electronic voice phenomenon (EVP), there is a great misunderstanding – and what I want to get across in this book is how dangerous it can actually be, and here's why.

When a medium connects with spirit on the other side, there is a direct connection that allows the medium to discern the nature of the spirit with whom they are connected.

If I drew a diagram showing spirit on one side and me on the other (showing our mind-to-mind connection), then there is an energetic connection - a direct connection between me and that spirit, like a "psychic wifi" connection. Now, with that direct link to your loved one or your spirit guide on the other side, you have a direct, inspirational, mind-to-mind or soul-to-soul connection between the medium and the loved one on the other side. Think of it this way – it's like looking through a peep-hole to verify who's knocking on your door. Without this direct connection, all you can do is say "Who's there?" and hope that the voice that answers is not lying.

But, with EVPs, you do NOT have that direct connection. You essentially take a box of electronics - whether it's a spiritbox or a simple voice recorder – and put that between the medium and the spirit on the other side. NOW, you don't have that peep-hole in the door, so to speak, to verify that the person knocking actually is who they say. All you get is a muffled voice and a promise.

Now, think of this:

If we then take into consideration the foreign object (that box of electronics) that is capturing phenomena or sound waves - you know people are using Tesla coils or who knows what else, spirit boxes and things – the foreign object is infil-trating and amplifying that energy in such a way that not only is discernment difficult – it's almost like you have established an energetic portal, or "beacon."

From what I understand from my own work and from my own teachings from the spirit world, in the hands of someone who is highly tuned, highly trained, dependent upon their level of vibration or their spiritual strength, EVP could be a good thing.

But, more often than not, we have nefarious and negative spirits or troublesome spirits able to interfere with us.

Why?

Because you have amplified the energy of the communica-tion- you have something foreign that's amplifying energy – whether it's the addition of a copper coil or crystalized prod-uct that helps to amplify that sound wave or that connection, it still is distorting the direct link you have between medium and spirit. And so it's very difficult then to discern.

And what happens is that the medium or the person in the other realm on this side is not able to discern whether that spir-it that they are communicating with is the real deal or not.

This is why it's very easy for spirit from the other side to be able to utilize this and lull the target into a false sense of security. Remember, all our energy – our auric field - can be read. I mean, it's very easy for negative spirits on the other side or playful spirits or what have you – to know about your uncle Tom whose passed and how he passed and what he did and all that kind of stuff because if it's in your auric field then they're going to be able to pick that up. They know more about you from this side over there than we do! You know, it's – you know, the knowledge is out there for them to pick up.

So, whilst I'm not poo-pooing the whole idea of EVP, I'm just saying that it is a very dangerous thing to dabble with, and in many, many cases in the past, people started using EVPs got lulled into a false sense of security in terms of grief, and you have people that think they are dealing with loved ones on the other side when it's nothing more than a mish-mash of sound waves and noise. I mean it's like if I said to you "Look at the sky, do you see the cloud that looks like a white horse?" And, if you stare long enough, you will basically conjure up that image of a white horse in the clouds in whatever ways, shape, or form you can, and then I hear "Yeah, I can see it! I can see it – it's THERE!" We see this a lot when mediums are attempting trans-figuration, and one of the sitters suddenly says, "I can see the face - it's coming!' and suddenly everyone else can see that face too, but it's only autosuggestion.

It's the same kind of thing with EVPs. Unless it is very, very VERY clear, distinct, and evidential, then I question it. When it's a class A EVP, then I'm more inclined to think "OK – let us go forward and let's investigate this further." But 99.99% of EVPs that I've heard are definitely not Class A quality. A lot of people that are grieving are hanging on to the fact that they've heard their loved ones through a recording but when I listen to it, it's not - it's just mish-mash; but, in their grief, they're hanging on to that and saying "Yes! I KNOW this is a DIRECT communication from the other side."

Now, where does the danger lie in this? If we have a negative spirit, and I'm not necessarily talking about demonic, here. I'm just talking about a negative-grounded entity that's got a not-very-nice past that finds a way of being able to be attractive to that person.

It's like with the adult at the kid's playground, years ago, you know, you'd tell your kids "Don't take candy from strangers" and stuff. But this is what it's like on the other side, they're tempting you with sweets, you know? You know, "come and have a ..." and that is how bad things happen.

Less-than-desirable entities are playing on the person who's grieving. Now, like I said, I'm not trying to be "All EVP work is bad." It's just very very dangerous. If you give me a thousand tapes of EVPs to listen to, I would probably only be able to verify only one or two. And I'm no expert, I mean I do know of cases where it's been utilized as a catalyst to actually introduce a negative, a demonic spirit or even a number of spirits.

We have recently had a case of a paranormal investigators who have had all hell break loose, because they'd been communicating with the other side and all things that were coming as a being of light turned very dark and sinister. The problem is that one doesn't have the power of discernment when utilizing a foreign object that's amplifying and interfering with the normal energetic patterns of a mediumistic connection.

In other words, you're making it easier for them to seduce you.

And that's exactly what they'll do and there've been many cases of possession or obsession that has happened through EVPs. You can find online tons of stories of grieving people who try it and things go wrong, or who have an interest in the paranormal and think, well, we can do some EVPs.

One thing: professional parapsychologists or paranormal investigators will not do EVPs in their home because there is such a chance of creating a portal or an energetic beacon that attracts low-level entities who otherwise would have no way to interfere with you. As they manipulate the energy of the recording device, they may have the opportunity to manipulate energy in your home near the device as well.

CHAPTER 35:

Grounded Entities

These are, by far, the most misunderstood of our spirit activity, and what may be seen and felt as evil and demoniacal, is in fact a grounded spirit who is trying to make him or her known to you. They almost always need help and causing phenomena is sometimes the only way they can get your attention. This can be quite similar to a phenomena called psychic vampirism, though the spirit has its own emotion and will, and has for various reasons decided not to cross over to the light. The spirit may have a fear of judgment, it may have unfinished business or may be materially bonded to the earth plane through the spirit's need to have their material possessions still around them. The spirit will want to make contact for various reasons and those of a sensitive disposition will feel the force of the spirit's desire and inquisitiveness. The reasons the entity may wish to communicate are:

- A desire to return home or to be connected with their loved ones on the other side

- Being angry or vengeful especially when someone else has moved into their home or area. This is normally because the spirit does not know they have passed.
- Never believed in an afterlife and have now found themselves caught in between lives, therefore they may need help. They are scared and shocked and need the communication to feel alive and to receive help.
- Have suffered a traumatic passing and fear has kept them from the passage of crossing over.

The biggest mistake that untrained mediums make, or indeed individuals of a spiritual discipline other than Mediumship, is the desire to banish the spirit from the place.

I once sat with a gentleman in Tokyo, who claimed that he was a bit of a shamanic ghost buster and that his job was to destroy or banish the spirit. I absolutely cringed at his words and felt such compassion for the spirits he may have came in contact with. This is out of order, and I am sure there is a Karmic price to pay.

Even the grounded spirit should be able to feel understanding, compassion and love, for it is with these three elements that you will be able to help the grounded spirit to return to their true home.

Remember, you are not a ghost buster, and you are serving the Great Spirit and humanity, so how would you feel if you were driven from a place that you considered was your home? These types of individuals that claim to get rid of ghosts very often cause further problems elsewhere or can cause the spirit to seek further revenge.

Obsessing Spirits

There is a great deal of conjecture concerning obsession, possession, diabolical possession and the difference between them all. One person thinks that obsession is oppression and another considers it to be just an influence with which you have your own power to thwart.

However, obsessing spirits are more serious than you think and can be the catalyst to something of a more sinister nature. Consider the necessity to make fire in a survival situation, if you don't have the oxygen, you won't make the fire and if all necessary aspects of what is needed is there in abundance, andyou fan the small flame with oxygen and other conditions, you could quite easily find yourself in the middle of a forest fire.

Obsession can start of as something small and innocuous, just like the initial spark needed for a flame, but with the right conditions it can quickly get out of control. In Carl Wickland's famous book "30 Years Amongst the Dead" he regularly talks to spirits who have obsessed individuals, and who clearly have no understanding of what the obsession process was and how it happened. A small influence may be harmless, but on the other side of the coin, it could be dangerous. I am not saying that all obsessing spirits are nefarious, but there are cases where an obsession turned into possession. Case in point would be the 1949 exorcism case of Roland as depicted in the Exorcist movie in 1973. A new book shines some light on this unknown case by Steven LaChance (Confrontation With Evil), which is excellent in its study and explanation of this ill-reported case, I read this twice and anyone who wants an understanding of the case should read it.) The actual target of the possession was in fact the mother and not the young boy. She was the individual obsessed and that became the catalyst to the possession of the young boy. I was chatting to Steven about this aspect and the case and his quote is clear: "Think of obsession as the hook which put the victim in the demonic line to be reeled in."

Let me reiterate that not all obsessing spirits lead to possession but they certainly with the right conditions and of course personality or weakness of an individual.

CHAPTER 36:

Hauntings

Normally the cause of what we would understand as a haunting is the spirit's desperation to control either the area they are in, or an an individual with whom they ar obsessed. It may be benign and could be spirit trying to make contact with the living in order to receive help. The spirits find very quickly they are able to manipulate energy, which will cause the experiences that a human being may feel within himself or herself, or in the home or area in which they are sharing.

It is also possible as aforementioned, the spirit may obsess the individual. Consequently from a medium's aspect it is important that the medium is compassionate to the plight of the spirit and will be able to communicate in such a way as to promote comfort rather than distress.

Simply banishing a spirit because you feel you are some kind of Ghost Hunter will not only cause you to take on some Karma and can make the spirit angry, but you could become the target of their anger as previously mentioned. You must remember they can manipulate energy far more than you and can also suck your energy, so why dance with them. I have seen this too many times when a mediumistic person claims they will banish the entity, without thought or compassion or will deal with a haunting and find themseleves very quickly out of their depth.

The entity is only asking for help and spirit may have brought you there for a specific reason. You could be an anchor of light and you may be able to help the spirit pass over to a better life.

Helping a Spirit Return Home

I wish to recount a personal story of spirit rescue. I hope this story will help you understand how you as a medium may be able to help the spirit cross over to the light.

Case 25: No Place Like Home

My wife and I went for a daytrip to a sleepy fishing village in south Wales. Now, we both like to visit coffee shops and the weather was turning for the worse. The problem we had is that we had no cash and only had our bank card. We tried to get into various coffee shops but everyone seemed to be there due to the inclement weather – so there was no room at the inn. Any coffee shops that were open did not take any cards and only cash was accepted – no cash machine in the vicinity. All seemed lost.

We continued to walk in the rain for a considerable time until I happened upon a bank machine. As I was standing there withdrawing some money, I noticed a small coffee shop just slightly adjacent to the machine. We were both very happy indeed. Something was a little unusual though, unlike the other stores, this was sparse and had very few customers. We walked in and smiled to the woman who was serving; she seemed delighted to see us and obviously felt this was better because she only had a few other people there and this was hardly a way to make a living. Jo and

I ordered our normal customary coffee and as Jo would say 'a little-little,' something tasty to eat with our coffee.

No sooner had we taken our first sip of coffee but we both looked to each other and stated that we could sense the presence of a little girl who was standing to my right and Jo's left. We both felt this at exactly the same time. Jo was amazed, and we both knew instantly this soul was grounded. Jo asked me to help and communicate with the young soul.

The girl told us that she died there in that building when she was young from Tuberculosis and that she remained there with her family, as she was too frightened to move on from them. Her family tragically passed and she had not seen them since. All she wanted was to see her mummy and daddy again.

She said she was sorry that she had upset people as she was desperately trying to make contact with anyone who could help her. She saw that we had bright lights around us and knew that she could receive some help in someway, which is why she took no time in appearing to us.

I asked my guide and my angel to help. No sooner had I put in this request that I viewed a beautiful angel standing next to the little girl and asking her to take her hand and look beyond the room. There in my spiritual sight, I witnessed the young girl's mother and father standing waiting on the angel to take her to them. This was such a beautiful sight to see.

The angel told us that without our combined light, they would not have been able to harness the energy to come and rescue the trapped soul. We were also told that business would pick up now that the energy had changed. All this went on silently without anyone knowing what we were doing and when we returned the next day, the tables *were full, yet the woman remembered us and asked us in. She stated that since we left something happened and the place changed. The proprietor had no idea who we were and we offered no explanation, she just knew intuitively that somehow we were involved.*

What I would like you to learn from this is that **you must show some kind of compassion and love for the trapped soul** and to have a high level of discernment. All you need is to discern the communication, and then you should ask the spirit to look beyond the area they are trapped in. Ask the angels and your guide to assist and to help move the spirit over to the light. Sometimes you may come across a trapped soul who is very angry. If this happens, you should try and calm the soul down by using kind and loving discourse. Try and explain what waits for them in the spirit lands and ensure they have no fear of judgment.

Just a word of caution though, only trained mediums should attempt this because they will be adept at spirit communication. Be aware that some spirits will not move and this is because they have free will. The spirit may still cause phenomena. They make themselves known by moving objects, rappings, showing themselves, cold spots in areas that have adequate heating. They may also actively play with your electricity around your home. However, one must have explored all other scientific explanations before accepting spirit activity. For example, a blown light bulb is just that, and is probably the result of a power surge. However, a flickering light in response to stimuli such as questions or other conditions will be the sign of a communicating spirit. Please ensure you take care and investigate all avenues.

Soul Rescue

Soul rescue is another new craze within spiritualism and the New Age movement, again another kind of Gucci bag syndrome.

I know of many individuals who claim to do soul rescue, and they are the ones who will embellish their stories dramatically. Yet, ask any of these individuals as to the nature of evil or the reality of darker entities, and they will skirt around the subject amazingly well.

Soul rescue is a specialized subject. It should not be taken lightly. The medium that dedicates himself or herself to this subject will have a true working knowledge of the spirit world and will know of the realities of evil. They would have extensive experience at dealing with problems of a paranormal nature that, though challenging, would be out of the comfort zone for evidential mediums.

There are too many unprepared mediums willing to do this type of service, yet the psychic debris they leave behind them is tantamount to a battleground. Soul rescue is done by the spirit team, you just anchor for them to work.

There is however, another type of soul rescue, which is more in tune with the developed medium's ability. That is, of course, the rescue circle. This involves a well-trained and substantially strong development circle that has gone beyond the basics and has dealt with advanced levels of communication to rescue trapped entities. This is predominantly through prayer and the use of our guides and higher spheres of angels. This form of specialized mediumship is very rewarding on a spiritual level, and is often done in complete secrecy.

The dangers of course, from this type of advanced mediumship is, that if you attempt this without the requisite training and experience, you will one hundred per cent come unstuck. The reason is that you will not be sufficiently strong in mind and body to be able to deal with the level of the energy needed, and which will be sent to you as a negative attack. Therefore, you will make yourself prone to spirit obsession and will endanger the other members in your group.

CHAPTER 37

Visiting Spirits

We have an area within the paranormal field that involves visiting spirits and these are normally family members, guides, or spirits from your own soul group. These spirits are relatively harmless, though to get your attention, they may let you know they are there by moving objects such as your keys from where you left them (this is called telekinesis or asport) or they may bring you gifts from the spirit world, which are known as apports. This is a present from spirit that you have not been previously familiar with. It is brought by the agency of spirit in a controlled manner from an unidentifiable source.

This is not meant to scare you - but to make you aware of their presence. They may also touch you or call your name, though never in a threatening manner.

However, there are spirits who are grounded and visit areas they know. If you are sensitive and have the ability to receive communication, they can interact and cause you to become fearful.

Case 26: A Neighborhood Visitor

I remember a time when I was staying in the USA, we were living in a house where the land was steeped in history and each house had a tale to tell. One evening while sitting quietly reading, I heard a voice call out, "Fuck you, I am going to get you when you sleep." Immediately I became rather agitated and all sorts of things started going on in my mind. Just when I asked whom it was and why they were here. My wife heard the same similar voice.

Immediately, we knew that we were in no danger because we already knew we were protected, and that this was merely a grounded wanderer. We ignored the spirit; there were no signs of anything else of a lower vibration, and after telling the spirit where to go to ourselves, he became rather amused that we could communicate without the fear.

Finding the underlying cause of it: he passed in the home not too far away; he was tied to the house and his family members through guilt. We eventually helped him to pass into the light.

Sometimes the visitors need help, and usually you will know them. They may just want to pop in every now and again to see that you are OK. Just as you would visit your family, they are visiting theirs; when you understand this, it can be a rewarding and comforting experience rather than something to fear.

CHAPTER 38:

Poltergeists

Poltergeists are troublesome and normally associated with adolescence. The word is derived from the German language that means 'noisy spirit,' the word "poltern," which means to "rumble", "bluster", or "jangle", and "geist," which means "spirit." "Poltern" can also be used in describing an act of speech, which normally can be heard on recordings of EVP (Electronic Voice Phenomena).

These types of entities can be the most frightening and are often misdiagnosed as a demonic entity. Probably the most famous case of poltergeist activity has to be in London in the UK known as 'The Enfield Poltergeist' and to date; there has been no evidence or scientific basis that can explain all of the paranormal events that happened there. Interestingly enough, even though there were many witnesses including general members of the public and public servants as well as scientists – skeptics still refute the case fervently to this day.

The distinguishing facet of this type of phenomena is how the entity is able to manifest and interact with the material realm, sometimes with increasing malevolence. No scientist has been able to discern if the poltergeist is in fact a grounded spirit or another type of entity but mediums throughout the world agree that the phenomena is down to spirit interaction.

Scientific analysis and research to this day still goes on to find out what the catalyst is for the phenomena of poltergeist activity. One hypothesis remains that repressed emotions from a maturing young person creates the energy, which drives and attracts the grounded entity, again this is a kind of psychic vampirism.

Other evidence suggests that it is not bound to adolescence due to the fact that other poltergeist activity has in fact occurred in places where there are no adolescent individuals present (Edinburgh Vaults). The hypothesis, however, is a bit of a paradox because we know that either it is based on repressed emotion of the individuals concerned or indeed of emotionally charged events of a negative nature that have taken place. This is known as recurrent spontaneous psychokinesis (RSPK) and could be a valid explanation for some poltergeist phenomena.

CHAPTER 39:

Ghosts

G hosts are perhaps misunderstood, for one person will explain it as a grounded spirit and another as something entirely different. However, most ghost experiences can be explained as a replay of emotionally charged energy similar to watching a DVD on your screen at home. (Residual Energy)

A great way to explain this is by giving you an example of sightings of ghostly activity. You can be guaranteed that at some point, someone will experience this type of sighting at a battlefield, castle fortress or within an old building which has a long history.

For 90% of the cases, you can be assured these sightings normally occur in the night, which also gives it that sinister air around it. The reason it happens at night is the lack of material energy of the day, and the fact the temperature will normally drop when moisture in the air is high – this is the optimum condition.

When all the conditions are right, which could be time, date, and anniversary; there will be a replay of energy, which can be seen by sensitive individuals. Think of famous battles such as Gettysburg in USA (Civil War), there have been sightings of ghosts of soldiers, and some people have claimed that they have witnessed replays of battles gone by. Obviously, you will deduce the energy that must remain there is emotionally charged. Think of how many people would have lost their lives and in the throes of the battle, how much energy, fear, hatred and all those emotions that charge the energy there.

Another famous battlefield where this phenomenon has been reported is in the north of Scotland – 'The Battle of Culloden' in 1746. I myself have witnessed the phenomena but I am a believer so it is interesting to converse with those of a skeptical disposition who have witnessed the unseen and scientifically their experience is not readily explainable.

Spirit Orbs

I am afraid that even as a medium, I am probably the greatest skeptic, and so find this relatively new aspect of the paranormal difficult to believe or explain. However, when one has discounted the theory that dust particles or moisture could be causing the phenomena on the digital device, then one would have to conclude there is spirit activity.

OK, so you want to know what exactly these are! Quite simply, when all scientific explanations have been discounted, an orb is a light and energy anomaly that appears on digital media such as a camera. These are normally seen on the image and cannot be seen with the naked eye. There is a great deal of conjecture surrounding what these balls of energy actually are and some would say that if you look close enough at the image when it has been magnified – you can see the face of a spirit. My opinion is that it is a load of BALLS.

There is in fact another scientific explanation within the realms of photography and I am more inclined to believe that, rather than the spirit energy hypothesis - that is the idea of light refraction when picking up pollen, moisture, or dust particles that cannot be seen with the naked eye.

The only time that I will conclude that something paranormal may have occurred is when the image is captured in response to an EMF (Electro Magnetic Field) alarm and responds to other stimuli such as questioning or conscious movement of its own volition. You can see distinct differences in these energy anomalies, and they have a different makeup from the particles that have been captured on the digital camera chip. So now, you would think that, OK! Hang on, that must mean there are real spirit orbs, and you would be wrong because science suggests and evidence from testing shows that each chip from each digital manufacturer replicates the light in varied ways, so no one orb will be identical to another from another digital processor.

This side of the paranormal still warrants further investigation, but for the most part, until there is adequate proof from the world of spirit that these orbs are in fact spirit manifested energy, I will continue to understand the scientific facts first. SO COME ON GUYS – THEY ARE ALL BALLS! Unless of course they are moving with a will of their own and subject to external stimulus. I will keep investigating, yet something does intrigue me, which may cause me to rethink the hypothesis. This is the anomaly of the energy glowing, this would suggest to me that some other energy makes it grow and glow and therefore that cannot be just one particle.

Fear Feeds Fear

Allow me to finish off this section with a word of warning and of encouragement. Throughout your development as a medium, your old beliefs and values will change. There will come a time when you will stop looking through material eyes, and will see through your inner eyes. You will come across subjects that will make you fearful and you will experience things that will build on this fear. The point is this, you will attack yourself through your own fears, and this, I am afraid, is inevitable and will be a part of your spiritual growth. You will have to face your fears in order to learn to control them. Notice I said control, and not defeat. Defeat has a kind of finality to it, and as with the yin and yang, balance is needed – how else would we spiritually grow? There would be nothing to learn.

Many of these fears will be the result of a catalyst that makes you think of them, and one thought will play out the other, and so you will go around in circles with the same fear that is attacking you. Perhaps you may feel that it is something outside of you, or of course some extraterrestrial being or entity. This thought creates further fear, and so you feed fear with fear. Irrational as it may seem, it is difficult to deal with, because it is you who creates it, and only you can control it. Switching the thought with a powerful affirmation is one way to do it and - of course – prayer. The fact that it is transitory should help you to come to terms with it – ask that your innate spiritual power be released to deal with the irrationality of the situation. This is a form of spiritual protection and of course atonement.

PART 8

"DANGER" You CAN Experience Very Real Attacks

W hile it can be such a rewarding experience to develop your gifts, I would just like to remind you of the nature of balance and that without one polar opposite, you would not have the other. Furthermore, you would be a fool to believe that a journey into the world of spiritual development was not fraught with its own inherent dangers and problems. These are in correlation to the problems that may show up in your everyday life. I would like to offer you a hypothesis, if you will, that shows that it is a simple case of awareness to be able to identify the psychic trends.

Many interested individuals dive into the Dark Waters of psychic development only to be faced with problems of a paranormal nature. You could open a Pandora's Box full of problems and throw your life into spiraling turmoil, if you ignore the basics and do not deny that of which you are fearful. What could happen? Well, you may be in danger of developing mental or psychiatric issues. Of course, you could make yourself vulnerable to infestation, attachment, and at the worst – full- diaboli-calpossession as we have discussed. That can happen, yet the frequency is small indeed, and a great many possessions are nothing more than psychiatric illness. However, the veil is thin, and offers up another theory for terrible events, such as murder, rape, abuse and other heinous activities. There are magnitudes of problems that are often ignored by untrained professionals.

These problems then cause a negative domino effect through-out life, and the student finds himself or herself drowning, not in a sea of tranquility, but a storm on the waves of negativity. This negativity will manifest itself in your life when you least expect. For the most part, you may not even recognize this phe-nomenon at all and just put things down to bad luck or your environmental circumstances. When most people want to de-velop their gifts, they do so normally for the wrong reasons. I also have to lay some blame on these overdone paranormal shows, which show mediums being taken over, and making it look almost like a ghost train ride at Disney. This is not the case, and if you think along these lines then you are being misguided; this in itself is a time-bomb waiting to go off.

It takes a great deal of energy, dedication and self-sacrifice to do the work that I myself, and other mediums, do on a daily basis. It is truly giving of yourself, and will not only tire you but also lessen your energy and your own vibrancy. Because oth-ers' emotions can affect you, if you do not take the necessary precautions, you could open yourself and make yourself vul-nerable to other influences. Besides, a true lack of understand-ing will make you delve into subjects without real training or knowledge. This is driven by the Ego and the need to look good, or to feed your material hunger or your wish for fame - to be viewed with awe. Just opening up without knowledge is tanta-mount to total destruction.

CHAPTER 40

Opening the Door

I f you owned a house, and all your worldly possessions were inside the home, it would be assumed that you would take necessary precautions to protect them. However, this is not always the case, and some individuals cause themselves much heartache, because of the lack of taking essential precautions. The type of protection that you would employ would depend on the threat that may be in your immediate environment, and the risk associated with it. You would use what is necessary to ensure that your home environment is a safe haven, where you and your loved ones could live.

However, what would happen if you left your door open? Perhaps nothing! Nevertheless, an opportunist thief, squatter or criminal may take advantage of your nature and your lack of diligence. This analogy is similar to that of your own body, which is the home for your spiritual assets. Though they may be contained in another reality, they are still a part of your divine essence. With this knowledge, you must learn to respect and look after your home, for within your physical body you house your spirit, which is aligned with your perispirit. Therefore, as aforementioned, it is a spiritual parallel of your physical body.

Further, if you do open yourself up and fail to take the necessary precautions, you may cause yourself more harm than good; and even though you may not be taken over by a malignant spirit, you could cause illness in your physical body through messing with your own inherent energy system.

Case 27: Black Magic and The Sins of the Fathers

Martin was a young man; he was married to a lovely woman, had one child and a Labrador dog that followed him everywhere. He ran his own painting and decorating business, which was establishing itself well in the local area where he worked, because of his dedication and good service. Everything for Martin was looking great, yet he felt something was missing and he wanted more, not realizing his glass was half-full and not the other way around. However, Martin was fascinated with spirit, psychic ability and anything almost magical and new age. He tried to meditate and read many books on the occult. He dabbled with tarot and began to use crystals and rituals to heighten his experiences.

He wanted to run before he could walk and was incredibly impatient. His impatience grew stronger, and the more he seemed to be failing, the more he would try new things to speed up the process of his development. He began to grow angry and upset at the lack of progress, and this anger began to spill out into his family life - slowly making its way into his working environment. Before long, he started to have arguments with his wife and found that he had little precious time for his child - constantly throwing himself at the desperation to develop his psychic ability. While trying to sleep one night, he explained that he was having difficulty to his wife lying next to him, and his wife was feeling his distress, which kept her awake too.

He remarked; "I decided to walk down to my kitchen to make a cup of herbal tea. I remember that as I walked, I felt a seriously cold chill run through me, and thought nothing more of it. I wandered to the bottom of my hall to turn the heating up, however, when I got there, the heating was at 25 degrees, and the first thought that came to me was that my heating system had developed a problem. The heating was on and I remember feeling so cold that I could see the steam coming from my breath rising and disappearing as soon as it left – it was so strange. I thought nothing more and had no inclination that it could be paranormal."

He then recounted another part of his story when after he had made his tea; he was sitting in his living room, just thinking. "As I sat there, with all sorts of thoughts going through my mind, I heard an enormous thump, and the ornament on the shelf fell off and smashed on my floor. I remember thinking that it was strange because the ornament was in the middle of the shelf, and the shelf was straight and very secure." Over the next few weeks, other strange events began to happen. Martin got increasingly fearful, his wife was beginning to see things and became rather inwardly depressed. A barrage of negative events consumed them, and the last straw came when his child began to talk to someone they could not see.

Martin approached another medium, the individual came around to the house spouting all sorts of nonsense, and telling him that he and his child were psychic, there was a grounded spirit who just wanted to say hi. You can imagine this exciting Martin, and now that he knew this was supposedly the case – he began fervently trying to contact the entity.

Instead of things getting better, it got worse, and now the young child was experiencing being woken in the middle of the night by an unseen presence. Martin's wife was also the brunt of the entity's affections in a negative way; she felt uneasy as if she was being watched and constantly felt sick – especially when she could smell putrid odors that had no scientific origin. Things would disappear, objects would fall without any cause, and the arguments in the household got so bad they considered divorce.

Martin finally came to his senses, after hearing me on a well-known American Radio show (The Hilly Rose Show), he contacted me. Now I know that I have explained a little of my con versation with him, and I will carry on from this point to explain the issues as I saw them. We chatted and he had said that he knew I could help in some way. He knew that if he was honest and told me everything, I would know what to do. I told him that I would have to meditate on this myself and asked him to send every piece of information that he could to me. I told him that I would do what I could, and that he should expect that I cannot perform miracles, so not to expect too much. I started to have incredible feelings of despair and felt that something else was wrong – he was keeping something from me. I needed to find the underlying cause of it soon.

I turned to my Guide for advice and asked that I be shown what was the root of the problem. As I often do, I meditate a little before going to sleep and ask certain questions of spirit - sometimes my questions are answered in my sleep, and other times I am refused a response. However, this was different, and as I finally fell asleep, I found myself standing over a group of people in black cloaks, chanting in what I could only imagine was Latin. There was a dagger on an alter-type table and I saw a brass chalice that had blood in it. I got so scared that I shocked myself back to my body, and awoke with such fear in my heart. I knew what was wrong.

I contacted Martin and said, "Look, I had a terrible experience and I believe that your house, or someone you know, is involved in Black magic." His voice shuddered a little and I knew I had struck a chord with him. "Martin, you need to tell me the truth, I will not judge but if I am to help, I need to know," I said.

He replied from a space of fear, I could tell this in his voice as his tone, speed, and general depth changed dramatically. "My home was given to me as a gift from my parents, they have moved on now and I met Angela whom I fell for, we were soon married and I became a church-going, God-fearing family man when my little girl came along. My father and mother were a part of a satanic cult and this is where my interest in all things spooky came from. As I had nothing to do with what they were do ing, I thought nothing more of it and in later years, it became less frequent.

When they moved, I was given the home, I thought nothing of it, yet my desire to learn more about spirituality, and the paranormal, was still there, and that fueled my passion further. So I began to study what I thought I knew, and that was an interest given to me by my parents."

At this point in the proceedings, I had started to think that I might be getting myself into something I could not handle. I asked for a little time to consider the case and see what could be done. Over the next few days, I continued to have nightmares and heard guttural voices calling to me and threatening me, swearing at me and showing me clairvoyant images that could only be described as evil.

I asked my guides and angels for guidance and prayed a great deal over the difficulty that I found myself in. I decided that I would show him how to carry out the work that neeed to be done on his home. I would like to say that as a medium,

I could go there and clear everything, returning him to some normality – I cannot. As a professional, I had to understand my limits and knew this was something far more sinister that I may not be able to handle. I decided to pass this on to professionals that deal with that issue.

I have to accept that my job is evidence of life after death, and not to battle with things that may cause my own death. I spoke to Martin and explained that he had unwittingly reopened a portal direct to hell; I know hell does not exist but he did not, and I had to be dramatic to make him listen. This was because of his desperation to develop, and that possibly because of the association with the black masses that were held in his home previously and his lack of protection, he unwittingly invited negative entities in to join in the dance.

I knew my limit and sent his case to clergy that specialized in this area. I was glad that I did not allow my ego to 'Dance with the Devil' and advised him to forget dabbling in practices which he was not trained for, and had no idea of protection. He had opened himself and his family to spiritual influences without protection, driven by his Ego's desire. I knew my limits and I know that he did receive help in the end. I receive requests for help like this on a regular basis, and some are simple and yet some require more than my limited knowledge. However, he caused the issues by opening the door.

Opening to the world of spirit and of the psyche is the same. If you do not understand or know what you are doing, you will cause problems for you and your family. Nevertheless, there are contrasts to the threats that lay in wait because of your lack of diligence. If you open yourself up without the right forms of protection, you are leaving your door opened for all to come in and cause mischief. It can be so subtle that you would not even know it would happen until it was too late.

CHAPTER 41:

The Door is Now Open

L et us assume now that you, the student, are a few cents short of a dollar and you have entered the world of spirit and of the psyche through your Ego's desire. I am now just going to give you a few examples of what you might expect from opening yourself up without understanding and proper training in protecting yourself. Some of what I am about to discuss will have been touched on before, but here you will find a far deeper explanation in order that you can learn from it and take the requisite precautions.

Energy Imbalances

Think of this analogy for just a moment. Imagine that you have just plugged your new computer into a socket, which is not set for the number of amps that your machine is designed to take. Too little, and there is not enough power to sustain it; too much, and there is far too much for it to handle, and each contrast has its own relative problems.

The same is true with your body. If you have too little, you will not have enough lifeforce energy to sustain your life, and again - too much, and you will have a total blow-out. This can manifest in physical ailments or psychological illness.

You must understand that you have to be able to balance and control your energy system, consisting of chakras and meridian points in the body. Imbalances within the energy system create havoc with the mind, body, and soul.

When you are open to the world of spirit, you are, in fact, plugging yourself into a powerful source, and even though this source is limitless and part of your innate potential and being, you can unintentionally overload yourself.

Even learning a little about clairvoyance, and then not knowing how to switch it off, could cause you to be bombarded with constant symbolism that will eventually confuse you. In the confusion, you will not be able to decipher between what is internally your own spirit or your conscious thinking, or another source that you cannot control. When this happens, you may feel that you have an enlightened perspective of a situation, and act on that intuitive thought or clairvoyance which turns out to be wrong. You would feel let down, and you may feel let down with your own divine nature – thinking that God, your angels, or your guides have abandoned you. The truth is much simpler and this is because of your lack of understanding - you have let yourself down and not taken the necessary precautions to control this energy.

Psychic Vampires

What if your energy was stolen? I wonder what might be going through your mind right at the moment, considering you have just read the words in the title above? Perhaps you can imagine a grotesque figure with fangs that protrude from the mouth – sinking them into you and sucking you dry of all your life-giving blood. Well, it is certainly not as bad as that, though the essence of the imagery is much in the same vein – pardon the pun. The difference being the entity is not that grotesque and has no fangs to sink into you before draining you of your life's blood.

The truth is that a psychic vampire can be anyone - your best friend, your family, your work colleague - and that is before anything of a paranormal nature should try to suck you dry. A psychic vampire is a social parasite that feeds on emotionally weak, spiritually or mentally and physically weak individuals.

I will break this down into two categories, the first being spirit attachment, one that deals with the personal and physical aspect of the earth plane. The second will deal with other planes of spirit and the reasons behind the vampirism from the spirit perspective.

Now the problem that you have when opening yourself up to external energies including those of the earth plane – is you may not know how to protect yourself, and therefore, you will soon find your energy imbalanced and out of control. Why is this and why does it happen so unwittingly?

Have you ever been so happy during a normal day that everything seems too good to be true, and then suddenly you come over all sad, depressive, and show other emotions such as anger and resentment? The chances are that you have just been vamped. I know that I am using a cliché here and forgive me, but for simplicity, I will use another example.

Let us say that on that day that you were happy, you perhaps bumped into a friend on the street or in the office. You do not realize or recognize that person's wretched emotional state within himself or herself, and so interact with them as normal. Spending time in the company of such a person like this is energetic suicide. Why is this? Because they are the ones draining you of your lifeforce energy, without you having any particular knowledge of it or experiencing it physically at the time. You will say your normal farewell and shortly after, you will feel drained, perhaps mirroring some of the deep-seated emotions they may be harboring, so suddenly you will feel out of sorts. You could be so tired that you have no energy to do anything.

So what has happened?

Your friend or colleague will be causing his or her own suffering and will be low in lifeforce energy; therefore, it can be likened to stopping at a gas station to refuel.

The problem is that you are the gas station, and you don't have an unending supply at that time – giving the energy away even unknowingly will affect you dramatically in some way. Your auric field is the pumping station, and what will happen is that your friend in their desperate need will unconsciously create a type of Etheric cord. This cord will attach itself to your Aura and your strongest chakra and will begin to draw the much-needed energy from your own electromagnetic field to theirs. There is a phenomenon called magnetic attraction, reaction and repulsion. These scientific laws act accordingly to the parallel in spiritual law, which works conjunctively with the subconscious need for the survival of the spiritual source within you.

If you do not take measures to protect yourself from this type of vampirism, and then if you constantly have these attachments, you will have manifest serious problems such as physical illness, mental illness and depression among others.

The same will happen with the spiritual levels; for instance, let us assume that you are living in an old house. Within this house, you will have what you consider a friendly spirit (I go into ghosts and trapped entities elsewhere). Those spirits have to sustain enough energy to remain in this earthly level. They will create those same cords to keep themselves topped up with the energy that is needed.

Case 28: A Dangerous Game

Fiona had called me to ask for help, she was feeling seriously depressed, and her boyfriend, Andy (who was skeptical), had seen the figure of a woman passing by his door, which made him sit up and take notice. He agreed to allow Fiona to call me in to have a look around and see if I could pick anything up. Their property was placed in the countryside with just a few houses in the surrounding area.

As I entered the house, I immediately felt the connection of a portly woman whose given name was Elizabeth - she told me she was known as Dot. I passed this information over to my clients, and they looked shocked when I came across with other information that confirmed that I was speaking to Andy's grandmother. Not so skeptical now, I thought!

The spirit told me that she was there in visitation and no other reason, but offered the explanation why Fiona was feeling the way she did. The spirit said two words - "Draining Friend." I asked Fiona if she had a friend who was going through a bit of turmoil. She explained that her friend Sal, who was close to her, was constantly breaking up with boyfriends, having money problems, and was facing losing her home because of the spiraling debt problems she found herself creating. She was constantly talking about her parents and their divorce. She stated she did not have a relationship with her father either.

This was a simple case of psychic vampirism.

Fiona was the shoulder to lean on and the ear for her friend, but the longer she was in her company, the more she felt drained. She would come away from her thinking negatively, and soon this blanket of negativity begun to subdue her own joyfulness.

I continued to counsel Fiona and taught her how to cut cords and how to protect herself. I also told her that she did not need to keep away but learn to protect herself from her friend, and to cut her cords of attachment regularly.

Cords of Attachment

Cords of attachment can be connected to you for a long time. They are not bound by time or space. They can connect through emotional ties, through intent, or just a deep need to feed on the energy or feel connected. I will use another situation from my own experience to show you how these cords can remain connected to you until you take it on yourself to have them cut. What is important to know is that you can create these cords by means of intent and a survival need for the spirit. These etheric cords will continue to affect you throughout your day, and night. They can be seen using the gift of clairvoyance. They are not tangible and do not exist on the physical plane.

Now imagine if you will that members of your family consider you to be a failure of some type, and are constantly praying for your salvation through their own ignorance and misunderstanding of spiritual law. They will create etheric cords of attachment to you that can last for a while. Slowly these cords can in fact block your natural progress in life – stifling your spiritual progress too. It is your responsibility to recognize this and take the requisite measures to control it. Your family members may actually be incredibly five-sensory and will be ignorant to the spiritual hurt they are causing you.

When they act in a willful way they consider being helpful, they will in fact hinder you because of their lives being cloaked in materialism. Therefore, their own desires and ignorance have harbored an unwitting intent to manifest these cords. Their joined negative energy can be like a smothering blanket over you and cause you to become depressed and have feelings of rejection, which will eventually hold you back. This similar situation happens to every medium because of the path they have chosen. Choosing this path is not easy, and the lack of support from your family will affect you in many ways. You may have always been considered as the black sheep of the family, and because you live a sixth-sensory existence, they will not recognize you with spiritual eyes. Instead, they will see you with the eyes of materialism and will judge you unfairly. Unfortunately, you have to deal with these family cords also.

Depression

With all of this going on, and the fact that you have opened yourself up to spiritual energies, you will become a candidate for depression and will manifest this illness through your own ignorance. Depression can come in all forms and varying intensities, from a light depression to a deep depression that can give you suicidal tendencies. This is another form of energy imbalance and it may have disastrous effects physically and mentally when not attended.

The fewer positive energies that you have within you, the harder it is for your emotional states to find the power to recognize or complete lessons that develop you spiritually. It is because of this that you will be in danger of falling into that deep depression.

All it needs is a catalyst to set the whole situation off, and if you have a lack of energy because all your life force is being used in other ways or by vampirism, you will eventually fall prey to the depressive energy that will engulf you. This catalyst could be the loss of someone in your life through death or separation; it could be another type of loss such as losing your job. If you do not recognize the spiritual lessons within, then you could fail to have the inner strength and will to fight and become victorious in your spiritual tests. When you open yourself up to psychic energy, you will be using a great deal. Therefore, if you have no control and tests such as the ones I have discussed above arise, you will not be able to deal with them adequately.

Hitchhikers

Hitchhikers, as I prefer to call them, are widely misunderstood, and many so-called spiritual teachers will offer differing opinions, especially those of a certain Christian dogmatic belief system. They will attest to the above as being a form of possession needing an exorcism. Hitchhikers are simply grounded spirits that will attach themselves to your auric field, to feel what it is like to be alive once more on the earth plane. It could also be to fulfill a material need that was not completed in their lifetime.

Let us just assume for a moment that you have entered a bar for a night out, and after a while, something does not feel right. If a spirit person has remained in that particular vicinity, the chances are that they would have been the type of individual who frequented places like this and enjoyed the effects of the alcohol. It would be correct to assume the spirit would love to feel that kick again. Therefore, as with the law of attraction, the spirit will be drawn to someone of a similar disposition. They will then attach themselves to an already weakened auric field, and begin to feel the earth plane effects of your desires and addictions.

As a teacher of the art of Budo (way of the warrior), I often meet many individuals who have their problems and need guidance, which is why I continue to teach Budo from a spiritual perspective. Sometimes they come to me when no one else will give them a chance and I help if I can – we all deserve second chances in life, though many will disagree, perhaps that's what compassion really is. Furthermore, these individuals will often receive help of a spiritual nature and not come to learn how to fight. The battle that is going on within them is even greater.

Therefore, I offer them training to protect the mind, body and the soul.

Case 29: Don't Pick Up Hitchikers

James had contacted me and wanted to come and train with me in my dojo. I normally interview everyone who wishes to train with me, so I can tune into them and see their true heart for myself. I agreed to meet him in Starbucks to have a coffee. When I saw James, I noticed that he had a negatively charged aura, and that he was full of anger, he seemed drained in some way. As we chatted, he opened and told me that he needed help with his anger; his whole life was falling apart because of his emotions, and he felt abandoned and alone.

As I tuned into his energy, his brother came through from the spirit world, he had committed suicide, and James was finding it difficult to deal with his passing.

It was his brother in the spirit world that guided him gently to me; he had taken to drinking too much and experimenting with substances that altered his consciousness to block out the substantial emotional pain he was feeling. He was finding it difficult to sleep and said that he felt like he was being told to do things that were not of his nature. He found himself getting into fights and felt like he was being coerced into attacking someone for no reason – he hated himself and who he had become.

I gave James a message from his brother in spirit to confirm his existence and to offer him the path to healing his grief. An immediate *weight seemed to be removed from him as a single tear ran down his quivering cheek.*

James was an incredibly burly man. He had a strong disposition, and for him to finally show emotion was a step forward.

Next, I had to explain to him that he had picked up a hitchhiker from somewhere and more than likely; this would have been in a bar when he was inebriated or in the act of intoxication through drugs. The spirit attachment would not be with him now because he would have known who I was and wanted to remain hidden. Nonetheless, James had to accept what I was telling him, that this was the spirit that was influencing his thoughts.

I turned to his brother once more to see if he could give me any information that would en lighten me to his brother's plight on the earth plane. He told me the spirit was attached because of the life that his brother was leading and the attached entity was having fun at his brother's cost. James' brother, who had passed, could not interfere as this was a major lesson, and the spirit was grounded, angry and insistent on remaining. Only James could get rid of the entity, and all it would take, was the correct free-will decision – to begin to live a clean life once again – he would have to choose.

Soon after that impromptu reading, he joined my dojo and trained with me personally – learning more of a spiritual way of being than a materially charged existence.

We have our problems and sometimes it needs opening your spirit to aid in the evolution of someone's soul. Many have wavered and cannot return to the soul path because of the continuous judgment of others. Unfortunately, in this plane of existence, you are constantly judged and forgiveness is just a word.

I also have a theory, hypothetical if you will, that this may be the reason individuals are cajoled into violent encounters and sometimes - even murder. Knowing this attachment can happen with various levels of influence will be challenging for the medium, because it offers a possible explanation into how spirits can influence susceptible individuals. Those that are developing their spiritual gifts can be coerced easily due to the direct communication from spirit through spirit to spirit. Learn to discern or as I like to put things, Learn, Earn, Discern.

CHAPTER 42

Dealing with Psychic Attack

I f you would visualize for a moment a target and an arrow. Imagine someone constantly firing these arrows at the target and being relentless in the task – constantly thwarting your advance by attacking relentlessly. This is what it is like for the psychic or the medium while under some form of psychic attack and it can affect the individual in horrendous ways, physically and mentally.

Either way, these attacks can come in many forms and can be a conscious attack, where deliberate intent is used, or of course, it could be one which is made unconsciously and without any form of negative intent.

As psychics and mediums, our sensitivity is so high that we can feel negative emanations easier than a five-sensory individual can. I am under no doubt that five-sensory people get these attacks regularly themselves, but because they lack the sensitivity of mediums and psychics, they would find them difficult to discern. Therefore, they will find some other plausible excuse for the way they are feeling and become skeptical of anything spiritual.

Psychic attack can have a tremendous effect on the sensitive. Consequently, it may be seen clairvoyantly if the victim knows

248

the person sending a deliberate attack. It can often manifest as a headache that suddenly appears without any just cause or a temporary illness. A feeling of dread and nervousness will often precede the headache too. Of course, you can just know that you are being attacked because of your own knowingness and inner guidance system – your intuition, if you will. Even loved ones that are close to you can psychically attack you without any intent, and this may just manifest because of inner anger and unbalanced emotions.

As mediums and psychics, we are in the firing line a great deal and I often find myself becoming the target of someone else's negativity. Especially when it comes from individuals who only understand their material existence and deny the spirit from within. Psychic attacks will affect sensitive individuals with more ferocity than other less sensitive people. Words can hurt and stab through you like a sword cutting through its victim, and the thing is – you do not need to be present. Even thought forms with negative intent towards you may have a detrimental effect on your own energy.

CHAPTER 43

Grounded Needy and Influential Spirits

These types of spirits are more of a nuisance. However, each will have its own level of interference and annoyance depending on the fear they can feed. This is normally what we understand as ghosts and hauntings. The grounded spirit is one who, perhaps through emotional issues and unfinished business, or perhaps even by materialistic attachment or fear of damnation, is too scared to pass over to the light.

They become attached to the material plane and are attracted to those with a similar disposition. They can also remain attached to a property or an area of concern to them when they were alive on the earth plane. They have a need to be nourished by the energies of emotion, and so can influence individuals who are less than spiritually awakened. This can often be the reason for many unhappy households. They will also be attracted to those who have an ability of communication and who become aware of their presence; this is associated with mediums. A word of caution though - trainee mediums will often communicate because of their own desire, and have not been able to discern the spirit. Sometimes this can have grave consequences as the spirit finds a free ride.

Case 30: Grounded Spirit Masquerading as a Trusted Guide

Marion was a developing medium who, in my opinion, was rather unbalanced. She had a desperate desire to meet her guides and even though others were talking of guides and angels, she felt rather put out at not having them. I met Marion on an Angel and Sixth-Sense workshop; while she was kind, she could not help but embellish what communications she thought she was receiving. Everything in her life was governed by spirit and she could not be in the here and now – living in the present moment.

I remember her once saying to me that she had a beautiful feather from the angels in the morning – she was sure that was a sign. I am scientific myself, but when you live by the sea-side and you bring me a white seagull feather – Hello! Wake up and smell the coffee; that is no more a sign than an angel manifesting with a placard.

Still, she was a lovely woman.

She called me, frantic and in desperation. "You've got to help me!" She said, "I have been seeing bad things, grotesque faces and voices in my head, my thoughts are almost evil and my guide has not been around. I have been meditating and I can't sleep."

What guide? I thought to myself, as I knew in her desperation that she would accept anything at all. I had an inclination this may be a grounded spirit playing with her; one who would have introduced themselves in a cloak of light.

I agreed to bring Marion around for a coffee and a reading to see what I could do. I poured the coffee and sat down with her – went into myself to communicate with my own guide Ellie, yet someone different was making an appearance. It was a woman who was obviously in the medical profession; she appeared quite clearly in my mind's eye and before I could even ask her the question of her name – she replied, "No need; that does not matter."

She then explained that she was Marion's guide and that in her desperation; a grounded male spirit had connected with Marion and began to communicate over a short time.

Marion, in her own desperation to meet a guide, took everything he said as gospel, and started to build a trust between them. However, she would often be taken along the wrong path and her meditative practice dwindled. She became depressed and the spirit would often bring others that would keep her awake at nights, this began to have an effect on her health. Her guide told me that Marion had no confirmation of the reality of the spirit and had a severe lack of discernment. Besides, she was happy to communicate with any entity.

The spirit was enjoying the fun and allowing others to play havoc with her, too. When I told this to Marion, she broke down in tears and realized what she had done. I told her the convention is to have validation from your guide on three separate occasions. Then, and only then, are you able to develop that relationship.

We cleansed her home, and I taught her how to protect herself with the use of crystals, salt baths, and white sage, but most of all – prayer and meditation. Soon she was back on form and a great deal happier; I only hope that her continued development is driven by spirit and not her own ego's desire.

Not just mediums and psychics can fall foul to these types of spirits. I have often known these types of entities to hang around places where they used to frequent when they were alive, such as bars, clubs, and other areas where negative energy exists. These spirits need to feel alive and will therefore cling themselves to an individual who is weak in spirit, to perhaps feel the effects of the alcohol or drugs that they are using at the time. If they were a particularly violent person on the earth plane, then they will very often be the instigators of violence from beyond the material realm in the world between spirit and earth. While remaining attached to the individual's auric field, they will often manage to influence their thought processes – goading the person into carrying out acts of violence.This reminds me of a particular time in my own life where I could feel and witness those negative spirits in a place that was frequented by my own family, and still is to this day.

Case 31: Negative Vibe Betrays Wandering Spirits

On this particular day, which was my nephew's Christening, we were invited after the service to go back to my uncle's bar for refreshments.

The bar is an old workers' social club, which is not the place I would frequent – especially now because of my spiritual lifestyle.

Anyway, the moment that I went into the bar, I felt an immense surge of negative energy, and could feel the emanations from wandering grounded spirits and their need to feel alive. My wife and I agreed that we should not enter here because of our own vibration and light, since grounded spirits may try to play havoc with us when they realize that we can see them and sense them.

I decided that rather than upset my brother; I would have a quiet word in my mother's ear to *explain the situation to her. In my own mind, I began to rationalize how I might explain this away. What do I do? Do I just go up and say, "Mum, we see lots of negative spirits wandering around and therefore we can't go in." She would think I was crazy, and as the family already questioned my sanity anyway for being a medium, I thought I would have to concoct some other plausible excuse.*

I decided to tell her that as we lived so far away and had to drive back rather than staying in a hotel, plus the fact we did not drink anyway, it would be prudent to make an early start and to let the others enjoy the event. Now I cannot remember if I said goodbye to my brother, or if I asked my mother to make our excuses. I am sure that I went with his blessing anyway.

Case 32: Grounded Spirit Makes a Poor Housemate

On another occasion, I was once asked by one of my students - who was developing in my Budo class - to visit a house of someone he knew. Seemingly, the house was haunted and the family who lived there was terrified.

As I walked in, I could feel the presence of a man who was telling me that his house was being changed and the people had no right to live there. I asked one of the family members if they had done any significant work to the house recently, and was told they had knocked down a wall to make the kitchen bigger, into a kitchen diner. This had also upset the grounded spirit and he began to use his own anger as a force directed toward the dwellers of his home. The problem was that he did not know that he had passed over and the home had been sold on. He still thought this was his home and they were obviously squatting.

The solution was simple; I had to try to persuade the grounded spirit that he had passed on and that his house was no longer his concern. It was far from easy because the spirit had grown accustomed to the atmosphere and the volatile relationship within the home, which he was adding to, and it was making him feel alive.

I knew then I had to ask for higher guidance and called on my guides and angels to intervene. I immediately saw clairvoyantly a wonderful sight of an angel bringing through what seemed to be his wife, who passed before him many years ago and was the sight that comforted him. He immediately felt safe and went into the light. The home had returned to normal and the problems that existed there had gone.

Violent Spirit Negative Spirit

I will base this on a hypothesis that violent spirits can influence the sensitive individual. I have thought for a considerable time that many spirits that are grounded can influence the mind of the individual. This is especially true for individuals who are sensitive or have opened up to spirit, either deliberately or unintentionally, due to dabbling in occult practices, alcohol or mind altering drugs that have weakened the Aura. I also believe those who may be spiritually lost or have turned away from the light are another particular target of these types of spirits.

Now I want to make a clear distinction here; I am talking about evil spirits that are human in nature and are grounded.

These spirits are dangerous and only a hop, skip and a jump to something more diabolical which I will discuss later.

These spirits have turned away from the light, and may have been of a murderous disposition or perhaps were criminals who carried out atrocious acts when they were incarnated on this earth plane.

It is true that when we pass over, we keep our same personalities and continue our spiritual development within the spirit world. So imagine then, if that evil spirit has not passed over to the spirit world for fear of retribution. They will remain grounded and will remain evil in nature, and when they find out they can influence weak individuals – they will, and normally with catastrophic effects on the earth plane.

There is a high likelihood that is why some people murder and abuse others, showing no remorse, and often claiming that they have been hearing voices. This also suggests the individual has Mediumship abilities too, though not developed in a spiritual manner.

Often these spirits can identify the developing student medium or psychic because of their spiritual light. This light will shine like a beacon for all to see in the spirit world. This is like attracting a moth to a flame, but not in a good way. The grounded spirit will only have mischief in mind and will quickly identify the individual's innermost fears. The spirit will play on those fears and aggravate them - even make the student prone to acting in a manner in which they would not normally act, and this can be a sure sign of being tampered with. The best way of protecting oneself is by prayer, and shutting down as described elsewhere in this book.

Case 33: Negative Spirit Means Trouble

Again, I received communication from another family who were seeking help because they tried to develop spirit communication without due care and attention. Further, they decided they did not need any help or advice from professionally trained mediums. This story is rather sensitive, and so I have continued in her own words after I had given her some advice. She is known as Mrs S and explains:

'I must report to you that my husband was physically attacked last night at approximately 11:30pm by an entity of some sort that left him petrified and withdrawn. My oldest son Mark who is ten years old has also suddenly fallen deathly ill and was almost hospitalized yesterday after-noon with an incredibly high temperature and for no apparent reason. Is this human or not human? Please let me know your thoughts.'

At this point you can deduce the family is con-sidering something more sinister than a grounded entity and suggests that it may not be of this world – perhaps demoniacal – read on.

I told Mrs S to gather some equipment that I would need such as I have discussed before; oil, salt, holy water and other holy items, she then tells me that she can't get some items and makes reference to her religion.

Now before you read the next phase in the story, there is something that you should know. During all this scenario over a period of a few weeks, I was having continual negative experiences and nightmares of a dark and sinister nature. Even though I knew I was protected, I could not help being consumed by fear myself. I continued to meditate and pray. My guide Ellie then enlightens me to the real reason this was occurring.

Mrs S continues; 'I do not know if this is of any relevance to you or not but I just thought that I should tell you since I haven't in ear-lier communications due to fear and for this I am truly sorry. My husband's family is into Witch-craft and black magic. We are not, but we are trying to develop our own abilities ourselves in our own way (we are Christians too and know this

*is against our rules). However, my mother-in-law
is a black magic witch, and that is why she is no
longer allowed to come around or contact us. When
my husband was a child all the way up to being a
teenager his mother would force him to practice
different types of witchcraft. He would partici-
pate in black masses and séances. Do you think
that anything that is going on here could be related to his past experiences with witchcraft?
My husband became a Christian back in 1997 when
he started attending church with the family. I
still am wondering if what is going on has anything to do with his past experiences with the
occult. What do you think? Please help us.'*

*I am sure that by now, you have the whole pic-
ture and you can deduce the seriousness of the
situation. This was getting out of hand and Ellie was spot on with all the information she had
given me.*

What would you do if you received this in your inbox? This is not an easy thing to deal with and you, as a medium or psychic, will come up against this issue at some point. You must be confident in your ability, and the way you conduct your life will depend on your effectiveness to deal with the situation because you will almost be going there blind. If you live a life that is questionable at best, then you are perhaps not the right individual to deal with a situation like this. It is important to have a scientific approach to anything, and having the right intent, and the correct back up such as an individual of science, is of paramount importance. You must be able to investigate from a scientific point as well as the spiritual.

A young developing medium will often jump at the chance to deal with issues of this sort as a sort of spiritual gauntlet if you like. The measure of his or her success in their understanding will come from how they think they have done. Very often, they will claim success prematurely, and will exacerbate the problems exponentially. Caution - do you not think that an entity will recognize where you are on your path of development and where your blind spots are? You cannot deal with this if you are not ready and you have to know your limits. Treading on a dark entity's lair unprepared is playing Russian roulette with your life.

CHAPTER 44

Demon Activity and Possessions

W hat is a Demon?
Many people attribute the reality of demons to only folklore and of course dogmatic religion. However, the word demon comes from the greek term daimon which is considered as a malevolent being in all spiritual and religious traditions. In reality, it is a name given to allow an understanding of that which is below and in opposite to divinity.

One must also consider that a demon (malevolent spirit) has never been incarnated upon the earth and is not borne of human influence, but exists in a non-physical realm. No matter what you call them - or understand them within a perception - there exists an understanding as being that which is in opposition to love and is intent on hate.

You may call it what you want, or even deny its existence, but that does not mean it is not real. Your choosing to deny the reality of demonic activity has no bearing on its reality as a negative force. Demonic activity does not rely on your perception or label. It is better that you will not believe than to allow the demonic influence to permeate the ignorant, for those who have knowledge also have the answer and the divine power to overcome.

I mentioned previously that by dabbling in the areas of black magic and the darker side of the occult, you could be inviting demons. Allow me to build on this. There are active covens, satanic cults, and other organizations, which are involved in the manifestation and conjuring of demons with a view to gaining paranormal powers and control over the forces of darkness. Remember I told you that all these were created by the great creator, and are therefore controlled by the will of the creator. They remain under the chains of bondage, and have a restricted amount of freedom to test and carry out God's Plan. However, dabbling in black magic using your own free will gives them an advantage and you can easily be tricked.

A demon can show itself in the form of light, yet it cannot by definition stand anything from the light, and if questioned will show its weakness. However, infestation can start slowly and develop into a full-blown possession without anyone knowing. There are five stages to Demonic possession:
1. Invitation
2. Infestation
3. Oppression
4. Obsession
5. Possession

Now as I have mentioned previously when I discussed a little about obsession. As you can see from the list obsession is the prior stage to possession, but, and that's a big but, it can happen earlier as obsession can also be a catalyst to the beginning stages of an attempt at full possession by a diabolical spirit. This stage can present itself, and in that case, it may run like this;
1. Invitation
2. Obsession
3. Infestation
4. Oppression

5. Deepened Obsession
6. Diabolical Possession

Even in our modern times, satanic cults are springing up everywhere, and though it may seem impossible to believe, the Vatican has been subjugated by satanic influences. So secret are the cults that they could be going on in your next-door neighbor's house without your knowledge. With that in mind, a war is going on right now in the unseen planes of the spirit realm, and this war is for the souls of humankind. Is that so difficult to believe, with all the negativity in the environment? Satan and his legion of demons are just waiting for the right invitation and dabbling in the occult for fun and without the proper training or experience is opening a portal straight to the nether world! That is the invite.

Hitler was actively involved in satanic worship through the Vril society, which was a fellowship that controlled the Nazi party. He took part in many séances and was led to believe that victory would be coming soon. Obviously, that never happened, which is comforting to know that Light will always transform the darkness. His desire for power and control is that same desire that exists within these negatively charged societies.

Psychic murders

From USA to Italy, Germany and Ireland - murder, rape, suicide and extreme violence can be attributed to satanic rituals and witchcraft. In Milan (Italy), groups of teenagers were dabbling in satanic rituals to invoke the power of demonic forces. Shortly after, they chose their victims, brutally murdered them and danced on their graves. In another case in northern Italy, another sect murdered one of their own members, claiming to hear voices.

Whether it is discarnate beings or evil entities, there is no doubt that negative influences have got so powerful that the will of the person is controlled, causing them to commit evil. They chose their victims and decided to murder them as human sacrifice. If you can imagine that the amount of negative energy in thought, feeling, and intent that is directed towards the victim is so intense and overwhelming, it is highly likely that the astral body or auric field would feel this bombardment of evil.

The individual (if aware through meditation and self-awareness) would have the keys to reverse the negativity through their own intuitive awareness, and thwart any malicious attempt against them. One survivor in Ireland stated that before he got close to the location that would have been his final resting-place, he felt an intense malice around him. Recognizing the evil intent, he left the area immediately – saving his own life. He later investigated the sect and raised the concerns with the Irish government – a mass investigation ensued.

Raising your spiritual awareness can save you from all physical malices, from outside influences that you can perceive, and all that you cannot.

Satanic Ritual Abuse and Murder

OK, for all you developing mediums and psychics, this is very real and very scary. Now let me remind you that I have said God controls all, and yet we have the ritual abuse and satanic killings by covens and individuals who have given themselves to the darkness through blood rites. The danger itself is not from the dark entities, but those who may be influenced by them are a greater enemy - for they have been subjugated by pure Evil, and exist to carry out heinous acts against humanity.

You as a professional medium and a warrior of the light may have to deal with the aftermath. This is worst-case scenario and possibly even more dangerous than spirit obsession or possession. This is why, in my mind, possession is relatively non-existent, because there are willing individuals who will happily carry out the work of Evil. I am in no doubt as to the reality that human sacrifice and child sacrifice exist - possibly even the reason why pedophilia exists. After all, there are plenty of cases throughout the world that have made the headlines. Very often, the individual who has carried out the work of the demon has no recollection of what has happened. Interestingly, these individuals often display psychic abilities, and that is what makes the possession or control easier from the Demon's point of view. The will of the individual has already been given over unwittingly.

One such case involved mutilations and murders of four teenagers that happened in Moscow, Russia. Russia has seen a massive insurgence in satanic ritualistic killings, as have other countries, including ours. To date there are thought to be 15 satanic cults in Moscow alone.

The murders in Russia all had the hallmarks of satanic rituals, dismembered body parts and charred remains were found in a ditch marked by a black upside down cross. This was the work of a satanic cult of which there were thought to be eight members headed by Nikolai Ogolobyak. The members held in custody showed no remorse and one stated that he did not expect to be punished, saying, "Satan will help me to avoid responsibility. I made lots of sacrifices to him." This is giving some support to my previous hypothesis, yet more worryingly another said he had got fed up with God for not making him rich and that "things improved" after he started praying to Satan.

This case itself gives credence to the fact that there are plenty of individuals who are giving themselves to evil willingly. Satanists as a religion put themselves before anything else, and core values include pride, indulgence, ambition, and meeting sexual desires. An offer of wealth and fame is sometimes the only dangled gift that it takes to cause someone to turn, yet I would assume that darker entities would have already been hard at work before the final crescendo. Another member of the same cult boasted he once dug up the body of a recently deceased person and ate the heart. This is another trait belonging to satanic ritualistic killings.

Another interesting point to note is the fact that a great deal of the murders are carried out by teenage Satanists. Perhaps it is because of the adolescent stage that psychic forces innate within the individual are particularly strong.

In another case of similar disposition and heresy, a couple that claimed to be vampires killed a man in a satanic ritualistic killing. Daniel Ruda and his wife Manuela had a dark and macabre history together. They claimed the Devil told them to do it and could not be held accountable, which seems to be another trait in all these heinous murders. The apartment where they lived was full of satanic symbols and equipment. The couple hit their victim over the head with a hammer and carved a pentagram into his chest. Rudas then stated they drank his blood and slept together in their own coffin. His wife, Manuela, claimed they were not alone in the apartment and that a dark presence was there with them constantly. She maintained that Rudas had "terrible, glowing eyes" before delivering the first blow. She also claimed that she was drawn to Satanism when she visited Britain and in particular, the Highlands of Scotland because of the drab, dreary environments. However, when she got to London, she worked in a Gothic bar and joined a group who were involved in worshipping Satan. She claimed that Satan contacted her when she was 14 and became involved in the Gothic scene. The group she was involved in regularly drank human blood at their parties and slept in graves, which they dug for themselves. (BBC World News)

I could go on forever citing case after case, and you would be shocked, upset, and scared. However, I will not because I feel that I do not want to bring energy to these cases, but I can assure you that it happens around the world far more than it should. Before I go into the reasons that you may come across this as a psychic medium, allow me to give you another example of my own.

If you can remember earlier on within the book, I told you of my past within the monastery. When I was very young, as well as being interested in spirituality, I was also fascinated by the occult too, and would discuss this with many of the brothers and priests, who believed that a healthy knowledge of the subject matter would be tantamount to protection.

Case 34: Surprise on the Hill

One evening, a friend and I decided to have a walk up on the hill behind the monastery, which was quite a distance. At the top of the hill was a stone table, much like an altar of worship, and I remember not ever liking it at all. On that particular evening when we went up the hill, we saw something that scared us terribly. Before we got to the area where the stone tablet was, we could hear chanting, and through the trees, we saw a number of individuals in black hooded cloaks with candles. Now I cannot tell you if this was a coven; a cult or indeed devil worshipers. I do know that I had to get out of there as soon as possible, and I tell you, it was the fastest I ever descended the hill. My friend and I were later found in the chapel praying and to this day, we have never discussed this till now.

A Medium's Perspective

Therefore, why this should possibly affect you as a medium or a student of development is important to understand; please remember that ignorance is certainly no defense. If you readthe stories again, you will see that there are constants, such as individuals, places, and buildings. Perhaps the individuals in that circle (or in its immediate environment), but on the outside of the circle may be affected and could end up on your doorstep. Allow me to reiterate the example I gave you when the wife of the young family contacted me to tell me their par- ents were involved in black magic, and that black masses were held in their home. These individuals came to me for help; they could come to you. What if you were called out to help a family who contacted you in desperation? They were experiencing dark sinister events of a paranormal nature within a home they had just moved to. What would you do? Of course, there might be a plausible and scientific reason but you must also assert that another darker element may exist, and you as a medium will have to discern this as well as offer some comfort and protec- tion. It is not all about giving evidence of life after death, which of course is our main priority, but you also stand as a warrior of light with the ability to discern between good and evil. There- fore, you can be of service in another way to your fellow broth- er and sister. You will not be able to help them if you are not strong enough in mind and body to deal with it, and have the requisite levels of protection around you.

Identifying the Activity

There are obviously signs and symptoms of diabolical activ- ity, and some of these will be more easily noticeable than oth- ers. You, as a medium, should acquaint yourself with all these basics. For instance, you may start to smell putrid odors such as rotting flesh and will find no cause for the stench. You may also note that religious icons that are near the phenomena may have been often removed, damaged, or defiled. Most satanic cults will be involved in defiling religious icons and symbols – hence the upside down cross which is mocking the cross of Christ.

The person who may be infested or obsessed will show a dis- like to religious artifacts and may react badly in their presence. There will be an increase in argumentative episodes or even violence when they are approached. Often, in cases that present evidence of demonic influence, there will often be heard noises of animals scratching or clawing and even growls not of this world, and this often precedes putrid odors. Furthermore, the individual who is under the threat or in the first stages of this type of attack will often hit very severe depression and will retreat from normal life. When the person is under the control of the demoniacal spirit, which may take years of oppression, they will display acts of superhuman strength and will often speak in languages that are unknown to them or anyone around them – especially Latin and ancient Aramaic. They may also show signs of prophesy and will know information not known to them. Now I know this sounds like a medium but there is a vast difference in the disposition of a medium and the extent of abilities and understanding as well as a revulsion to anything remotely from love.

The signs and symptoms of possession can be very subtle or right in your face. If you experience any of these, consult a professional immediately. However, one must also understand there is a fine line between possession and psychiatric illness. I remember studying a supposedly real case of demon possession, which had concluded the person was levitating and speaking in foreign tongues, which would be a real sign of paranormal activity of a negative nature. However, upon studying the evidence, a colleague and I were able to conclude that it was merely an episode of epilepsy and nothing more.

Real cases of possession are rare, and we must remain scientific in our approach in order that we are fully aware and have discounted all other avenues. There is, however, a real danger to the medium of spirit obsession, which I have discussed previously. We have no real evidence of levitation, to the point that a host of whom it is claimed has been levitated, has never been witnessed on video or camera, and most phenomena can be readily explained. Except within a séance and physical circle where these phenomena, under the right conditions can be witnessed. Again, there is much conjecture surrounding this aspect of mediumship.

In Catholicism, it can take many months of investigation before it is finally confirmed that diabolical possession has indeed taken place and needs to be dealt with through a formal exorcism. This investigation will involve a great deal of scientific research and an interesting point to note is that mediums are used by the Catholic church to be able to discern spirit – this, of course, is normally denied.

What is also interesting is that many other religions do actually contact the Catholic exorcists for help rather than dealing with it in-house. Why this happens is not entirely clear, but it is thought because if the success with the rites of exorcism. In contrast, though, there are real cases of possession which have caused controversy, such as Annalise Michelle – a young woman born in Bavaria, Germany and devoutly Catholic, but suffering from epilepsy, and one would wonder; why would God allow such a travesty to a devout individual. However, there remains controversy regarding the epilepsy.

The answer is simple, which is because of God's will to teach a real lesson to humanity. There are many restrictions on a full-blown possession, and it can only occur through the will of the creator or through the individual playing with black magic, and taking part in rituals of that nature where blood rites are used. Therefore, free will has had a part to play. The individual could be a drug user or abuser of the spirit and the light, and therefore succumb to spirit obsession, which can lead to possession. For the most part though, it is not that prevalent and as one is leading a spiritual existence and works in the light, you will be protected as long as you take precautions.

Remember your spiritual self is different, and I discuss the reality of protection in another chapter. There are an increasing number of demonic cases throughout the world, and

I am certain the reasons are the numbers of individuals who get involved in Satanism and who dabble in the occult without knowledge and training and of course, ill-informed, untrained and ignorant developing mediums.

Another recent case was in the USA, and unfortunately, the woman who was possessed cannot be named for legal reasons. The history surrounding the case has the typical hallmarks, and she herself was primarily involved in satanic worship over the years. She herself called for the exorcism and scientists and Catholic priests were involved in the exorcism. The case was documented by Richard E. Gallagher, M.D. who is a board-certified psychiatrist in private practice in Hawthorne, New York, and Associate Professor of Clinical Psychiatry at New York Medical College. He is also on the faculties of the Columbia University Psychoanalytic Institute and a Roman Catholic seminary.

He documented the case to offer evidence of a real case of possession in the modern day. True levitation was witnessed and the possessed individual would often enter into a trance-like state and show evidence of prophesy, while objects would often be thrown around the room. She would speak in foreign languages, and often hurled abusive comments to the clergy there – showing distain for anything remotely religious (Gallagher, 2008).

This case again shows all the hallmarks of a true possession and again there are underlying factors.

I have discussed various dangers of psychic development but as we move forward into the development of various levels of mediumship, there are other dangers of which we should all be aware. Of course, we can become affected by the odd psychic vampire or through emotional imbalances; yet perhaps the greatest danger however is spirit obsession, which does have a kind of demoniacal feeling to it, and can in fact be a step towards this. Nevertheless, to the medium, it is merely the danger from negative or wandering grounded spirits or as I mentioned previously – influences that are subtle in nature. Yes you have power and authority and free will, but often and, dependent on conditions, this may be suppressed. It is better to be ready than caught off guard.

Spirit obsession, when not recognized, can cause psychological imbalances within the medium and can eventually have the gravest of consequences such as suicide or possession? However, this is worst-case scenario.

What I would like to make clear is that your soul or spirit cannot be possessed, but mainly the vehicle that you use for your earthly expression can, and mostly because these spirits only wish to live again or complete unfinished business. Get that fear out of your head now, and you are one step closer to being able to recognize and deal with this issue - should it occur. Unfortunately, we live a life that is governed through fear - fear of not having enough, fear of losing what we have, fear of no success, and so on. Hudson Tuttle attests that a deficiency of will power, induced by physical conditions rather than mental, is the cause of spirit obsession, though in varying degrees.[12] The gateway has to be open or such an influence cannot enter or take place, no matter how hard it tries. There has to be a weakness and this can be a severely depressed sensitive or an inharmonious circle or, evidently, the desperation of the medium to develop too quickly. Psychological imbalance or illness and damage to the auric field through destructive practices can also be a catalyst.

The physical body, when in a state of disease, is also prone to this attack, which is then reflected on the mind, and therefore, the mind soaks up these impressions like a sponge. Now here is a modern scientific skepticism. Obsession can be thought of as schizophrenia or other psychological disorders and many

12 A Guide to Mediumship and Psychical Enfoldment by E.W. and M.H. Wallis (Office of Light)

sufferers are institutionalized unnecessarily. I remember being told of an example of a medium that was greatly respected in the community where he worked. The problem that he had was the fact he could not shut himself off from the desperation of those spirit beings that wanted to communicate with him. The constant barrage of communication came to a crescendo, when soon enough psychologically he became imbalanced and the voices would not stop. He ended up being committed to a psychiatric hospital where he ended his days still hearing voices. He was clearly obsessed by a spirit who kept the gateway open. Another example was when I was once called to a psychiatric hospital to meet with a nurse whom I had previously read for. I was to meet with a young woman who had been committed by her parents. Instantly, I could see the young woman was a natural medium and was so sensitive that she remained close to the Borderlands (spirit realm). What she was experiencing was spirit obsession, even though she was not a developing medium; nevertheless, she was still a medium. It was not long before she was taught how to deal with her problem, and when she left, she attended a spiritualist center and learned to control her gifts.

Spirit obsession is therefore the main danger to a developing medium and as I have stated before, it is better to start spiritual protective practices now before you are faced with the issue. Remember though, that the spiritual self will not be obsessed or harmed, it will be the conscious self, and recognizing this is the first stage of dealing with it. A spirit obsession can be incredibly influential on a person's life, and in many respects obtrusive. This is why it is important for the developing medium not to communicate with anything and everything, because before too long you could be obsessed if you are slowly being eroded. This would be a spirit so desperate to communicate, they would not let you rest. In that regard, another sign of obsession can be emotional upset, and a severe insomnia with the fear of sleep being the catalyst.

In shamanism, the shaman would consider the only way to get rid of a spirit who does this would be to communicate with the spirit, and sometimes I would agree this would be necessary. However, in my opinion, I consider it necessary that one should be able to increase the psychic defenses from within, as this weakness was the reason the obsession had taken place in the first instance. Drinking, drugs and taking part in events or indulgences that damage the mind, body, and soul are a sure way to become obsessed. It is even easier for a medium to become obsessed, should they take part in the aforementioned indulgences.

Like anyone, and especially those in the military or police services, I drank and had a good time, but when I started to develop my mediumship properly, I stopped all of those indulgences to remain as clean as possible. Now there is nothing wrong with having a drink or two but as a developing medium, you should be aware of the consequences with over-indulging.

Clearances

You can take part in as many clearance rituals as often as you like, but the truth is, if you are infested with diabolical spirits, it will take more than a simple cleansing to be rid of the influences that surround your family, your property, and your own life. A clearance using ancient remedies, for example sage and cedar, will only work in certain occasions such as a grounded or trapped entity that is looking for help, rather than being the cause of mischief. If you attempt to use a clearance on a darker entity, you will only anger this spirit, and you will cause far more devastation and destruction than you realize. The truth is that Prayer is your best weapon until you can reach out to a suitably qualified individual. I am one of those individuals that will investigate the case but have found myself out of my depth at times and always have to revert to the Catholic Church or a suitable expert that I trust to take over. There is no honor in trying to be a hero. Sometimes it is better to change tactics than admit defeat.

The truth remains that evil is more prevalent than you would think and forewarned is forearmed. As I have said, there is another hypothesis that exists, and that is the fact that possessions are less likely due to the fact, there are many who have already sold their soul in order to gain material advantage in this world. This means that we have a possible cause for murder, ritualistic abuse, and pedophilia. You may have to deal with the aftermath as a medium, and you may be called to the aid of a priest or other clergy, so you had better be prepared and recognize the dangers, how to discern them and deal with them. You must ensure that you have the maximum amount of protection around you. *Recognize the innate divinity and power within, this is the secret.*

The Two Selves (Secret)

Here is a bit of good news; did you know that you are two people, right here, right now? That may sound a little bit crazy and you would be forgiven for thinking that you had a split personality. What I am talking about is the real you and the physical you, which are two different individuals, and this is where your ultimate protection lies. Having an awareness of something is the first step to releasing your innate spiritual authority to deal with situations. Your divinity can never be extinguished, and your free will is restricted according to your spiritual growth and realization of your innate spiritual power. The real you is driven by the Divine spark that is your soul and your replication of the essence of God; the physical part of you is driven by your ego and succumbs to fears and the maladies of material existence.

When you have an acute awareness of the reality of your spiritual duality, you will know that goodness and divinity resides in you, and your spiritual authority is that which is in line with all spiritual forces. Therefore, nothing evil may touch you and you can call upon your spiritual authority, which is the parallel of the Christ consciousness to protect you and to deal with negativity. Darkness always fears the light, and you are abundant with this light right now in the present moment, you have that same authority. Recognition of this is all that is needed.

Getting it wrong

There is also perhaps a greater danger that exists, and that is deluded self-proclaimed religious leaders and evangelical indi- viduals who tar everything with demonic influence and possession. You know the kind – you are depressed because of a demon. You lost your job because of a demon, you like the wrong music because of a demon and your psychological illness is because of a demon. You can witness them doing over-the-top, so-called exorcisms, which do far more damage to the person than good.

There is a need for caution in this area, especially important at a time when untrained non-professionals, or worse - public ministries - may unfortunately mislead or even exploit believers in this area, turning to blind faith in the ministry itself for help. You only need to watch TV or search on the internet to find self-proclaimed professionals offering to deal with these issues for a fee, and some people find themselves bankrupt because their own fears have been played upon, and through this desperate need for help, they have given everything up – feeling they are damned and acting through fear.

Ask yourself, who is more in need of divine intervention? Some would say the ministry or self-proclaimed clergy is in need of far more in the way of spiritual help.

Psychics and mediums often get it wrong too, and there are many who will dive into these dark waters thinking they can adequately deal with the situation because they think they know it all. After all, they communicate with the dead and display spiritual gifts! Who are we to argue? I am sorry, but these people are deluded too and self-absorbed. They show no fear and will often deny the truth – claiming instead to believe that the phenomena are just a nice grounded spirit or spirits that needs guidance. I suppose this is rather like an angler claiming the one that got away was huge and offered a terrible fight, which you lost.

You need to wake up and smell the coffee and realize the danger is very real, though very rare; you still have to have the knowledge and be prepared. What if a Catholic priest came to you and asked you to help in the carrying out of the Rituale Rominum? You probably would have no clue what that is. The Rituale is the rite of exorcism, as used in the Catholic Church by trained exorcists ordained by the Vatican in Rome. It is far better to equip yourself with all the knowledge you can now and have a just-in-case attitude.

Another word of warning that I should offer to you as a medium, and you can deny this all you like. Do not challenge the entity; the dark spirit is far more superior in knowledge than you are. It is able to play on your innermost fears and weaknesses very quickly that will have the desired effect on you - should you be weak in constitution. It is important that you be prepared for the unexpected, never question the entity in such a way that you show weakness, or can be used against you. I hope that you as a medium never have to deal with anything this sinister, but if you do, you should take solace in the fact that God has chosen you for a higher purpose, and therefore, you need to recognize the power of your divinity. And for those of you who think it's all a load of baloney, remember that even though you can't see gravity, it **will** affect you if you fall, trip or crash.

Casting Demons

Unfortunately in today's world, claims of casting out demoniacal spirits, exorcisms, or any other rite using spirit ability is said to be the work of Satan and his legion of satanic demons. Even in the time of Christ, there is evidence of the same problem when he was accused of using black magic or Satan's power to cast out unclean spirits or demons from the possessed. Furthermore, this is replicated in the modern day and many on the spiritual path are hated and jeered for the work they do. Accept that you are also a target, for when you take up the cross of being of service in this field and as a medium, you will also be targeted, and it is important that you are able to discern between good and bad as I have mentioned before.

If indeed, there is credence to the claim and understanding that the opposite poles are that same mocking of the Christ presence such as the witching hour at 3am as I have previously mentioned, how then, can Christ or true lay exorcists be acting on the command of Satan rather than the power of God? If the darkness hates and rebukes everything the light stands for, and Jesus is casting out demoniacal spirits that are part of Satan's subjects, how can one who shows so much compassion and love, be acting in the ways understood as evil?

In contrast, the claim that demons can imitate messengers of light is a foolhardy statement, and one that we, as spirits ourselves, should be a little cautious about. Perhaps this is another reason as to why we would question the entities three times. Rather like surveillance – we draw out the targets by breaking down their weaknesses, and the weakness of a demonic spirit is its strength and belief in the conviction of hatred for God and Christ himself. Dark spirits cannot disguise themselves to other spirits who have the gift of spiritual sight, and perhaps this is what may be understood collectively as discernment for the medium – it is more than mere clairvoyance.

It is true though that they can cloak themselves to mere mortals but cannot maintain the bravado for long, as what is done by them comes not from a place of love, therefore a demonic presence will show almost instantaneously. Nothing can be done in love and light and manifest itself as a loving spirit if it cannot stand the light.

A good analogy for this would be as follows:

Visualize yourself in a dark room, where no light exists, everything is pitch black and you cannot see anything in front of you. There are no windows and no lights around. However, in your pocket you have a small torch, or flashlight. You fumble around and find your torch, your flashlight – pull it from your pocket and locate the switch. Just at the instance that you push the button, the light comes on and lights up the whole area. Now you can see everything in front of you. Immediately, you feel safe and secure.

Let us now look at the opposite scenario. Now find yourself in a room full of light. Try to bring in darkness to make the light dissipate. It is impossible and cannot be achieved, no matter how much science you involve. The light will always transform or transmute the darkness and turn the negative to positive. The same cannot be said of the dark, because it cannot transmute the light, and hence where light dwells – no darkness shall prevail.

Exorcism

Exorcism gains in popularity the more and more we see it on the TV and in the media and that results in many people who dive into this field of service without knowledge, faith and, most importantly, Divine Power. There are so many people who claim they have dealt with the demonic and yet the reality is that it's just their misguided ego talking. If you really had dealt with this, then you would never be the same person again. Your life would forever bear those scars and what you thought was reality would be gravely miscalculated. Even if you don't believe in the existence of the demonic, you would not know a polar opposite had you not experienced the polarity. To know health, you must feel or witness illness, to know light, you must witness dark, and so the story goes.

Why Is the Catholic Church Considered the Expert?

Exorcism exists in all beliefs in some form or another and one does not claim to be better than another, but perhaps the Catholic Church has the edge due to the methodology behind it, the focus it was given and the reality that the rite was actually developed through the gift of mediumship and not as revelation as some would assume, divine transmission through the gift of the spirit. The Catholic Church would then develop its immense study into the reality and need for exorcism rites due to the intercession by mediumship transmission.

Perhaps The Most Terrifying Case Of Exorcism To Date

We are going to look at one of the most terrifying cases of demonic possession in history. The possession of Anna Ecklund of Earling, Iowa, began when she was fourteen, and did not end until she was 46 years old. One of the most widely documented cases of possession of the twentieth century (the identity of Ecklund was often protected by reporting her to be named Emma Schmidt), this was the case that was to rock the very foundations of historical exorcism within the Catholic

Church and is widely studied today. The exorcism, witnessed by outsiders of the Church, included such phenomena as levitation, prophecy, speaking in languages unknown to the host, and a disdain and hatred for anything remotely religious.

The Exorcist

The main exorcist on this case, Father Theophilus Riesinger - a Capuchin friar from Appleton, Wisconsin - was assisted by various individuals including nuns from the local convent. It is said that Father Reisenger carried out over 20 or more exorcisms in his capacity as an exorcist, but his first case was Anna/Emma in 1912. This particular case was written about in a document titled "Begone Satan" by Rev Carl Vogl and quickly became one of the most widely talked about cases of its time. The document was actually banned by several religious organizations. The author William Peter Blatty is said to have used this case when writing "The Exorcist."

> *"You cannot imagine the terrible symptoms and feelings that possessed persons have. Strange cats and dogs talk to them in the night. They cannot perform their religious duties, they are kept away from the sacraments, they are exceedingly unhappy." – Father Theophilus Riesinger, 1936*

The Parents

Anecdotal evidence suggests that her father and step-mother (or perhaps her step-aunt Mina), suspected of dabbling in witch craft and occult practices, were the first to cause the possession because of their religious beliefs. Although as a young girl, Anna was pious and devoted to the church, her father Jacob was the opposite and was known for his negative behavior and alcohol abuse. Her step-aunt Mina was considered to be a witch, though this is not documented evidence and is mere conjecture at this point. However, it has been suggested that the Aunt was unkind to the young girl, cursed her and used poison or some kind of herbal potion against her.

Anna was 30 when the first exorcism was performed by Father Riesinger and she was considered to have been possessed over a period of 16 years. She was unable to enter holy places and displayed other elements of possession. The first exorcism was successful, but when the aunt supposedly caused the repossession in 1928, things exacerbated. It is said that repossession is more dangerous and harder to deal with due to the reality of the strength in possession. Mathew 12:43-45 alludes to this reality within biblical teachings:

> *43.“When the unclean spirit is gone out of a man, he walketh through dry places, seeking rest, and findeth none.*

> *44.“Then he saith, I will return into my house from whence I came out; and when he is come, he findeth it empty, swept, and garnished.*

> *45.“Then goeth he, and taketh with himself seven other spirits more wicked than himself, and they enter in and dwell there: and the last state of that man is worse than the first. Even so shall it be also unto this wicked generation.” (King James Bible)*

From many studies and transcripts over the many exorcisms in history, we can see the truth within this scripture as it has been made clear by the questioned spirit that not only one returned but legions and so the repossession is often the worst possible case to deal with.

1928: The 23-Day Exorcism

This apparently was the only case in history that was witnessed at the time by many who can validate the accounts as being real and true to their depiction by Rev Vogl and who were of no substance within the church at the time.

"As soon as the priests invoked the names of the trinity, the woman flew up off the bed" and her body, carried through the air, landed high above the door of the room and clung to the wall with a tenacious grip." (Vogl, 1935)

During the exorcisms, she spoke in many languages of which she knew none, she vomited and excreted terrible foul substances even though she had not eaten anything. She showed tremendous inhuman strength and the demons showed prophecy – even attacking the priests and nuns and foretelling of terrible events. Father Reisinger is said to have aged over these events.

It must be noted that she was examined by doctors physically and mentally and they could find nothing mentally wrong with her at all. However, one major clue of the demoniacal possession was that she could not even say the name of Jesus Christ at all, it made her convulse and when she was blessed with holy water, it was recorded the demons spoke as if in pain.

At the mention of the name St Michael (the Archangel), it was noted the woman convulsed and recoiled. When the name of Jesus was mentioned, the demons were forced to come forward and be known.

This alludes to the necessity under divine law to be able to question the entity who has no way to hide from the questioning in the form it takes. This does not mean that you question with words of rote or an unprepared heart.

This was important for the father to gain control. Many times, the poor woman would scream vile, evil threats in order to frighten those who were present. Voices were heard within - and without - the poor woman and those who heard them shook with fear. This was further exacerbated by the hideous beastly animals that were heard writhing in pain. The excreta from the body continued in inhuman amounts and at times was aimed at the exorcist. However, this was in vain as it seemed the father was definitely protected by a heavenly power.

Why the Possession Happened

According to Vogl, when Father Reisinger began to question the demons, one claimed to be Anna's father. It became clear that he had been damned because of his own acts and way of life. The reason his daughter was possessed was because of a curse he placed on her whilst forcing her to commit incest. She had thwarted all attempts and in a torrent of rage he cursed and asked that all hell take her and force her to commit acts against her chastity. Understand that he could have sought forgiveness but, either through his will or the control by demonic spirits, he did not do so and was therefore damned by his own doing.

Another lesson to take from this, forgiveness is a divine right of all who seek it and is not refused but by your own hand.

Anna's step-aunt Mina, in league with the father, also condemned herself because of the murders of her own children, which she willingly carried out. She had disdain and hate for anything remotely of the light.

Let me also make something clear, the exorcist was not the only religious person there other than nuns from the faith but was also accompanied by a pastor who took part in the exorcisms and doctors who examined her – as aforementioned.

As reported by Vogl, during these exorcisms, Anna's whole body would become distorted and convulsed in inhuman ways with her stomach often being hard as iron and her face and eyes taking on grotesque forms. At one point, everyone was convinced that she would explode with her body being so grotesquely bloated and her facial features being disfigured.

A Unique Experiment

At one point, a piece of paper was placed on Anna's head that had a prayer written on it from a pagan ritual. The demons within remained quiet and unaffected. The interesting thing to note in this experiment is that no one knew it was being done.

Another piece of paper, this one with a divine blessing of the Catholic Church and sprinkled with holy water, was placed upon Anna's head. At that moment, the demons became enraged.

Anything that is remotely divine in nature and pure has an effect on the demonic entities and they react as if they are being tortured.

St Michael: The Secret Weapon

"St Michael the Archangel, defend us in battle. Be our safeguard against the wickedness and snares of the devil. Restrain him, O God, we humbly beseech thee, and do thou, O Prince of the heavenly host, by the power of God cast him into hell with the other evil spirits, who prowl about the world seeking the ruin of souls. Amen"

This prayer also came about by spiritual faculties such as gifts of the spirit with mediumship mechanics. Pope Leo XIII, once in conference with the cardinals, suddenly fell to the floor. Doctors were called, they thought he had died as there was no pulse or sign of life to be found. Suddenly, life was restored upon him and he woke to the revelation of a clairvoyant vision he was given or perhaps of him being taken to the spirit to witness objectively for himself the battle between Michael and the fallen. He was witness to what was going to happen to man and the evil that would befall, but Michael The Archangel appeared and cast them once again to hell, or what you may understand to be a place of such torment. This gave way to the pope using the prayer forever more and at the end of each mass. Another point to note! During the exorcisms, there are a lot of claims but the church has never validated any such as the validity of Judas as a demon or being in hell, though it has been alluded to in other exorcisms. Knowledge of divine law is your protection and prayer is the weapon.

Causation of Disasters In The Material World

There is often a great deal of conjecture on whether or not an inhuman spirit can cause physical suffering or harm within the material world, and the truth is that it is possible. During this exorcism case, the pastor and others were physically attacked and prophesized of impeding problems and threatened to be affected in the material world and these events occurred, though perhaps divine protection thwarted the desired outcome. It was even alluded to by the demon that disasters within the world were at their hands. This would make sense and is a possible hypothesis to the permeation of evil within the world.

A demon will aim to trick someone or influence the host to get a desired outcome. This was especially prevalent during this case. It is clear from the notes and written text that many influences of a negative nature touched the physical world. However, protection was granted on a divine level and the demon was unable to finish what it started because of a higher guiding force.

Finally After 23 Days!

This exorcism took 23 days of continuous prayer, battling an unseen force and was finally concluded and the woman was set free. The events that happened in the convent and outside of the holy environment made this a holy battle to be reckoned with and whether or not you believe it, the witness accounts gave credence to the case. You can't see the air you breathe, yet it exists and keeps you alive.

Good Psychic Practices

In order to navigate the dark waters well, we must employ a daily routine of psychic practices in order that we remain grounded and fully protected. This is of course without the normal psychic protection exercises previously discussed.

First, one of the most important psychic practices is to learn how to shut down your psychic centers. I would normally begin by visualizing each chakra as a particular flower - for me, I chose lilies, or sometimes I use orchids. I visualize each one of these closing their petals tightly together and by using this visualization with the proper intent, I can shut myself off from unwanted outside psychic emanations.

Second, I ensure that I try to remain in a state of gratitude, and I try to be thankful every time I eat or drink something. This state of mindfulness raises the vibration of the soul and spirit, making it difficult for negative emanations to affect you. I also ensure that I try to eat in the light or to be aware of high vibrational foods. Think about it, if energy is positive and negative, then it is safe to assume that something that has been treated in a negative way is the energy you will ingest.

Another good psychic practice is to be aware of the way you speak to others. This is a mindfulness practice. Ignorance is no defense, and as a spiritually enlightened individual. You should be aware of what comes out of your mouth. You know how negative energy affects others. Therefore, how you speak about someone, or how you react to someone is of paramount importance. Remember two wrongs do not make a right, and it is often the highest form of spiritual growth to show compassion to another's ignorance.

What you take part in can be the difference to your spiritual growth. You can hinder yourself by taking part in idle gossip or by what you watch on TV or the internet, the best you can do is to have an awareness of how you water positive seeds or negative seeds.

A High Note

Now all this may sound quite scary - and in reality it is if you judge wrongly - but one thing that you should take from this is that the realm of spirit and psychic ability is not an easy task to take on. A great many students never take on this reality.

I remember sitting in an Angel workshop and the conversation actually took a dark turn. Instead of teaching the students the reality of what could happen and the truth of the modus operandi of darker spirits, the teacher decided to negate the questions and circumnavigate the subject matter, choosing to remain in the light or so she thought. Think on this though; don't you think that heavenly angels know of these issues? Remember – know your enemy.

Like all things in life, there is the great balance of positive and negative and if you do not understand the balance of its nature, you will surely fall into a dark abyss that can be difficult to get out. Keep a true heart and study under a reputable source. Realize there is a negative and a positive, and prepare yourself for all eventualities. I know there is a lot that will make you think. I am aware that you may become a little scared of what I tell you, but realize that in His name (God, Jesus), you have the power. You could do what I do, realize your limits and do not get involved if you think you may be out of your depth – contact a real exorcist.

PART 9:

"DO" Develop Your Mediumship

First of all before you decide this is for you, it is important that you take your time and consider all the options and realize how important that choice will be in your life. It will change your life dramatically and there will be no turning back, for once you are developed – that's it. Developing any form of mediumship takes patience, understanding and a willingness to run through a very hard gauntlet. Nevertheless, it is also a wonderful blessing and one that will see you being of service - working for the divine Spirit for the benefit of humanity. I live by my code that I learned from spirit and I have this saying on my site: **'Place service first and self last.'**

So you have decided that you do indeed wish to develop your innate gifts for psychic mediumship, and though many believe it is your own decision which dictates your path, you are following the will of the creator and are being called to service by the Great Spirit. Therefore, even though you may be desperate to work in this field, you have to accept that your calling may actually be elsewhere. I never asked for it. Spirit called me - in spirit's own way, and I was made to listen to the calling. This is the case with so many mediums. Furthermore, when called, you have to accept that you are about to tread an even more difficult path than you have before. Mediums, you see, are born and psychics can develop.

Unfortunately, when you take up the cross of mediumship, you become a target, and you must accept this. You will be hated, jeered, laughed at, called a fraud and a fake, but even through this persecution, you must develop the faith that spirit will guide you, and try harder. People who have not yet awakened will attack you for your belief, and as far as they are concerned, you are damned to hell for eternity. Losing family and friends through this path is inevitable, and you will become more sensitive to all sorts of energies. Unfortunately, in this world, you are guilty until proven innocent and when innocent, you are still guilty.

Being a medium is not an easy path to walk and this is before you realize that you are a target from the lower realms of sprit too. It is like living two separate lives and trying to master both at the same time – mountainous terrain that you will have to navigate and where the conditions are as changeable as the weather. However, all this becomes negligible when you see the fruits of your labor.

When you are able to bring comfort to the parents who have lost a child or the wife who lost her husband – it all becomes worthwhile. No matter what you experience that is negative in your life because of your chosen path, there is always a blessing to be found and one of the greatest gifts that you can give is the ability to help ease someone's suffering.

Now I do not mean to sound negative here, but I have found that mediums, by their very nature are incredibly moody. Even so, this is not because of the personality they have. It is my opinion that due to our heightened sensitivity, we tend to be a bit emotionally challenged, and can notice vibrations all too easily. Anything that a normal individual would feel emotionally can be exacerbated to such a high degree that it affects the medium far more than normal. Obviously, awareness of this is necessary in order to control it.

Another point that I should make is mediums are not very good at being around other people, especially those of a 5-sensory nature, so they gravitate towards people that are more creative and intuitive. Family members laugh because they know that I am not a people person, and that I do not really like mingling with others much, but that does not mean that I am ignorant in any way. It means that I am aware of energies and choose not to submerge myself in energies that will affect me in a negative manner.

As you develop spiritually, so, too, will those that are not of your vibration will get distant from you. This is not to be looked upon as a negative thing. As I am now a professional medium and have dedicated the rest of my life to working for spirit, you will not now see me in a bar, a nightclub, or in areas where there is excessive noise, as I used to be in earlier years before I developed.

When I was opening up again later in life, I used to work in a situation that involved crowds of people. The more sensitive I became; the more I needed to get away from that atmosphere. I wonder if you guys reading this book feel the same way. For instance, I have written most of my books in coffee shops, bookshops, and my mother-in-law's house but I have to admit that even these atmospheres can sometimes become excessive for me. There have been occasions when I have sat down to write in Verdi's coffee and ice cream parlor in South Wales. I begin, and then it seems the noise has increased, and the more aware I become, the noisier it got. I end up having to stop or leave for a while until I have acclimatized myself once more.

This level of sensitivity is the burden I must bear, and I am sure others of a similar disposition experience the same. I am incredibly sensitive, and that makes us more vulnerable to energy attack than a 5-sensory individual, therefore it is good to keep a clean house and stay on top of things with regular spiritual cleansing.

So now to development; You can develop in a circle, in a church, with your friend or even on your own. The important thing has to be your desire to serve. Secondly, there has to be some psychic potential and this will already be manifest in your life in some way, from hunches, dreams, visions and warnings and perhaps a sense of foreboding. The constant that remains with all of these types of mediumship is intent and meditation at regular intervals. You need to understand there will be highs and there will be the inevitable lows, but each is a deep learning process. Most true mediums that are called to service will have experienced difficulties in life, and will have gone through some suffering in order to feel empathy.

Types of Mediumship

What type of medium will you be? You can't be a Jack-of-all-trades. There are many expressions of mediumship, and you may become adept in a few of them, but not all.

For instance, someone may express his or her particular gift through art - being able to draw the communicator when the connection is made. You may be able to demonstrate high levels of mental mediumship, or be adept at trance channeling, which many claim they do, but are certainly not trance channels. You may later develop other forms of mediumship that will be expressed after you have been in service for a considerable time. You may even develop physical mediumship at some point in your service, which is very rare and only a few true physical mediums exist in the world.

Physical mediumship is the ability to become a channel for spirit to materialize in the material world and give various forms of evidence. This evidence can be as unique as full materialization of spirit forms through the manipulation of ectoplasmic energy.

DEADLY DEPARTED | 293

You could develop direct voice, which is another form of physical mediumship, or you could be like the great Harry Edwards and use your gift for healing purposes of a medical, physical, and mental nature. Nevertheless, you must realize there are many expressions of mediumship that we shall discuss now.

Mental Mediumship

Mental mediumship can be considered as the blending or connection of two minds. One mind belongs to the spirit communicator, and the other belongs to the mind of the medium. The spirit will communicate in images, words and phrases, and the medium will have to interpret what they perceive within the limits of their developed spiritual gifts.

The only issue with mental mediumship is that a medium may allow their own thoughts and feelings into the message, which therefore detracts from what spirit wishes to convey. As I have mentioned, some mediums cannot discern their own ego from spirit communication. It is important to find your feet and develop your gifts to a level that you know without a shadow of doubt that you are receiving spirit contact. In any case, I recommend you do your own research and study the lives and experiences of the great mediums of the past that I mention in this book. One of the greatest mental mediums of the past is a woman called Estelle Roberts who was considered at the top of her class in the world.

One of the best evidential messages of mental mediumship had to have been Arthur Ford, who was the only medium to successfully pass on Harry Houdini's agreed prearranged code to his wife from the spirit world. Harry had agreed a word that he would send to his wife from beyond the grave. But this word would be in a cipher code, and only Houdini would be able to send it from the world of spirit and his wife would be the only one able to understand.

After many mediums tried to do it and failed dismally, Arthur Ford sent the cipher back to his wife and the code was broken – the word was 'Believe.' However, this was not a simple word that was to be sent but was a coded list of ten words that made a phrase. It is too complicated to explain here, but it was the best evidential message that was passed from beyond the grave, and especially because it came from Houdini himself during one of Arthur's séances.

Mental mediumship is perhaps the first form of mediumship that one would develop. It is important to understand that you will develop one spiritual gift more than another. For instance, I am predominantly a clairaudient (clear hearing) medium, and though I will use the other gifts, clairaudience is the one I am stronger in. Another medium may be more developed in the gift of clairvoyance (clear seeing) and so will be better at using this spiritual sense.

No matter what your strengths are as a medium, your gifts will be developed according to your particular strengths.

Trance Mediumship

Trance can be considered as an altered state of consciousness of varying degrees. A pet peeve that I have is the plethora of mediums that claim they are trance mediums or channels when, in reality - they are not. You can tell that most of what they channel or trance is essentially their own personality. Furthermore, when someone is in trance they should be in true trance. In my mind, there exists only one level, that is deep trance when the medium has no recollection or physical control of the body. In addition, there should be evidential messages that come through deep trance, and if one (who claims they are in trance) shies away from questioning – they are not in trance. I have experienced this at all levels and witnessed some good and some who are deluded. Allow me to explain the trance condition. Trance mediumship and channeling are very different from each other. However, like so many other forms of spirit communication, it is a very misunderstood practice. I have noticed with much dismay that many mediums have called themselves "trance channels," when, in fact, they were not working in a genuine trance condition. This is evident not only from the communication but the level and understanding of Trance Mediumship.

A medium has to link with the spirit, and the spirit has to reduce their own vibration sufficiently to link with the medium, but only if the medium can raise their vibration enough and allow the level of control through his or her own will. This can take a very long time to achieve. This may be the reason that the supposedly controlled medium thinks they are in the condition when feeling the energy of spirit – they begin to talk gobbledygook, which comes only from their own mind.

When the guide or control connects with the medium, the spirit communicator exerts various degrees of control or temporary possession of the human vessel, or overshadows the consciousness of the medium through the auric energy field. Certain sensations may be felt within the body before successful trance is attained such as the twitching of muscles or a change in the breathing patterns. When this state is successfully achieved, after the session, the medium should have no recollection - should be sensory-deprived - and this is not always the case. Of course, there is another lighter level of trance and the medium may be aware to some degree, but he or she has no control over what is being said, and this is discussed further on. The conditions required are particular and bound by intent and ability of the medium and of course the ability of the spirit control. During my own trance sessions, I am told by those in the spirit that many spirits will be present within the séance room and that there are many chosen spirits that attempt to learn how to control the medium. This is nothing to worry about and all a part of the process – the best spirit wins and so your main spirit guide will have chosen the right one for the Job.

Of course, I can only give you what I have learned over the years, though I know I have much more to learn. The medium then has to be willing to come under the control of a spirit entity and to have no fear of this process, and this is not an easy thing to do. Perhaps this is one reason why the level of trance and the communication is so poor in the modern sense, as there seems to be a distinct lack of evidence.

Trance is considered the strongest degree of control over the medium. There should be sensory deprivation or no real recollection depending of the degree of control. It should be noted that when in the correct trance condition, the individual would not respond to painful stimuli or environmental factors. However, there are various degrees of trance control: from a semi trance state, which is not understood as far deeper light trance to a very deep trance.

Deep trance is used primarily in physical mediumship, and physical mediums will have no recollection or sensory control. Deep trance can be considered a form of physical mediumship, though there remains a great deal of conjecture surrounding this.

There are many factors which indicate genuine trance control, and parapsychologists and other researchers have used various tests to determine whether, in fact, a medium is under trance control, and, if so, to what degree. Genuine trance is a strong sharing of mental and physical energies and consciousness between the medium and the spirit communicator.

With trance, there is generally -- although not always -- manifested within the medium, the following:

- A slowing of the heart rate
- A slow, deep, and steady breathing pattern
- No rapid eye movement, or REM
- A lowering of body temperature

- A greatly reduced reaction to touch and pain
- Various degrees of unconsciousness
- No conscious recollection
- Change in speech pattern

The voice patterns will change considerably and may take on several personalities, the spirit should be able to provide evidence. Furthermore, because in the trance condition, the spirit communicator is speaking directly through the consciousness of the medium, the voice pattern, inflection, and general manner of speech differ from that normally exhibited by the medium.

Finally, much research has been conducted around the language patterns of dialogue exhibited during trance communication. There is very often a broken speech pattern, a reversal of sentence structure, and an overall change in grammar usage. This is very evident in the Cayce readings, the Seth material, in other famous trance mediums such as Ivy Northage, Leslie Flint, Stewart Alexander, and Kai Muegge.

It should not be considered that possession occurs in its truest form. One of the dangers associated with trance is obsession at a lower level, and this can come about through the desperation of the medium to prove they are in trance, which makes them open to spirit obsession.

There are a few real trance mediums out there, who I can put my hand on heart and say are genuine, and there are far too many who think they are trance mediums, who clearly are not under any influence from higher level spirits who have come to teach.

I would certainly recommend little known individuals such as David Thompson (Circle of the Silver Cord), Tom Morris (Yellow Cloud Circle of Illumination), and Kai Muegge (Felix Experimental Group), and Scott Milligan. These individuals are the new pioneers who can stand shoulder-to-shoulder with the likes of Maurice Barbanel, Leslie Flint, and Ivy Northage, to say the least.

Direct Voice

Direct voice phenomena are considered the highest form of physical phenomena, and the most evidential. It is so rare, that very few mediums have developed this ability. Direct voice communication between individuals in the séance condition gives rise to the highest levels of evidential communication, because it is so intimate and personal between the communicator and the listener who does not need to be a medium.

Leslie Flint was perhaps one of the best Direct Voice mediums of the last century. Leslie was tested under the strictest of scientific conditions, often gagged, and it was noted that several voices could be communicating at the same time, which negates the claim that Leslie would simply mimic voices. Next, the level of evidential information that came from the voices was absolutely startling. How could this possibly be fraudulent? A lot of you will be wondering how this can possibly take place. What happens is quite in-depth, and we only know a little of the process. An Ectoplasmic rod is created between the medium and by the spirit team. This ectoplasm is taken from within the medium and mixed with other elements that are available. The ectoplasm is then fashioned into a kind of voice box that replicates the vibrations that is required on the physical plane. The spirit is then asked to come forward and speak through the ectoplasmic device.

Physical Mediumship

Mediumship has been around for thousands of years, and I am not going to tire you with tales of the Fox sisters, because my belief in spiritualism stems from the time of Christ and not, as some would think, the Fox sisters. What has died and risen again is the development of physical mediumship, which I am glad to say, is coming back into the modern day. Perhaps because we live in a world governed by deadlines and timescales e caused the death of physical phenomena from the past, yet the spirit has obviously decided they need the physical phenomena to come back to waken us once more to the basis of our reality.

Physical mediumship was especially prevalent in the early eighteenth century and involved the medium sitting in what is understood as a cabinet in dimly lit conditions surrounded by various sitters. The sitters would be chosen, and the medium would be securely strapped to a chair to ensure there was no opportunity to cheat. However, that was not completely effective and many so-called mediums were proven fraudulent. Perhaps this was because of the spirit boom during those times, when séances were a means of entertainment. When the conditions were right and the intent of a higher order present, spirit would manifest in physical form or through direct voice, which is another expression of physical mediumship. Soon after, and with the introduction of the Fraudulent Mediums Act[13] physical séances died out.

Now in the modern day, physical mediumship has made a resounding comeback, thanks to scientifically-minded individuals such as my friends Robin Foy and Kai Muegge. Robin was the orchestrator of the Scole Experiment held in his home in Scole, England. The success of this particular physical mediumship experiment has resulted in new methods of achieving the

---

13 Fraudulent Mediums Act -- 1951 Act of Parliament of the United Kingdom --An Act to repeal the Witchcraft Act of 1735, and to make, in substitution for certain provisions of section four of the Vagrancy Act, 1824, express provision for the punishment of persons who fraudul ently purport to act as spiritualistic mediums or to exercise powers of telepathy, clairvoyance or other similar powers. Private Members Bill introduced by Walter Monslow, applying to England and Wales, and Scotland. Royal assent, 22 June 1951; repealed 26 May 2008 by Consumer Protection from Unfair Trading Regulations, 2008

old phenomena, without putting the medium in the same danger as when using the old methods. Kai is the only medium in the world who has full materialisation in red light.

The Importance of Sitting Regularly

It is important that you sit with some kind of regularity. You make an appointment with spirit, and you should honor that appointment no matter what. I know there will be times that may change when it happens, but as long as you put a thought out to the spirit world, then you are still keeping your part of the bargain so to speak. Ensure that you keep your appointment the next time.

During this sitting with the spirit world, it is not about communication in the first instance or just meditating. It is a process of allowing yourself and your spirit team to get used to each other as you both learn of each other's vibrations. Your spirit helpers or guide will work on you to get used to your mind, vibration, and if you are developing advanced levels of mediumship – your physiology. It is important that you sit for a minimum of one hour at least. This may be hard at first but stay with it. You may also go a long time without results and this is to be expected - the spirit world want to see your dedication. I sit as regularly as I can, and if I cannot keep an appointment, I send out the thought to spirit. At first once a week is absolutely fine, but if you want to develop trance, physical or direct voice, you should sit at least 2-3 times per week in a development circle as well as on your own. Allow spirit to develop you and do not push your development yourself.

If you seek a teacher to help you develop, allow spirit to guide you to the right people. This is important; your mediumship teacher has to be the right person for you. You could sit in circle and the medium who is running it will be the only one wanting to develop and will hold you back. This is especially prevalent in spiritualist churches. Now notice that I am not singling out any church as like anything in life – we have good and bad. Even so, there are a lot of mediums that will want to ensure the spotlight is on them only. If you seek to develop, a true spiritual teacher will do their utmost to ensure that you reach your full potential.

CHAPTER 46:

Spirit Communication Takes Many Forms

I am sure all of you by now know how we as mediums communicate, if you do not, you are finding out in this book.

Divine communication is something that I am passionate about. Nevertheless, many mediums unfortunately are a little misguided, and I know this comes from their ego - they claim the communication they are having with the spirit is better than it actually is, which provides a sort of false sense of security to the grief-stricken individual. This happens a great deal when the medium is on the rostrum and this type of message offers a kind of false sense of safety and purpose to the sitter. It is a pet peeve of mine when a medium claims they see the spirit person standing or sitting next to the client. If this were the case, the medium would be able to offer irrefutable evidence of an aesthetic nature and therefore quell the idle talk from skeptical onlookers. Mediums who claim they are receiving the clear communications, as if you and I were speaking, are also misleading their sitters and readers.

The truth is that 95% of mediums 'see' subjectively, perceiving something inside themselves and therefore, communicate in a subjective nature, whether through seeing, hearing, or feeling. These are the main methods of communication, and of course, one must be able to discern the quality of the messages that are offered in content and evidence. I always try to ensure that spirit will give me enough evidence that can be validated much later, and therefore, be evidence that can also be thought of as scientifically valid in nature. If the sitter cannot validate the information instantly, and they have to investigate family information, events or dates - if the information turns out to be 100% accurate - it is difficult for even a skeptic to refute. I have to admit that although I make a living from the work I do - a great percentage of my readings is given on the spot through need for the spirit to offer comfort and healing to the sufferer, and I never charge for this. What I ask is that the person will say a special prayer or offer a donation to their favorite charity, if I do give them an on the spot reading.

Case 35: A Post-Reading Validation

This happened with a man called Nicholas, who was attending one of my martial art seminars. This message below has been unaltered and unedited, and the author has provided an affidavit to qualify the content's authenticity.

"This information is true and accurate as I experienced it.

"Jock dropped off another student and told me I would be getting a reading sooner than I would expect as he was receiving communication from someone belonging to me. We pulled up at the side of the road. Straight away one thing after another and it started with my gran's nickname

*Bunty, then Elizabeth, and then Beth. I was going
to call my boy Beth if he'd been a girl after my
Gran, my Gran was with Jack and William which he
had told me, I told Jock they were her brothers,
my son's middle name is Jack after her brother.
He then said William was chopping wood, my Gran
had told me a story of William, or Uncle Will as
my mum and her cousin called him, he used to chop
kindling and leave it at my Gran's door in really neat bundles. Pops was there with his pipe;
my gran said she could smell his tobacco in the
hall a year before she passed. My gran was watching over Tyler my son, and she spoke to him. I
often walked past Ty's room and found him mid-way
through a conversation with thin air. I never really thought much about it, he was even answering
questions and correcting. Jock could see a rain-
bow and said I'd been through a lot and that my
Gran was proud of me and my mum, and especially
my mum who has associated rainbows with my Gran
since she passed. My mum saw a double one and
since then has just associated them with my Gran
just after her passing. She was also grateful for
the tidying up I did around the house and when
she was in hospital, Jock said she appreciated
the wet sponge. Only my family knew about this
and that I did it, the nurses left little sponges
on sticks that could be dipped in water, I don't
think they paid much attention to my Gran; she
was always really thirsty and really appreciated the sponge. She also said she knew I found
it hard to see her the way she was, my Gran was
starved for three days thrashing about, and bang-
ing her arms of the side of the bed. It was hard
and I thought it was a terrible way to let your
loved ones go. It just wasn't right the way it was
done. My mum was mentioned next, February (her
birthday), then her middle name - Marie, my Gran
wasn't happy with a family member, he was abusive
to my mum and drank, that sounds like my dad, my
Gran wasn't keen on him, but was always polite
and welcoming. I was to tell my mum that Gran*

loved her very much. Jock said he could see a family bible, a big one with gold sides; this was my Gran's and is now in my living room. He also saw an ornament on a mantelpiece or a fireplace that had broken recently and I should not feel guilty, again I had some of these ornaments, one of which broke recently and I did feel guilty about.

"Before I go to sleep sometimes I think about my Gran and tell her I love her and miss her, Jock said I talk to my Gran sometimes especially at night and that she could hear me and that she sings to me. I'm rubbish at dates but I always remember my gran's birthday, Gran told him this too. Jock then asked about an Elspeth, and said she was a dear friend of my Gran's and would visit and have afternoon tea and scones; Elspeth was a neighbor and lived close by. All of it was accurate and true, Elspeth lived across from my gran and they were good friends, I was to tell Elspeth my Gran was grateful and thank her. Jock told me my Gran liked traditional Highland music and The Corries, which she did, and the Corries were played at her funeral.

Many dates were mentioned but I was not sure of them, I asked my mum later and she said one of them was my gran's parents' anniversary and others fitted later. He asked me about a broken fireplace, I've had 2 broken heaters, one of the bars broke on each of them for no apparent reason: Jock asked if my lights flicker and they have been, Jock told me these were my Gran letting me know that she was around and watching over me. Jock had said my Gran liked gardening which she loved and different types of roses, which she did. My Gran had a few of these types in her garden, he also mentioned that Gran was a great cook, I loved her cooking! Jock told me she had a big pan of Goldie soup cooking for me and that was my favorite! I was shocked he used this name as only my Gran and I called it that. Was this just another way of letting me know it was definitely my Gran, which by now was irrefutable, or do they cook in the spirit world?

She thanked me for the kiss on the head, something I had always done and I did it the last time I saw her.

But what came next truly floored me, Jock mentioned a letter that was on or at my gran's grave, I was shocked about this, as I knew there was none there and I could not think; she thanked me for the flowers.

Jock dropped me off and contacted me later on when I was at home to make sure I was ok as I was very upset. My Gran was a big part of my life, always a safe place, and an escape from some of the negative things in childhood. I have not been right without her; I never knew you could be affected like this by losing someone important.

I knew it would hurt but I did not know I would lose direction and an important part of my identity. This has been gnawing away at me for four years, Jock's helped me start to heal and hopefully get back on track, I'm extremely grateful towards him, he has the gift to help people heal and come to terms with the loss of their loved ones and move on with their lives positively…

"Amazingly, the day after the roadside reading, my mum picked me up and took me to her home. My uncle and aunty were on their way too. We were going to visit gran's grave. I noticed when we got there, next to her gravestone was a laminated letter, we do not know whom it is from but it has been there for a while. I was amazed to see it and mum had totally forgotten about it, it said mum on it but it was not from my mother or her brothers, it was next to the pots my mum and uncle had just filled with fresh flowers."

- Nicholas

The most important point within this statement is the fact that the information which was passed from the spirit world was validated later. No one could remember or had any knowledge of the letter that was on the grave, until later inspection it was found to be entirely accurate. This is an example of spirit communication that could not be validated until a later time and therefore, transmitted by intelligence with its own consciousness, a spirit that has its same personality as it did when on the earth plane such as a loved one who passed the information to the medium.

CHAPTER 47:

The World of Spirit

Now, I feel it would be prudent to give you, the student, an overview of the levels of the spirit world, and how these may be understood. I describe them as levels, as there seems to be a great deal of controversy, primarily through the teachings of religion and pragmatic dogma. Within most religious traditions, and especially in Christianity, there is only heaven, hell, or purgatory - three levels that are greatly misunderstood. Jesus had already alluded to the different levels within the realm of spirit when he claimed, "There are many mansions in my Father's house." What do you think he was saying?

The truth is, of course, that the house was an analogy of the spirit world, and the mansions were an example of the difference of the levels within that realm – each one being a different mansion and higher in vibration. So each spirit replicates the vibration of the particular level or mansion to which he belongs - a kind of like-attracts-like. Spirits who pass are therefore attracted to the level that matches their vibratory emanations.

What's it like?

I am asked this question time and time again, and I find that many clients who come for a reading with me often have the same question. I suppose it is a blessing to be able to live in a dual existence, and that is the way that I prefer to describe it to the layperson. This is because, as mediums, we are often given glimpses of the world of the spirit, and when under the trance condition, we are able to interact in this world of the spirit.

The first level is that of the etheric, and is very much like the world we live in here, except far more beautiful and with no negativity. To many individuals, this is known as the first sphere of the spirit realm. There are flowers of such beauty and magnitude, and the waterfalls are spectacular. There are forests and majestic mountains that are beautiful beyond our material comprehension. There are colors that are beyond your wildest imagination, and which no words can be used to describe them. My own father - Big Al - tells me that he has his own home, which is very tangible. He tells me that many on the other side go to learn how to be of service to others and my father is no different. From my father watching me work, he decided to train to help grounded spirits cross over to the light.

Big Al has moved on in the spirit, and he often comes back to tell me what he is doing. He talks of the world as it is here and how so much more beautiful it is there. Each time I speak to my father, I feel that he has progressed even further, and he often comes to give me other forms of evidence through my wife and this confirms what he has previously told me. I know that he has met with old friends and made new friends. My uncle who also passed often pops in to see me when he is not so busy.

My Uncle Tom was a monk and now continues in the same vein. He is training to become a guide for those in the material realm. My father tells me that service is the most important commodity in the world of the spirit and that to be of service is the most wonderful gift that you can ever give anyone no matter from spirit or on the earth plane. Many advanced spirits often return from the higher spheres to be of service to humanity.

Now that we understand there are many levels, you have to conclude there must be higher and lower levels. These are what may be understood as heaven and hell. Now the reality, my friends, is that you have nothing to fear from hell, as this is a place that is non-existent in the context it is meant. This is a place that your conscious mind will create for itself, making it seem very real indeed. Even when Our Lady talks of hell, it is a symbolic understanding of the spirit realm that is lower, and where tormented souls go. Do you think she would have called it this if she were appearing to a Buddhist? I know there is a place where evil spirits are held, and I know it is a lower-spirit realm (perhaps even segregated from, and separate in nature) that houses these evil entities. A separate vibrational level wherein like attracts like as I said before. If you understand that this is hell - then so be it.

If I may just reiterate a point that I have made: everything that we receive from the world of the spirit is of course incredibly symbolic, which enables us to search deeply within to find the answers. A great many scholars will refute the idea that much of what is in the modern bible is symbolic, and that many deeper meanings lie hidden beneath what seems to be a simplified surface truth, which is why those with blind faith will follow according to the letter and without question. I refer to a statement by Emanuel Swedenborg (Swedish Scientist and Mystic):

"Immediately after the suffering of those days, the sun will be darkened and the moon will not give its light, and the stars will fall from heaven, and the powers of the heavens will be shaken. And the sign of the Human-born One will appear in heaven, and then all the tribes of the earth will lament. And they will see the Human-born one coming in the clouds of heaven with power and great glory. And he will send his angels with a trumpet and a loud voice, and they will gather his

chosen ones from the four winds, from one end of the heavens all the way to the other end." (Matthew). (Swedenborg, 1758)

So, what does this mean? Well, firstly let me explain exactly who Swedenborg was, He was a scientist, but was also a renowned medium and was known to pass on prophecies, teachings, and messages while in the trance state. These messages were followed to the letter by Royalty and leaders of nations with great results, and information was validated and clarified. The meaning of the statement above can be understood when breaking down its symbolic content. Individuals who read the Bible would only believe, and adhere to, its literal meaning. Therefore, the above statement alludes to elements of the final judgment, and yet, if you study the symbolism deeper, you can arrive at another intuitive understanding.

The meaning of the statement is very deep and profound yet entirely spiritual in its nature. The sun will be darkened is in respect of the meaning of the Lord to Love, and the moon means the Lord in respect to faith. The stars suggest the insights into all truth and what is good with contrast to love and faith. The Human-born One is the understanding and coming of divine truth. The wailing tribes of the earth mean what is good and true, with respect to love and faith. The Lord's coming in the clouds of heaven with power and great glory suggests his presence in the word, and revelation. The clouds refer to the literal meaning of the word and the glory to its inner meaning. The angels with a trumpet and loud voices mean heaven, which is where divine truth comes from. This enables us to see the deeper meaning of the word of God and its inherent nature, not from a conscious understanding, but a deeper meaning of the truth.

Therefore, we can deduce there is a symbolic aspect to this nature of mediumship. This has been discussed in many trance addresses, and we must understand that messages can be distilled and misunderstood. The path to mediumship cultivation is not an easy one and is a life-long journey, not to be taken lightly. Therefore, we must understand what a medium believes, and how they communicate, as well as discerning the real meaning of the symbolism.

Survival Hypothesis

Man has always held onto the hope that there is something more after the death of the physical body. Primarily, this clinging to hope is fear based. To think that there is finality in death has terrified untold millions of individuals, yet even ancient civilizations have always had an inclination that there was more. The idea they courted was the heavenly realm where good men, women, and children go, and this is what they clung to. No one could have imagined there was a life after death, and that communication within our realm could take place between the living and the dead. The truth is that we do survive the process we call death. Now say this to yourself repeatedly. How empowering is it to know that you cannot die?

When we lose a loved one, we go through so much turmoil because we feel those bonds of love that once we shared are gone. It then sinks into our minds that perhaps we never measured up to the person they thought we should be. You begin to feel that you never told them you loved them enough, or that you wished you could have done things so differently. Oftentimes, the individual who faces the veil we call death, will feel like they have failed their loved ones and so the real grief sets in between both parties. It is such a blessing to be able to offer words of comfort to the bereaved, to help them through the process called grief as grief can be so debilitating.

This is why I will mainly only work with those who suffer from grief, and that I made the decision not to attract those looking for future predictions rather than evidence of life after death. We will discuss this later, but the most important thing that spirit wants to impart is the love they still have for us, and that they are around us constantly interacting with us but unknown most of the time. They wish to come back to prove they have not died, and they are very much alive and in the peak of health and vitality.

Case 36: Fiona and Donna's Story

Fiona and Donna were sisters, Fiona was somewhat skeptical of life after death, and though her sister was in a better place with it - her skepticism was surfacing due to not having real evidence from sittings they experienced in the past. Fiona was recommended to come and have a sitting with me, and explained that her sister also wanted a sitting as they had both lost their mother to cancer when they were younger. I agreed to see them both, and even though I knew the mother was in the spirit, I also knew that others would be waiting to communicate. I agreed to see them both and because spirit was urging me to do this soon, I gave them an appointment as soon as I could.

This was a Saturday evening, and I would not normally see anyone at weekend's as those times are sacrosanct for me to relax and enjoy myself with my wife by having a nice meal and chat or perhaps go to the cinema. The evening came and I never had enough time to meditate or go through my normal process due to the girls being nearly an hour early.

I knew immediately who was coming through as I had a dream just before I got up in the morning, and a woman called Margaret came to me in my dream and thanked me for seeing her girls. She asked me to send them a kiss from her and gave me some evidence for the girls. I noted this down on my phone. Just as the reading began, I recounted the dream and gave the girls the message telling them that mum was excited and waiting for them. The evidence they received was very strong, including identification of items they had personally chosen that day, conversations and information pertaining to them and their family members. First Names, second names and addresses were also imparted.

Margaret provided startling evidence to both of them and allowed other spirit friends and relations to come in and validate their lives. Messages were passed to others on the earth plane, and all were validated. This reading was very special and indicated to me how the spirit of their mother would go to great lengths to prove she was very much alive and around her girls. Margaret was a wonderful communicator and this will be one of the loveliest readings that I have witnessed from the spirit world.

AFFIDAVIT:

We can validate that the evidence Jock Brocas has given is accurate. Names of family members and friends, dates of birthdays, anniversaries, street names were accurate. He gave instances of conversations and experiences from our past. He very accurately linked family and friend connections. It is all true and amazing. We have been left stunned but reassured and happy by his reading accuracy. Thanks again Jock. --Fiona and Donna

As a medium, I believe that one must keep a skeptical enquiring mind. One happens to think along scientific protocols when considering the science of mediumship. Moreover it could be suggested that the person who is reading for a client may actually be receiving the information in a telepathic nature from the sitter, rather than from spirit. How can we refute this theory? Allow me to offer a rebuttal to this theory by using an example of one of my own research cases.

Case 37: Communicators Unknown

I sat as the medium reading for client 44a.

Several members claiming to be the loved ones of the sitter came through, the information was recorded, and nothing more was heard. Only one member of the family was validated - four members of the family were not validated due to the sitter not knowing them and, with no living family left, no way to validate the information.

The sitter took it upon herself to contact a relation who was adept at researching genealogy. The family history was investigated thoroughly and the missing family members were all placed correctly and were validated as those in the spirit that communicated with the medium.

Now this shows that the information could not have come from any other source other than those in the spirit world who were communicating with the medium. The interesting thing to note is the sitter had no idea or any information to validate the evidence that was given. The sitter had to contact a third party and have that third party investigate the evidence thoroughly. This shows that telepathy through the sitter could not have played any role in the information that was received.

Case 38: Xenoglossy

The next case is that of a woman who originated from Peru and who wanted to hear from her husband who had passed to spirit the year previously. The reading progressed as normal and at the beginning the sitter had already said that her husband was not of foreign descent. As the reading progressed various forms of evidence was presented and validated.

However soon the spirit person began to communicate words and sentences that were heard clairaudiently, not understood by the medium, but presented. These words and phrases were indeed validated but the remarkable thing was that they were given in the native language of the sitter who claimed at the end of the sitting that her husband spoke fluent Spanish and they agreed to communicate this way. The medium had no knowledge of the Spanish language and could not normally communicate in this language.

This is another example of communication from the spirit world. One could presuppose the information could have been telepathically communicated from the sitter. However, it is important to remember the medium could not communicate in the foreign language, therefore the information could only have come from the spirit communicator who wanted to prove his continuation of life after leaving the material plane.

I understand that a pseudo skeptic will always find holes in research such as this and even though no holes may be present, they will create them. This research is intended to provide evidence of the existence of the continuation of consciousness in a fair and enquiring way. Only one who is willing to have their own beliefs and perceptions challenged will accept the evidence as presented.

Let me offer you a quote from Arthur Ford, medium who broke the Houdini Code; I think the quote eloquently highlights this problem:

"Physical Science has a great deal of know how, but very little know what or know why. In analyzing a note, it loses the symphony; In studying an atom, it misses a universe. As a result, it spurs us to do with greater and greater efficiency, things that have never should have been done in the first place."

I now offer a letter by way of affidavit that will confirm the story above in Case 38 as being 100% true on all accounts.

Saturday 5th of March 2011

I would like to share my personal experience of how I met Mr Jock Brocas and what my meeting with him was like. My husband died and three or four months later for no particular reason I found myself looking for web pages which could talk about life after life and the possibility that people who passed away may be able to make some sort of contact with living people. I found quite a lot of different kinds of mediums and spiritualists. Suddenly I clicked in Jock Brocas' web page. I focused on reading what he had to say about the afterlife. He seemed to me quite honest to say that a medium's mission is not to tell people their past life or predict their future but to transmit messages from people who passed away to their loved ones here in the physical world - to have certitude that those who left the physical world did not disappear, that they are real entities in a different plane of existence. What I was reading sounded very logical to me and I had the impulse to contact him although I had no idea where he was and although he mentioned that he rarely accepts an appointment with someone who contacts him with no reference from a known person.

I wrote a little note telling him that my husband died unexpectedly during the night, I was at home but that night I decided to sleep in the spare bedroom beside ours to give him space to have good rest because he had been feeling bad during the day. I requested Jock if he would make a reading for me because I wanted to know if my husband had something to say to me.

Six or seven months passed when one day I found a mail from Mr Jock Brocas asking if I was still interested in having a reading. This was a big surprise because I knew I had no chance to have reply from him. I replied yes, I was still interested but I wanted to know how it would be. He answered that it was up to me to have the reading by phone or personally. It was when he said that I could have a reading personally when I asked him where he was. What a big surprise it was when he told me that he was in Inverness for a short time. This was very good news to me because I was not sure whether I would be able to maintain this kind of telephone communication because my first language is not English and I find very difficult to communicate by

318 | JOCK BROCAS

phone. However I did not tell Jock this, I just told him that it would be great if I could meet him personally because I was in Scotland too and it would be easy to me to go to Inverness. We agreed on a date and time and finally I was there attending a meeting with Jock something which was not meant to happen because everything was against it. He explained how the dynamic would be and I asked if I would be able to talk to him. He laughed and said 'of course, we are going to have a conversation all the time it is just that during our conversation I will say things which will have make sense to you now or later even when I do not know why I say it'. He added that maybe it was not going to be an easy communication because we were from abroad and I made it clear that I was from abroad but my husband was British. Then we started. He affirmed I had a photograph of my husband with me, true. He mentioned straight away my husband's mother's name, with no doubt, his father's name, brother, niece, his best friend, all of them were mentioned clearly, I mean they were not similar names Jock mentioned family members by using their proper names. He mentioned the name of my father in my language, Spanish, my grand-mother's in Spanish again, my sister's name. He mentioned the first letter of my dog's name which is also a Spanish word. What called my attention the most was that he mentioned the nickname of my dog, a word, which is not even Spanish but a distortion of a Spanish word which I use to talk to my dog. Jock did not mention exactly this name but he was amazingly close, he said "babuchi... gaguchi..." I said to him it is "Papuchi"..... My dog's nickname, my husband used to make jokes of the way I talked to the dog by using this nickname. Jock described perfectly the sitting room of my house, a room with a big window through which a lot of light comes and makes the room very bright, he described me as standing in front of that window watching outside and thinking of my dear love which is absolutely true. Jock added that my husband wanted to let me know that when I am there he is beside me. Jock was telling me something which was not new to me in my heart because sometimes I think or better I feel when I am in front of that window that he is beside me as it used to be before when we were together.

Jock said that my husband knows about a letter, a letter which I wrote, true. I wrote a letter to him the day of his birthday when I was on my way back home after visiting his grave. I did not remember what the letter said; the only thing I remembered was that I was very sad. When my meeting with Jock finished and I was already at home I looked for the letter. In general terms I was telling him that I wanted to write to him although I knew he never would read nor know what

I was writing. At some point Jock was a bit disorientated because he was trying to reproduce words that were not familiar to him but I was able to recognise them. It was at this point that I told Jock that my husband spoke perfect Spanish and we communicated each other mostly in Spanish. Actually Jock had no idea where I am from because I never mentioned it; I did not even mention that my first language was Spanish, maybe that is not difficult to notice but anyway I never mentioned it.

I could tell in detail all what Jock said but it would have meaning just for me and that is not the intention of this testimonial. What I would like to say is that during the two hours that my meet-ing with Jock lasted he described how my everyday life is since my husband died by using separated words and ideas, from look ing after the rose bushes which we planted together up to kiss his picture before I fall slept in the night, everything in a way that seemed to be so natural but at the same time it was not natural because Jock knew absolutely nothing about me before that after-noon; I explained to him afterwards what he was saying and why. -- Martha

There are of course instances of mediumship that are questionable, consequently, I also asked Robin to write down some cases that involved fraudulent practices, which I have included below:

Case 39: Robin Foy on Fraudulent Mediums

All three of these instances happened while I was the Chairman of the Noah's Ark Society (NAS) for Physical Mediumship (which I founded in 1990). It was an educational Society for the development, demonstration, and safe practice of physical Mediumship and its phenomena. The soci-ety is now defunct.

As the recognized authority at that time on the subject, we had a number of oddballs from all over the world contact us and declare themselves 'the best physical mediums in the world' from time to time. They wanted us to promote and endorse their Mediumship. Some that approached us were genuine

and good physical mediums, but those in this cat-
egory rarely boasted that they were the best. The
ones who did usually turned out to be frauds and
fakes, and must have thought we were as green as
grass to even consider their claims to such amazing Mediumship. However, we did make the effort
to have trial sittings with those who persisted,
and were rarely wrong in our initial assessments.

1: There was one woman who wrote to us to declare that her male partner was an 'amazing trumpet medium'. We agreed a date and they came to
visit us at Scole, where we promised to sit with
them in two initial sittings to assess the medium. Both these sittings involved just Sandra
and I, as well as the medium and his partner.
We were informed that the medium's spirit guide
would levitate the trumpet, and that the trumpet
would spell out letters in the air in answer to
any questions we might pose to the guides.

The first sitting got under way, with the
trumpet (complete with luminous tabs in the
darkness) standing upright, reasonably close
to the medium. Before long, there were gurgling
noises from the medium, which sounded as though he
was being strangled. Soon, his partner announced
that he was in 'deep trance' and that the trumpet
would shortly levitate. Indeed, the trumpet did
so, moving in close proximity to the medium.
A question was asked, and – sure enough – the
trumpet moved so that it spelled out a short non-
evidential answer. We were not too impressed at
this point, and asked if the trumpet could perform
any unusual maneuvers. The trumpet duly nodded
a 'yes', and off it went, moving only near the
medium. At one point, it seemed to move forward
beyond the medium's immediate vicinity but – at
the same time, we heard his labored breath move
from the chair towards Sandra, so realized he
was not where he should have been. Immediately
afterwards, the wide end of the trumpet pointed

towards Sandra, and was then screwed painfully into her breast area.

For anybody with the smallest experience of genuine trumpet phenomena, with the accompanying graceful movements all over the room, they would have realized immediately that on this occasion, such brutal treatment of a sitter from the trumpet could not possibly have been the result of genuine spirit activity.

Since we had promised it, the second test séance took place the next day. This time we had moved the trumpet well away from the reach of the medium. The trumpet did not move at all! We had proved our point.

2: This was the result of a chap who claimed to be 'the world's best physical medium'. He was from the Spalding area, as I recall, and he invited me to meet him at his home there. As soon as I entered, he showed me the 'amazing apports' he received on a regular basis. These consisted mainly of cheap 'New Age' jewelry and some large children's style marbles. He told me how excited his children were when he placed frozen peas into a dark airing cupboard; and they discovered the next morning that these had turned into the 'glass alley' style marbles by the power of spirit apportation! His wife just happened to let slip that he had a shop in the town where he sold crystals and New Age products. I made a point of calling in on my way home while he was not in the shop. Surprise, Surprise! Every one of the 'amazing apports' he had shown me was there amongst the stock he had in the shop.

He contacted us shortly afterwards and had the cheek to state that I must have been impressed by his amazing Mediumship. Therefore, he wanted to arrange for himself and his wife plus their children to visit us and stay free with us for a 'working holiday' where he would duplicate his *amazing feats and restore his mediumistic power. On the provision that we also arranged for two free sittings with an accredited NAS physical medium - oh, and we were expected to babysit for him and his wife as well while they witnessed this medium's phenomena!*

3: This case was a little different. The NAS bought two infrared video cameras to use during sittings with society mediums. Shortly afterwards, we were contacted by another 'best physical medium in the world' who claimed he was a transfiguration and materialization medium. Our technical officer contacted him and he agreed to do a test séance for the society, which would be filmed in total darkness by one of our infrared cameras. He stated he would have to sit in a 'cabinet' (enclosed space) for this test séance; but he did not realize exactly what the cameras would pick up!

The video film was duly made (there is still a copy around somewhere). The 'sitting' lasted for about 1 hour. The medium sat down in the cabinet with a hood on (rather like a monk's hood). Surprisingly, as he sat down, there appeared to be a shape under the hood that looked suspiciously like a large nose. The medium closed his eyes for a while, but never went into any recognizable form of trance apart from a few 'mutterings'. This went on for about 20 minutes. Then the medium was seen to bend forward, out of the range of the camera. When he sat up again, his face had changed totally! It looked very ugly and had a large prominent nose. Surprisingly, the shape of a nose under his hood had vanished. The medium just sat there. There was no attempt at speech or communication at all.

After another 20 minutes or so as 'mask man', the medium once again bent forward out of the range of the camera. When he sat up again, his features had returned to normal but - once again

- there was the definite shape of a large nose under his hood! I often ask myself why they do it. Perhaps it is just ego, or the lure of making easy money by fraudulent means. Fortunately, 37 years' experience of the real things allows us to sort the men from the boys, so to speak!

These are just a few cases that Robin was involved in, and another reason why, as mediums, we remain targets for many who would seek to destroy legitimate messages from the world of spirit. Have the old ways gone?

I am delighted to say the ancient methods have not died. A group is enjoying great success demonstrating physical phenomena to the public using the old ways and achieving full form materializations in red light. The medium, Kai Muegge, the Felix Experimental Group (FEG) is the only physical medium alive today who demonstrates effectively in public and in full red light and who has been tested under strict scientific conditions. Other mediums exist, though in relative secrecy, such as David Thompson, Scott Milligan, Tom Morris, and one name that should be mentioned above all here is Stewart Alexander who is a renowned physical mediums with phenomena that spans a lifetime.

There are other mediums of note whom I have tested personally and at the time offered legitimate direct voice phenomena such as Warren Caylor, and since then I note these mediums have developed even further with phenomena and under varied test conditions in other parts of the world. Scott Milligan is another physical medium to note and has also delivered highly evidential information as well as physical phenomena under test conditions and continues to lecture on the subject. Many other mediums exist and who are continually developing their phenomena. One thing to note is the time it takes with development and how dangerous the afterlife can be when dabbled with without the proper training and development.

New groups are springing up all over the place due to the growth in interest of physical mediumship, and I do have a fear that the attraction to physical mediumship will be another fad that will lead to the inevitable - individuals attempting this form of specialist mediumship through their own ego-based desire and who are ill prepared or insufficiently trained. Even so, there are groups that are starting, and it will not be too long before there are problems of a spiritual nature within these groups. As I write this book, I have already dealt with several cases within small groups. However, for the groups that are developing in the right conditions and with the highest of intentions, I believe that we are on the borders of the most exciting development in spiritualism today as we blend science and spirit as one. Nevertheless, we need to know both sides of the coin.

There is, of course, a grave danger within this expression of spirit communication and as long as there are highly developed professional mediums controlling and running these circles, we are relatively safe. That is not to say that I mean everyone who has trained in a spiritualist circle or church, as there are sufficiently trained and professional individuals outside these settings. A stark warning, though: mediums that are untrained, and not of the right caliber, are beginning to dabble in this aspect of spiritual development. Robin recently alerted me to a medium who was insufficiently developed yet was doing sittings. The medium's phenomenon was real, but he had attracted lower-level spirits, and the phenomenon that was witnessed was not of a high order. I want to ensure that you develop along with the right intentions and guidance from those of the highest order in the world of spirit, and I believe that I have given you more than enough information in this book to ensure that you become as professional and successful as you should be and that you serve humanity with the highest ethical standards.

PART 10

"DO" Strive for Professionalism

When Should You Decide to Work?

This is a hard question to answer, because the reality is that you will begin to work when spirit knows you are ready.

There are many individuals that will begin to work way before they are ready and have not developed their gifts enough. This will usually tell by the way they work and the messages they impart. You can find that most of their messages do not come from the spirit but from their own ego. It is important that you keep this part of you in check.

You know when to work when you have developed your gifts enough that you can communicate with your guides effectively, and that you have had proven and validated evidence from your guide or guides. Only then can you consider that you may be ready to make the next step, but you have to be aware that it will not be your decision.

This decision will be made by your spirit team and you will know when it is made. I cannot tell you how, I can only tell you that they will do it and you will know.

Tremendous Responsibility

As a developing medium or psychic, you have a tremendous amount of responsibility upon your shoulders. This responsibility not only covers the clients whom you help but also to the spirit world and yourself. By now you should have gained a great deal of information on how to remain safe and how to deal with situations as they arrive. One thing you should never take for granted is the spiritual law and the most important to the medium is of course the law of responsibility. There is a plethora of dangers as we have discussed, but when you move into the world of the professional, there is more responsibility. In all areas of industry and business, you have your professionals, your ignorant persons and your frauds. Unfortunately, this is the same in the psychic industry. While there are honest hardworking individuals and groups, there are also your unscrupulous individuals. However, there are more honest individuals and dedicated spiritual workers that work tirelessly in service than there are frauds and fakes, and this is an excellent thing. It is such a shame that good people can be tarred with those that bring a bad name upon what we do. The problem we have is that man's inhumanity to man means that the bad things in life tend to make more lasting impressions than the good. I am sure you have heard the saying "You're only as good as your last Job," this is true. Look around you; all you see is negativity in the news, in the media, and most people hang on to what is bad in the world or in their lives than what is good. I want you to be as ethical and professional as possible, so that you can stand shoulder to shoulder with the professionals and help to maintain the standards of a needed industry. This is also the work of our new society – the ASSMPI.

Mediumship, as a profession, is a specialized niche of the billion-dollar metaphysical services industry. However, who are the winners and losers in this industry? Sometimes it is the ethical medium who is the loser.

Listen closely and you will hear the cries of individuals seeking help because of the position in life they are in, which they co-created of their own volition. Listen for the cries of the person who has lost a loved one and who desperately needs some closure and guidance, or a catalyst to begin healing. Listen closer still and you will hear individuals crying out fraud; fake; con-man and even evil Bas***d. I have had to endure this myself, and yet we carry on working harder to pass the message of the spirit world.

There are many people that suffer through grief. They are so desperate in their need, that to continually help those that need it or want it, we have to make the decision to not only make it a career, but our lives and livelihood, and so we can no longer have what is termed a nine-to-five job.

Sometimes people will need longer than the one hour you have allotted them, and for the most part, true mediums and psychics will not put financial rewards before anything else.

But we do have to pay our bills the same as everyone else, and we take on far more responsibility than the average person does, and we put ourselves in the firing line. It's not an easy job.

Wait! I hear you shout, there are frauds and fakes out there, and I agree. There are those who will target the weak and the grieving, and the fearful. Fear is a strong ally for this type of person, who stalks their prey as a lion stalks the antelope on the plains of Africa. I cannot offer words of caution to those who have already been caught, and neither can I rewrite the past, but what I can do is offer you, the medium or student, advice on how not to fall into the trap as others have done.

Remember, awareness is of course the first step. There is a striking difference between professional mediums, psychics, or healers, and non-professionals, and this is in the way they present themselves. Professionals know what they are capable of doing for you. They will offer you nothing more than guidance or communication from loved ones.

CHAPTER 48:

The CERT Process

We (as professional mediums) communicate on a professional level through a particular process. This is called the C.E.R.T. process. There is a great deal of conjecture surrounding who coined this, and it is said that one well-known medium in the UK was perhaps the one, his name is Stephen O'Brian. He was a major celebrity many years ago and continues to be a major influence in the field of spirituality today.

Case 40: Demonstrating the C.E.R.T. Process

I once worked in Stephen O'Brian's center by a sheer fluke when my wife and I were invited to an open demonstration. It turned out the individual who had the chair was an acquaintance of ours and who was a member of our spiritualist church in Swansea.

Tony unexpectedly, and in front of the congregation, told Stephen who we were, and we were asked to demonstrate on his platform. To say we were scared and nervous is an understatement, and I had never seen my wife shake in her shoes before as she idolized him as a youngster. Anyway, after the demonstration, Stephen approached me and said he recognized that we were trained in the C.E.R.T. Process and this was one of the ways of not only identifying a professional medium but also ensuring the connection was real. Wow, I thought, Stephen liked us and my wife was blubbering like a schoolchild.

So now, I know that you wish to know what the process is. C.E.R.T. is the unwritten standard for most if not all mediums, and it is a simple mnemonic, which stands for:

- Contact
- Evidence
- Reason for Return
- Tidy

You can clearly deduce who has been trained using this unwritten standard and if not, then you can see where the parallel will lie. Not everyone will know of this process and in fact may use it perhaps under a different understanding, but the constant is there and the real path to evidential Mediumship. The fact of the matter is that most mediums will use this process if they have been trained professionally.

When I first started to train, I was a member of a spiritualist organization in the UK. I soon found out that the organization (well, the church I was involved in) was incredibly cliquey and suffered from jealousy - ensuring that anyone who had a natural gift was kept back. The other thing I noticed was the same people were always the ones who got messages. It was not until I met my wife Jo, who was a medium and ran her own Christian Spiritualist church, that I really got the professional training that I required. I started demonstrating in churches with my wife soon after we met.

The medium will work on a mind-to-mind connection and will relay messages that are being shown or told to the medium, using whichever gift is stronger within the medium's own psychic/spiritual faculty.

There are individuals who, even though they have an exorbitant amount of fame, clearly cannot discern between psychic information and contact from the realm of spirit. Furthermore, in most cases, this is only pure ignorance and lack of understanding combined with a mountainous ego. However, there are certainly a few cases where this would be deliberate and a misuse of the gift. I will recount an event that my wife attended recently when she went to see a famous psychic in the UK and who also claims to be a medium. I will call her Debbie and will try to be honest without making assumptions based on the facts as I was told.

Case 41: Pardon Me, But Your Motivation is Showing

This well-known psychic was demonstrating at a charity event, and apparently had more ego than anyone my wife and her friend had ever met. The comments that went around the table was that she was not very good, rude and loved herself too much. Suffice to say, the evidence she gave was not evidence at all and she had more misses than hits. She went to one woman who had lost her son through suicide. The psychic gave her no evidence and no comfort. In fact, most of what she said was wrong, and she even stopped the reading in mid-flow to answer someone else.

It is also important to note that she would allow individuals to ask one question that she would answer for a fee. Now ask yourself this: what is her motivation? Is there compassion and love with a wish to help the grief-stricken individual, or is it a purely financial exercise?

Scientific Testing

A true medium should never shy away from being scientifically tested. However, there has to be a limit to how much testing we do that gives us the same results time and time again. In testing the same things, we are perhaps potentially missing all the new evidence and structure to our universe that is out there.

I have put myself forward and have worked closely with scientists regarding this science of discarnate communication and spiritual awakening. I have a passion for the correlation between science and spirituality, and will continue in my endeavors to mold the two as one, which is why I like to work with scientifically- and open-minded people, to investigate the continuation of consciousness and the abilities we have out with the material world we live in.

I suppose this makes me somewhat skeptical in terms of having to understand the processes and the realities. Consequently, this also allows me to identify the frauds and the fakes of the paranormal world, though I have been tarred with these titles myself from the hate brigade, but then again haven't all true mediums.

Scientists are excellent when open-minded, but you must remember that a branch of science exists that refutes everything because it does not conform to their own ideas. I guess you can't even call it a branch of science really, let's suggest it has its own cult following. Surely though, ideas are not proven to be correct unless tested, and this is what we try to do with the science of spirituality.

How far does science have to go before the evidence is accepted? Conversely, how much testing can we do? For instance, if many mediums and psychics have been tested and the evidence far outweighs the hypothesis – how much do we test using the same protocols to achieve the identical? It is a never-ending cycle of mistrust and abuse in which we miss the bigger picture so to speak.

In his latest book (Alexander, 2010), Stewart Alexander alludes to this same problem. He spent many years being tested by legitimate organizations. He then came to the conclusion that they were testing the process and medium time and time again with the replicated results and the replicated protocols. The very nature of physical mediumship is dangerous to the life of the medium and therefore continual tests by some who are not qualified in the science of physical phenomena can cause injury. It is my opinion that we have had enough information to crush skeptical analysis and we should move to the next step, not stay on the same one we have been on for a hundred years or so.

There are organizations that continue to study and try to expand their understanding of the spiritual world and the supernormal abilities that some individuals display. These abilities are not just Mediumship but also include healing, spiritual awakening, communication, telepathy, telekinesis, ghosts and haunting, remote viewing and much more, so much, that I could go on endlessly.

Mediumship has now become a science of its own as a new science has emerged from this mediumship phenomenon. In our modern-day world, scientists are expanding the boundaries of consciousness and science as they begin to tread upon the realm of the spirit. Scientists such as Julie Beischel, Gary Schwartz, Russell Targ, and Dale Graaf are constantly challenging our materially driven beliefs. The hypothesis is that life continues with the same personality and personality traits after the death of the physical body, and that we have an innate intuitive power, which, when developed, can enhance the way we live within the material realm. It is an interaction between spirit and earthly existence. It is the duty of mediums to offer the evidence that supports this hypothesis.

Paranormal research and scientific models are helping to break down the skepticism that exists, which of course not only challenges the scientific belief but also creates a new skepticism over our world religions and the way we conduct our lives. The medium, then, is the conduit between these two worlds, and is still to this day largely unaccepted by humanity. Many mediums are constantly under attack and will continue to be. I suppose this is just the nature of things. This is man's inhumanity to man – lack of compassion and forgiveness.

Dale Graaf - who was once one of the directors for Project STARGATE, the US Government's psychic spying program - is still heavily involved in the science behind these anomalies and gifts. Dale has written books and published articles in scientific Journals. It is with Dale that I hope to study the correlation between Mediumship and remote viewing in the near future if he can spare the time. Other organizations, such as the Windbridge Institute, the Monroe Institute and the Rhine Institute, continue to study the advancement and parallels between spirituality and science. As I have previously mentioned, there are many areas under study now. All of them are of particular concern to me, but two stand out, which are the science of Mediumship, and the science of intuition or the sixth sense.

When it comes to examining the phenomena, it is important to have in place certain controls that will ensure the validity of the experiment; consequently, it also ensures there are no methods by which fraud could possibly take place. There are blind, double-blind and triple-blind methods used to ensure the medium or psychic is working under the correct conditions - to measure the communication and/or intuitive methods.

A blind reading would be when the sitter is not known to the medium or psychic and is hidden from the view of the reader. A double-blind reading would be where the third-party has passed an image or a name, or both, to the medium and no information is given. A time and date for the reading is arranged, and is normally conducted in separate areas such as other countries and different states etc. Not merely different rooms. A triple-blind reading is when the medium is relaying information to the third-party and that information is then validated.

I have done all three of these, though I have to admit, a scientific professional did not conduct the third method. This was a reading I conducted for a group in India and over the phone, and all I had was a name and telephone number. The information was relayed to the third party and was confirmed by the family in question. I have to admit to being a little skeptical myself, and am passionate about the science behind our spirituality. However, when the discarnate entity wishes to thank "the person standing to the right of her sister for looking after her" and names him, and who turns out to be the Doctor and not a family member, you have to be a little shocked and wonder how that happened. Spirit continues to amaze me with the accuracy they give, though only if I interpret the message properly.

Another eminent scientist who probably first pioneered the research into mediums and consciousness - certainly in the media - was a man by the name of Dr. Gary Schwartz PhD, professor emeritus at the University of Arizona. He is also the author of many scientific papers and books on consciousness research, and continues to this day.

A new organization also exists to support the standards of mediumship and its associated scientific investigation. The ASSMPI (American Society for Standards in Mediumship and Psychical Investigation) is a non-profit organization that exists to uphold the highest ethical standards in mediumship and psychic science. If you wish to become involved with the ASSMPI[14], please refer to the website www.assmpi.org.

---

14 As of this printing, the ASSMPI is anticipating a name change to reflect the global appeal of the organization. Begun some years ago in the United States, the "American" appelation no longer truly represents the scope. Directors of the organization are now located in Australia, France, and the United

If we are to move forward in this world, in the search for peace, harmony and understanding - or the three spiritual lessons of love, forgiveness and compassion - we must join spirituality and science as one to a kind of new spiritual science and enhance our connection between mind, body and spirit.

It is important that we bring science and spirituality together if we are to move forward with our spiritual progression. It is important to understand that we all have a desire to live safe lives, and lives which are blessed and abundant.

The problem is that we live through our eyes, and yet much of what we need is beyond our physical perception. It is therefore important that we feed our desire for knowledge by bringing a new spiritual science into being. So many skeptics are all too ready to mock and try to destroy that of which they have no understanding. They will always find a way of finding fault with scientific protocols, even when they have no ammunition and no target, and can't explain anything themselves.

Probably the most important research organizations so far would have to be the Center for Consciousness Research in Arizona, and the Rhine Institute, which is respected throughout the world, especially in the scientific community. I keep in touch with developments and scientists so I may play my small role.

I do support the work of organizations such as SCEPCOP where noted researchers, and Vinstonas Wu (Founder of SCEPCOP) and others have been exposing the unfair modus operandi of Pseudo Skeptics. These exposed individuals do not rationalize or understand a true scientific approach to the afterlife and the paranormal. We, who are professionals in our field, should not only support scientific research into our work, but in addition, organizations such as the aforementioned, which can stand with us to investigate and prove the afterlife or para-

Kingdom, thus the organization will soon be known as the International Society for Standards in Mediumship and Psyechical Investigation (ISSMPI)

normal science in a respected and professional manner - should be accepted.

Lynne McTaggart's book, *The Field*, explores research by scientists re-examining quantum physics and its extraordinary implications. The equations they came up with stood for Zero Point Field – the quantum field generated by the endless passing back and forth of energy between all subatomic particles. The existence of the Field implies that all matter in the universe is connected on the subatomic level through a constant dance of quantum energy exchange, that is something that enlightened individuals and mystics have known for thousands of years. (McTaggart, 2008)

Why then are we compelled to only accept and begin to investigate this now? On a more basic level, each one of us is made up mostly of energy that pulsates, moves, and binds at different frequencies. This is perhaps a good understanding of the concept of interbeing, and that all in the universe is connected within this dance of quantum energy. Interbeing suggests and supports this hypothesis and is a belief within some religious traditions.

CHAPTER 49

Psychic? Medium? What's the Difference?

N ot all Psychics are Mediums but all Mediums are Psychic. How many of you have heard this statement? I am sure a great many of you that delve into these murky waters of development have heard this repeatedly. The difference is vast indeed. I know that many 'mediums' are not mediums in the true sense of the word. They continue to work in a world of generality. They do this by reading energy and not receiving mental or telepathic communication from a discarnate spirit or intelligence. Very often the information they impart comes from their own deductions based on what they see physically if they are sat in front of a sitter. They can also impart information they think is correct and that comes from the medium's sense of what things should be. The information will be general in nature and therefore holds no evidence.

Case 42: Trouble at the Rostrum

I remember being in the Christian spiritualist church that my wife and I were married in. We were there for the divine service on a Sunday evening. One of the aspects we discussed previously with other mediums was the lack of professionalism in our industry and the need to raise the standards.

One particular gripe I have, even to this day, is that divinity seems to lack in the service, and this is from a public point of view. Individuals go there for a show, and not for the right reasons. Furthermore, many individuals that desperately need messages from loved ones miss out because of what I call Link Thieves. These individuals will make any link fit their situation, even though you as the medium know where the link is going. They will create problems with your link through their own selfish desire. Sometimes the spirit will give up, and another will come in. This makes the job of the medium very difficult indeed. Though when the right link is placed, it can be a wonderful experience.

Anyway, I digress slightly; on the night in question, we had three mediums on the platform, and the general standard was dreadful. I am not in the position to judge as I understand how difficult the job can be. As a professional, however, you must have a good idea of what is expected and how it should be delivered. The first medium stepped forward and addressed the congregation. "Can I come to the gentleman in the second row?" and pointed to a rather elderly man who had seen more years than I care to describe with a sense of authority and a hardened gaunt looking face. He looked pale and had problems breathing.

The medium remarked, "I am told that you have been under the weather, and that spirit is bringing you healing." Well duh! That's obvious. "You have been either at the doctors or the hospital *lately, and I have your father here saying that he was with you, keep your chin up and know that spirit is around you, thank you for working with me." The man thought it was good and possibly took a little comfort from it.*

Any skeptical person would rip the medium apart, and that is one reason that we have such a negative reputation. Standards have been low; they are only now beginning to get stronger because of the dedication we give to spirit and the dedication they show to those that understand the true path.

Just to reflect on the reading; there should have been far better evidence such as names, dates, death, times, places. Accurate descriptions of events and information that cannot be validated until a later date would be irrefutable. It is important then, that we as mediums and psychics should employ the highest standards, and not rush because of our ego's need. There are of course stark differences between a Mediumship reading and a psychic reading. Normally, the psychic, if not working from the heart center, will give misleading information and general information that are similar in feeling to the aforementioned.

True psychic ability, and of course Mediumship is different according to the vibration, and the evidence that ensues is so strong that it would be difficult to deny. What is even better, is if the evidence cannot be validated right away, and has to be validated days, weeks or even months later. Allow me to give you an example of how this evidence could be so accurate, it would be difficult to refute - especially after the information potentially saved a life.

Case 43: An Ounce of Prevention

Phillipa's sister had a reading with me over the phone and suggested that Phillipa should have a reading with me at some point. Now normally I do not like doing readings for various family mem-

bers as there are always high expectations, and sometimes the information will be similar, especially if they are hoping to hear from the same deceased entity. However, I agreed and nearly six months later, Phillipa had her reading.

Spirit was fast to come through, and as well as giving comforting evidence from the world of spirit; they wanted to discuss her husband. They told me to tell her that her husband should have his heart checked and that he should see someone before it was too late – as a precautionary measure.

Phillipa is more skeptical than her sister is, which I always feel is a good thing. She denied that anything might be wrong with her husband. "Sometimes he gets stressed at work but other than that he's absolutely fine," she said in a non-believing tone.

A few weeks had passed and I received a call telling me that Phillipa's husband had gone for that health check. It turned out that his blood pressure was so high; he was within the danger limits of having cardiac failure. Apparently, the reading had saved her husband's life.

I wish to get something straight here right from the onset. If you heard a warning over the radio or on the telephone, would you consider those inanimate objects to be your savior, if the warning had averted a potential disaster? Of course not, that would be ludicrous. So why think that a medium or a psychic has done it either? We are only that radio and the telephone, it has been the spirit world that has averted the disaster – perhaps give thanks to them and God for doing it, and show gratitude to them for finding you the right medium.

Most of us have demonstrated on the rostrum and do not have a need to advertise constantly, though we may do so discreetly from time to time, and we will not make claims that we cannot substantiate. My opinion is that the one big sign of those you need to be aware of (and forgive me for being general, as I do know there are professionals who do promote themselves in the manner I am discussing), are the individuals who allow you to ask them questions, in order that they can tune in, to give you guidance.

In addition, those who offer potions and spells are not of the professional standards demanded by the spiritualist movement. Any such ones who claim they can fix your life, or bring back your loved one after they have run away with someone else, are deluded and are only after your money. Unfortunately, though, there are those who are in the industry who make gold their God and do not see the plight of the needy. The following story is an experience that I had myself.

Case 44: One Bad Apple

When I was training and developing, I needed to have a reading myself to have some answers, and I chose an Angel Intuitive. I am not tarring every angel therapist with the same brush; instead I will only give you the example as I experienced it with this particular individual. I had arranged my appointment and was told that I had a slot, which was a one-hour appointment with an Angel-healing at the end. The cost would be around 80 dollars.

I went for my appointment, and to say that I was given evidential content would be a lie - in fact, much of what I was told was very general with no substance whatsoever. I was then talked into going on a workshop; the reader chatted with me for a little while, and then asked me for nearly double the fee because I had gone over the allotted time.

Unfortunately, this is a common occurrence within the industry, and it instills hatred and skepticism toward those others who do it for the highest good.

Case 45: Outright Fraud

Another woman contacted me in desperation, saying that she was scared. She had been to see a medium in the area that told her - she had a bad spirit attached to her and this was the reason that her husband had left. The medium would be able to get rid of the spirit for her but it would cost several thousand dollars. She contacted me after hearing me on a local radio show and asked how much I would charge to get rid of the spirit. I was disgusted at what this poor soul was going through, and felt an inner anger toward the person who was deceiving her. She seemed terribly shocked when I told her that I would not charge a penny to help her. I proceeded to talk with her and to calm her, making her aware that she was being conned. I managed to help the woman - who was not being haunted by a spirit.

Nevertheless, many fall prey to these fraudulent people through sheer desperation. Perhaps this is one of the fundamental reasons that many individuals in humanity hate mediums so much.

Another trait that a fake psychic will show, is when they ask you for your date of birth, where you were born and your name – just for a star chart, but these facts are all you need to find out background information on someone.

It is also important that you do not deceive anyone while you are giving a reading. This has happened on occasions to people when the reader becomes privy to personal and private information. You must remember the law of responsibility and be aware of the law of Karma, for those who deceive cannot escape the Karmic Law. You must uphold the highest levels of integrity.

CHAPTER 50

Preying on the Vulnerable?

Awoman, not knowing that I was a medium, once asked me at a dinner evening if I thought that mediums and psychics all prey on vulnerable people. I went quiet inside and asked my own guide. The words that were put in my mind instantly were, "You are all Vulnerable." This got me to thinking about our natural vulnerability.

The truth is that we are all vulnerable in some way.

You cannot go through this life feeling that you are invincible; this would be a complete illusion and a face of untruth. From the moment that we leave the womb, we are vulnerable. The word vulnerable (adjective) comes from the Latin word vulnerabilis, which means *to wound*. The dictionary terms explain that vulnerable means susceptible to physical or emotional attack or harm, i.e. "we were in a vulnerable position" or "an animal is vulnerable to predators." When used in the correct manner, it suggests that a person may be open to some form of attack which suggests a predetermined act against a potential victim whether this is physical or emotional. Predator suggests that a person or animal stalks their pray to a point that a successful assault can be made.

The fact is that *professional* mediums and psychics do not stalk anyone or attack either physically or emotionally. I wouldhave to say that no, we do not prey on vulnerable people. The word prey also suggests that one would be in fear of a predator. Anyone who is seeking help from a medium or psychic is coming to them of their own free will, therefore one cannot claim truthfully that we prey on vulnerable individuals. Instead, through divine intervention and gifts, we offer solace and com- fort to the recently bereaved by offering evidence of the world of the spirit.

Let me go back to the reality of our vulnerability. I mentioned that in some way, we are all vulnerable - and that is a truism of life. We all have weaknesses that make us vulnerable; it could be from a failed business, a relationship, or even injury. Yet does that vulnerability measure more or less than someone who may be suffering the pain of a lost loved one. If you have problems in your life, you may turn to a Doctor, Surgeon, or perhaps a counselor if you suffer from depression. No matter what, you will obviously turn to someone who may be able to ease your burden in some small way, to offer you that missing comfort, or to ease the suffering you are experiencing. No one is right 100 percent of the time, particularly when it comes down to understanding and communication. We even turn to religion to ease the vulnerability and yet one man's understanding can be misjudgment and so the real meaning becomes lost, yet we rarely condemn our physicians or religion. It is easy to condemn that which we fail to understand. Our vulnerability is what keeps us searching for inner truth and comfort. Furthermore, we will cling to someone else's ideals and beliefs without real evidence.

Free will cannot be taken likely, and so one who will seek out a professional in our field is not being taken advantage of because they seek the help from the divine gifts that may be bestowed on that chosen person. If the medium or psychic then uses their free will to extrapolate financial rewards or to cause hurt - they have then exploited the situation. This does not make the person any more or less vulnerable.

Nevertheless, we believe that spirit will guide those that most need help to the right conduit, and that may not be a medium or psychic, it could be a physician, friend or third party. Mediums and psychics are only another doorway to the spirit or to comfort and understanding - merely a catalyst to begin the healing process.

There are unscrupulous individuals that will cause suffering from ignorance and there are always those that will prey on the weak. But to tar the entire spiritual community is simply ignorance of the highest degree. This is some kind of paradox, for we do the same thing with religion, politics and in our daily lives. Man truly is inhumane to man, and it seems the in thing is to revel in someone's misfortune and suffering, then cloak our guilt by helping financially. Perhaps it is time to wake up to where the vulnerabilities lay and who truly is predator and prey.

Psychic Phonelines

I will begin by apologizing here and say sorry right from the start: I do not like psychic phone lines. You know the kind I mean, the ones that will answer all life's questions on your relationship and your career and so on, and just for the sum of 1 – 3 dollars a minute, how cheap that sounds! These people will keep you on the phone as long as possible - they will empathize with your situation, and in your own desperation you will feel that you have a friend on whom you can rely. The only friend they have made, however, is your wallet, and they want to make that acquaintance as much as possible. I know of an individual who experienced this, and unfortunately ended up in serious amounts of debt because of it. I suppose the problem really is like smoking or drugs, when you are offered a little comfort, or the reader tells you what you want to hear, you become addicted.

I am sure there are phone lines out there that are ethical and do use professionally trained people, but I am afraid they are rare, and their motivation is money. Suffering people will come back time and time again to them. These companies are just that - corporate machines interested only in the amount of money they can separate from you and they have no care whatsoever for what you may be going through. If you wish to remain at the top of the tree, do not prostitute yourself out to psychic phone lines and trust spirit to bring you the right individuals.

CHAPTER 51

Referrals are Best

I f you really want to ensure that you operate at the highest ethical levels, then I would offer you this advice, and I will use myself as an example. I have a strict policy of only doing referrals (this is when someone whom you have helped recommends you to someone else in need). This ensures that the person really needs the reading. I am not interested in your need to have a reading because your mate says it was a great experience, and that things are coming true.

You have to look at the authenticity of the need for the reading; do not look at the money aspect before anything else. Remember that your faith should be in the Great Spirit to guide you, and to bring to you the requisite individuals who need help. In addition, it ensures that you are not set up in any way, because there are many people who would love to set you up, in order to defame you or to destroy your reputation; and some individuals, as accurate as your reading may be, will claim otherwise.

In addition, those who wish to do this are taking the place of someone who possibly needs help desperately. There are, of course, occasions where you have to use your intuition; sometimes I get individuals contacting me and I can tell they really need help, so I may on this occasion accept them or pass them to someone else. I never do internet appointments, and will not offer readings by e-mail or advertise this on eBay. I am not saying that advertising your services on eBay is wrong. I just choose not to do it because it appears that you are interested in finances more than anything else.

Another thing you should be aware of is that spirit will let you know who really needs the help and will ensure you listen when the need is great.

Case 46: Referral from Spirit

I once had a woman contact me for a reading, and as she was not from anyone I had read for before (that is, not a referral), I was considering refusing her until I had my spirit guide tell me that I had to read for her. This was mid-flow of me sending back a refusal letter. Turns out, one of her family members had been murdered and the family were seeking closure.

CHAPTER 52

A Reading - What to Expect

A s a professional, you should know what constitutes a good standard and a bad standard of reading. This is not you being judgmental at all, this is you recognizing what is right and wrong, and will ensure that your standards remain high and completely ethical.

Is it possible that a true psychic medium could negate the necessity of going to another professional such as a counselor, mediator or psychiatrist? If you had the choice of paying one of these people on a continuing basis to help you with your depressive state or the downward spiral of life - could you take a chance and consult a respectable medium? The consultation is only once, with the cost being a one-off for their time – so would you? If you knew the chances of healing yourself through the power of your spirit were true – would you choose that route to health? Would you continue to pay for someone who often has no more experience than reading the theory in books? Would you trust spirit from where you came or put your life in the hands of materialism?

It is a sad fact that many individuals continue to search for happiness and healing through others, without pinpointing the root cause of the trouble. With a medium, it can happen within minutes, rather than days or weeks. A medium provides evidence of life after death but also facilitates the beginning of the healing process within one's life. Grief can become just another hurdle to get over, and the knowledge that our loved ones are still there can facilitate the healing instantaneously.

Furthermore, let us look at another form of depression or emotional illness.

Case 47: Spirit Therapy

For instance, client A came to a medium for a reading because of the depression that he was going through, as well as the issues in the marriage that were causing undue stress. Now, to this client the issues of depression were fundamentally down to the problems of the marriage and the arguing within it. He never had a reading before in his life and his idea of a psychic reading was to tell the future. In his mind, he believed that psychics were nothing more than entertainment but he was so desperate that he would try almost anything – he wanted to know if the marriage would survive.

The reality, of course, was different. As he sat down and the medium tuned into the spirit world, an uncle came through to talk with him. The evidence that he had from the medium was compelling; in that it left him with no doubt that it was his uncle. Such information as names, dates, places, and important events in his life were brought forward.

As you can imagine, this evidence shocked the skeptical man – yet the best was still to come. Another person came forward asking for forgiveness, and to say that they had unfinished business that drove them apart on the earth plane. The client had failed to say goodbye to his late father, they were estranged, and the guilt that remained with the client was destroying him, emotionally, materially and physically. The tears rolled down the client's face and further evi-

dence was given, that the father was near to his son – he watched over the family – he was sorry, and most of all, the spirit identified the problem in the marriage.

At the end of the reading, the client expressed his thanks and said that he did not believe in life after death and that communication from this world to the next was impossible. He told the medium that he would have to rethink his beliefs as the evidence he had was compelling, but most of all, he believed that he had a new lease of life now that finally his demons had left him. He could get his life back on track. The healing happened all within the time of his reading. He is now happier and the depression has been resolved.

How long could it have taken another professional to arrive at the conclusion that the problems within his life were the result of the relationship he had with his father, who passed before they could make amends? It would have taken a long time to get to the root of the problem and - at the average price of $100 an hour per session would have resulted in a great deal of money being spent unnecessarily.

Not convinced? Allow me to cite another example on an unrelated subject.

Case47: *Spirit Therapy, Again*

Client B came for a reading with the same medium – hoping to hear loving messages from those who had crossed over. She said nothing about her life, and yet the message from the spirit world was very different to what she wanted to hear. For years, she suffered with depression, anxiety attacks, and financial problems. She had gone to counselor after counselor and had suffered in three marriages.

*The medium quickly identified the problem was
related to the abuse that she suffered as a child.
The client had not spoken to anyone about this,
and the revelation from the spirit world brought
her to tears. Spirit had told the medium of these
issues and that those on the other side were
aware of the suffering. They had also confirmed
the individual who caused this suffering was busy
making reparations for the mistakes made on the
earth plane.*

*The client learned the gift of forgiveness was
the most powerful form of healing that could happen. By accepting the events, forgiving herself,
understanding the bigger picture of life and forgiving the perpetrator, she could learn to move
on and heal herself through the power of spirit.
Now she is off the antidepressants, moved home
and made radical changes in her life that have finally brought her happiness. She is back studying
to learn to help others in a similar situation.*

Client B had gone to counselors, doctors, and psychiatrists
for seven years, yet no one had been able to lift her out of the
depression she suffered. No one knew the root of the issues
and yet once again, spirit did all this within an hour. I am not
saying the only way to heal is through a psychic medium, for
the other professionals have their place in the grand design of
the universe. What I am saying is, there are other avenues to
consider. Very often the powers to heal are inherent in every
one of us – we can heal ourselves. When seeking the counsel
of a medium, we are only allowing the medium to channel the
necessary information from the spirit world. The spirit is the
catalyst for the healing.

Disease is a dirty word and with it is held the negative vibration that affects us emotionally. Emotional unbalance is revealed in physical disease. From abuse to causes of cancer – all
is manifested from an imbalance within the mind, body and

spirit. That is why the route to all healing is through the spirit – from spirit, through spirit, to spirit. Occasionally a psychic medium can effectively and quickly get to the root of the matter through channeling information from the spirit world.

During a reading, you should expect to perhaps have a nice relaxing time. I remember once, a man came to me for a reading and said, *"I have to admit, I never expected to have a reading that was like sitting and having a coffee with your best friend."*

CHAPTER 53:

Establish Boundaries and Avoid Problems

I want you to stop and think for a few moments. You will have your appointments, possibly have many different people coming to you, all with different levels of desperation and at different stages of their grief. What do you think will be the energy that exudes form their auric field? How easy would it be for them to create a psychic cord to you?

Consider if the individual has lost a child or a loved one through tragic circumstances, the emotions would be rife, and I have often heard other mediums say that their client brought them to tears, and they could not stop crying.

STOP!

This is wrong, I have already explained that you have to remain detached to be able to carry out the reading professionally, but you must also stay detached in order that you do not soak up the negative emanations coming from the sitter.

The Problems of Prophesy

Is it right to prophesize or tell the future? That question causes a great deal of controversy within spiritualist circles. Contrary to popular belief, the future is not set in stone, and free will does play a very important role. If you wish to remain professional, then you should decline to give predictions. The reason is because the only time a prediction will come true is if there are a series of events already in motion that have only one ending place. So, the only thing that you can offer is probability based on what is in motion within the present circumstances. I know there will be many of you shouting at me and saying but I have predicted this or that. Yes, I agree, and I have had high accuracy with predictions too, but only because the wheels of life circumstance had already been set in motion with no possibility of stoppage or diversion to a new road.

So, prediction is like a road that you travel upon, if there are areas to stop and turnings that take you in a different direction upon another road – you have freedom of choice to take that one. This means that it is going to be impossible to predict the outcome. However, if you are on a road with no options because of the decisions you have already made, and then the outcome becomes more inevitable.

A Law Suit Waiting to Happen

That says it all. Whenever you work with people, you are always one step away from a lawsuit - unfortunately, this is the world we live in. Many individuals have expectations and live by these expectations most of their adult lives. Some people will expect everything to go their way, others will expect everything to be handed to them on a plate, and another may expect that everything will go wrong for them. People live by what they expect, and this is no different for the medium or psychic – primarily because people will come with expectations.

Fortunately, if you are worth your salt, you will not tell your client what they want to hear, but will instead tell the person exactly what message spirit needs to impart to them for their highest good. This may be to nudge them into leading a more fruitful, spiritual life, or to help them along the path they have chosen – even to guide them with gentle loving kindness onto a new path.

Remember, it is not entertainment, as some would suggest; it is better adding a disclaimer that would say something along the lines of it being a scientific experiment, though you must ensure the individual knows they are not paying for anything more than your time (just the same as they would a therapist). It is also important to note that in the modern age, defamation, libel and slander is rife. You as a medium also have the law on your side, if you are being ethical and professional.

Changes in various laws around the world, and one in particular in the UK - 'Fraudulent Mediums Act' - means that professionals have to ensure they are covered. It is important that you add a disclaimer to your website, or that you have each client sign a legal disclaimer, ensuring that you abide by ethical standards and that you protect yourself from individuals who would like to set you up or do not like what you tell them. You can take other measures, though it all sounds a bit James Bond, such as recording your readings. How sad it has become, that we must take these precautions! We live in a world where suing is just a handy way of trying to extort money.

Confidentiality

The confidentiality between you and your client is absolutely sacrosanct, and is a three-way agreement between you, the client, and the spirit communicator. It is important to realize that you cannot discuss anything that you are party to within the reading. You will be privy to personal information, and you will have so much responsibility upon your shoulders. As a spiritual individual, you will have a great knowledge of what is right and wrong and perhaps more in-depth. If you break this confidence you will receive instant karma and you must realize the client has placed their trust and faith on you. Keep everything sacred and you will not go far wrong.

Blockages You May Face

Don't think that you will do a magnificent reading every time you sit. As I have maintained throughout the book, good mediumship is all about the requisite conditions, and here is the shocker – you are one of them. Your state of mind and how you are feeling will also be a deciding factor that will determine how good or bad the communication is. The sitter who comes to see you may be a negative person and someone that you might take an instant dislike to, though it is rare for this to happen. This instant magnetic repulsion will cause you to reduce your own vibration and cause issues with the level of communication you may receive. The communicators will not be able to get through to you.

If you argue with loved ones in your home or your colleagues in your environment, this can leave an emotional trail of energy that will reduce the conditions necessary for effective communication to happen. Similarly, if you have a lot of phones, computers or electrical items in the room, you will cause far too much electromagnetic energy that will distort the messages you are receiving or make it difficult for the spirit to communicate. The individual who has seen other mediums and psychics, may come with a skeptical attitude or may think they know it all. They may have had a bad experience with other mediums and psychics and so you will be made to feel bad just by their demeanor. Your fear will ultimately hinder you, and at this juncture you just need to take a deep breath, relax and allow your spirit team to interject.

Worry is one major emotion that will block your communication. If you overly concern yourself with things of the material plane, you will cause this fear to dominate your mind, and that will cause your focus to be on that fear. The spirit communicator will find it difficult to get through. It will be like trying to break through an impenetrable fog. It is therefore important that you should try and remain as happy as possible, keep your vibration elevated and you will allow the right conditions that will help the spirit communicator connect with your vibration.

Why Charge?

Ok, so that brings us nicely onto the reasons why we charge for our services. A great many people would suggest that because we have a gift, we should be giving the service free. Where would be the value in that? The fact that so many individuals are in need of help makes it impossible to just offer this for free. It is about valuing something - of showing gratitude for the service, and of course, we all have to make our way in life by paying our bills, and surviving in a world that is governed and controlled by money. So why is it so wrong for individuals to make money from spiritual work?

There are psychics who only do this part-time and who are supported by another income from himself or herself, or indeed a partner. So, they have no need to charge a great deal. However, these individuals are not dealing with spirit on a daily basis, and a plethora of clients with varying degrees of issues.

A person who dedicates their life to working for spirit has to be able to make a living; they have to pay bills and taxes like everyone else. They will also need somewhere to work from, so may need to pay for an office where they can see their clients. The medium in this case, for instance, very often has had a great deal of experience in dealing with all sorts of individuals with different issues. Therefore, one could assume they would be more attuned to the spirit world due to having to do the work - day in and day out. That is not to say that one would be better than the other. Spirit will bring to you those whom you can help the most, and the full-time mediums may not be able to help the person any more than the part-time medium. We all have to make a living though, and sometimes the professional will offer a great deal of time to help someone, meaning that it's not a conveyor-belt reading.

Contrary to what people think, we do not do hundreds of readings a week, or a minimum of 10 or more a day. That is saved for the side-street psychics or those at psychic events. Instead, we may only do one or two, and dedicate our time to helping that person and clearing the energy around us when they leave. This, of course, does not offer much time to run other errands or turn up for your usual job. Also, full-time mediums and psychics are in a position to help many more people and this is a factor. It has been reported in the media that mediums make 200 dollars an hour, and how terrible this is. I say how inaccurate this is, for as professionals, we do not do that many readings per day, and as it takes a great deal of energy to be able to do this, we have to have time to recuperate. However, what about the lawyer who charges up to a thousand dollars an hour? What can you say to that? Are they wrong too? You may hate them and talk about how much of a rip-off they may be, but rest assured, when the time comes, their services would be well received. This is a parallel.

Telephone Readings

One surefire way of maintaining a scientific approach is the offer of telephone appointments. This takes out the visual sensory information that a skeptic could claim you are using for cold or warm reading. Most of the readings that I have done from around the world are like this. It ensures you cannot use one of your physical senses to make judgments; moreover, you can't be accused of cold reading. Sometimes, I even blindfold myself and have done this with students. The important thing that you should do is to ensure that all you have is the basic information, and carry out the reading at a mutually convenient time. Make statements and not questions; ensure you impart only what you are receiving; and do not fish for information.

I have been known to give the client a telling-off because they offer me more information, when they have validated some of the information I have already given them. This is what we call 'feeding' the medium. You are professional and ethical if you stop that in its tracks, and remain as scientific as you can.

CHAPTER 54:

Preparation for a Reading

I am not sure what other professionals do in preparation for a reading, but we all have our own little quirks and ways that set us apart from others. It is important that you develop your own preparation routine. John Edward prays the rosary and I have known other mediums who will have a sleep before. For myself, I have a rather more elaborate preparation before I do a reading, and do this as and when I can. Sometimes, I actually start to pick up information before the client arrives, and normally I will remember this information. On a few occasions, I have been visited by their loved ones in the dream state, then wake up and frantically take notes on my phone. As I am writing this section, I have a reading for a client in 3 hours. Therefore, I prepare as follows.

I do not eat anything 3-4 hours prior to doing my reading. This ensures I have all energy available for spirit to use in order to communicate, and I am not using energy for the digestion and assimilation process.

I have a shower or a wash. When in the shower I have an active meditation whereby I clean my auric field through a series of visualization techniques.

I stop at least 30 minutes before the reading and I go to my reading area to sit in silence.

I pray.

I breathe to release any fears and nervousness.

When the client arrives, I meet them with a loving and friendly tone and I talk to them about the process. I tell them what to expect and tell them the scientific way that I work.

The reading begins when I feel spirit make the connection.

You should develop your own way and stick to it as much as you can. Be aware that you are only a vessel to pass messages of love and the continuation of consciousness. Know that spirit will never let you down and work with an open heart. Be the best you can be and do not be hard on yourself. You will have good days and bad days and you will meet many people with many expectations. Just do your best and know that you are working for the highest good.

Your Client's Expectations

Inevitably, you will have a diverse clientele coming to see you, and mostly they will be guided to you from loved ones in spirit. However, there will be those that come because they have heard how good you are. Now there could be a few things to consider here.

They are being sent to you for a reason that is beyond their reckoning and spirit want to reach them – either to awaken them or to reach them for a very important personal reason.

They are coming to hear about the future and have no interest in life after death or they do not have anyone in spirit. You have to consider that it might be a waste of time for you both and do not just consider the financial loss. I am never interested in prediction and only interested in proving life hereafter.

They do not understand the process and are looking for blood. What I mean is, evidence that is like bank account detail-sand even more or they want to be told what to do. Spirit will only give advice if they can see the results of your decisions. They will do it out of love and never out of a need for control. They need to understand how you will receive the information and how it can be placed. Never make anything fit and always strive for the highest level of evidence.

Many individuals will come to a reading with a psychic medium - full with expectations, and sometimes have an idea of what they want to hear. You must realize that the medium will only give what spirit wants or what the sitter needs, and not what they want to hear. In contrast, many people are misinformed about the differences between psychics and mediums or how the communication works. What you must remember is that to be ethical and professional, you will provide your sitter with evidence of the continuation of life after death – so this is what you should aim for as a student. In the words of my friend Robin Foy "Jock, It's all about the evidence."

When those in the spirit world have created that bridge of communication between the spirit and the medium, loved ones in spirit can give help and guidance to the sitter that will help them in the next phase of their life path. A medium is not a fortuneteller and very often those that purport to be mediums are only reading possibilities that may exist depending on the free will choice of the sitter; this is a psychic reading.

Many people will want to know what is coming up for them, and yet the spirit world may have another plan, which means that the medium will accept and carry out a reading depending on what the spirit world wishes to impart. There are those who only want prediction, and while that is possible depending on the flow of future conditions, there is too much at play. It is important that you understand those in the spirit world are more interested in communicating love, compassion and forgiveness than foretelling the future, yet be aware that spirit can see what path you are on, and what may be the result of your choices.

They will only advise in this instance. As a psychic medium we exist to end suffering through bridging the communication between our two worlds.

Bibliography

About Page: Joanne Brocas Spiritual Healer. (n.d.). Retrieved November 11, 2016, from Joanne Brocas Spiritual Healer: http://www.joannebrocas.com/joanne-brocas/

Alexander, S. (2010). An Extraordinary Journey: The Memoirs of a Physical Medium. Beaconsfield: Saturday Night Press Publications.

Birch, S. (1938). Teachings of Silver Birch. (A. W. AUSTEN, Ed.) Oxshott: The Spiritual Truth Press.

Cayce, E. (1971). SPIRIT COMMUNICATION - A compilation of Extracts from the Edgar Cayce Readings. Virginia Beach: Edgar Cayce Foundation.

Chesterton, G. K. (1924). St. Francis of Assisi (14 ed.). New York: Image Books.

DORIS STOKES, Celebrated Medium and Clairaudient, fondly remembered... (n.d.). Retrieved November 10, 2016, from The Mediums' Hall of Fame - Renowned Spiritual Workers Remembered . . .: http://website.lineone. net/~enlightenment/doris_stokes.htm

Family, T. L. (n.d.). The Secret of Fatima. Retrieved November 7, 2016, from The Fatima Project: http://www.thefatimaproject.org/the-secret-of-fatima.html

Foy, R. P. (2008). Witnessing the Impossible. In R. P. Foy, Witnessing the Impossible (p. 584). Diss, United Kingdom: Torcal Publications.

Foy, R. P. (n.d.). A Short History. Retrieved October 30, 2016, from Scole Experiment: http://www.scoleexperiment.com

Foy, R. P. (2008). Witnessing the Impossible - The True and Complete Story of THE SCOLE EXPERIMENT - Book Summary. Retrieved October 29, 2016, from Scole Experiment: http://scoleexperiment.com/

João Teixeira de Faria. (2006). Retrieved November 11, 2016, from The Friends of the Casa de Dom Inacio Abadiania Brazil - João Teixeira de Faria: http://www.friendsofthecasa.info/index.php?page=joao-teixeira-de-faria

Marie, D. A. (1917). The Message of Our Lady of Fatima (Selections). Fatima, Portugal.

McTaggart, L. (2008). The Field The Quest for the Secret Force of the Universe. New York: HarperCollins.

Ruffin, C. B. (1982). Padre Pio: The True Story. Our Sunday Visitor.

Shankar, R. (n.d.). Biography. Retrieved October 30, 2016, from Sri Sri Ravi Shankar - "My Vision is a Stress-Free, Violence-Free World": http://srisriravishankar.org/

Tolkein, J. (1965). The Lord of the Rings. London: HarperCollins Publishers.

Welcome To The Official Helen Duncan Website. (n.d.). Retrieved November 13, 2016, from The Official Helen Duncan Website: http://helenduncan.org/

Who Were the Essenes? (n.d.). Retrieved November 10, 2016, from The Essene Spirit Web site: http://www.essene-spirit.com/

Appendix A

Prayer to St. Michael the Archangel

In the Name of the Father, and of the Son, and of the Holy Ghost. Amen.

Most glorious Prince of the Heavenly Armies, Saint Michael the Archangel, "Defend us in our battle against principalities and powers, against the rulers of this world of darkness, against the spirits of wickedness in the high places" [Eph. 6:12].

Come to the assistance of men whom God has created to His likeness, and whom He has redeemed at a great price from the tyranny of the devil.

The Holy Church venerates you as her guardian and protector; to you, the Lord has entrusted the souls of the redeemed to be led into heaven. Pray therefore the God of Peace to crush Satan beneath our feet, that he may no longer retain men captive and do injury to the Church.

Offer our prayers to the Most High, that without delay they may draw His mercy down upon us; take hold of "the dragon, the old serpent, which is the devil and Satan," bind him and cast him into the bottomless pit "that he may no longer seduce the nations." [Rev. 20:2-3]

Recommended Reading

Powers of the Sixth Sense by Jock Brocas (O-Books 2008) www.jockbrocas.com

The Book of Six Rings by Jock Brocas (Tuttle 2011) www. jockbrocas.com

Feel the Vibes by Joanne Brocas (O-Books 2009) www. feelthevibes.org

Psychic Children by Joanne Brocas (O-Books 2010) www. feelthevibes.org

On the Edge of the Etheric by Arthur Findlay

A Guide to Mediumship and Psychical Enfoldment by E.W. and M.H. Wallis (Office of Light)

Practical Occultism by JJ Morse (Carrier Dove 1888)

Peace is Every Step by Thich Nhat Hanh

The Miracle of Mindfulness, Rider Books, 1991

Living Buddha, Living Christ, Riverhead Trade, 1997

The Miracle of Mindfulness: A Manual on Meditation, Beacon Press, 1999 Anger, Riverhead Trade, 2002

The Spirit Within – Chan through the Trance Mediumship of Ivy Northage. (Eye of Gaza press).

Teachings of Silver Birch . Spiritual Truth Press.

Spirit Intercourse by James Hewitt McKenzie (New York 1917)

Fifty Years a Medium by Estelle Roberts

Heaven and Hell by E. Swedenborg. (1758).

The Mechanics of Mediumship by Ivy Northage (Spiritualist Press)

What is Mediumship by Horace Leaf (Spiritualist Press)

In Pursuit of Physical Mediumship. Published by Janus in London. Still available direct from www.januspublishing.co.uk or from www.amazon.co.uk.

Witnessing the Impossible. Self-published through Torcal Publications. Available direct from www.scoleexperiment.com

Note: This book is the definitive report of the Scole Experiment, from its inception in late 1992 to its unexpected demise in 1998. Much has been written about this amazing, pioneering experiment since then, and it has become somewhat famous in the field of physical mediumship and its phenomena. 'The Scole Experiment' typed into Google now produces over 54,000,000 hits!!! Most comments and reports have not been accurate. This hardback edition contains the only true and complete story of every sitting of the Scole Experimental Group - from start to finish, as it is a genuine eyewitness account by one of the only two people in the world who witnessed the whole 1,000 hours+ of continuous physical phenomena and spirit communication over the five-year period of the experimental sessions.

Index

CPSIA information can be obtained
at www.ICGtesting.com
Printed in the USA
LVHW091008120519
617530LV00001B/270/P